Y0-CBA-928

solutions@syngress.com

With over 1,000,000 copies of our MCSE, MCSD, CompTIA, and Cisco study guides in print, we have come to know many of you personally. By listening, we've learned what you like and dislike about typical computer books. The most requested item has been a web-based service that keeps you current on the topic of the book and related technologies. In response, we have created solutions@syngress.com, a service that includes the following features:

- A one-year warranty against content obsolescence that occurs as the result of vendor product upgrades. We will provide regular web updates for affected chapters.

- Monthly mailings that respond to customer FAQs and provide detailed explanations of the most difficult topics, written by content experts exclusively for solutions@syngress.com.

- Regularly updated links to sites that as our editors have determined offer valuable additional information on key topics.

- Access to "Ask the Author"™ customer query forms that allow readers to post questions to be addressed by our authors and editors.

Once you've purchased this book, browse to

www.syngress.com/solutions.

To register, you will need to have the book handy to verify your purchase.

Thank you for giving us the opportunity to serve you.

SYNGRESS®

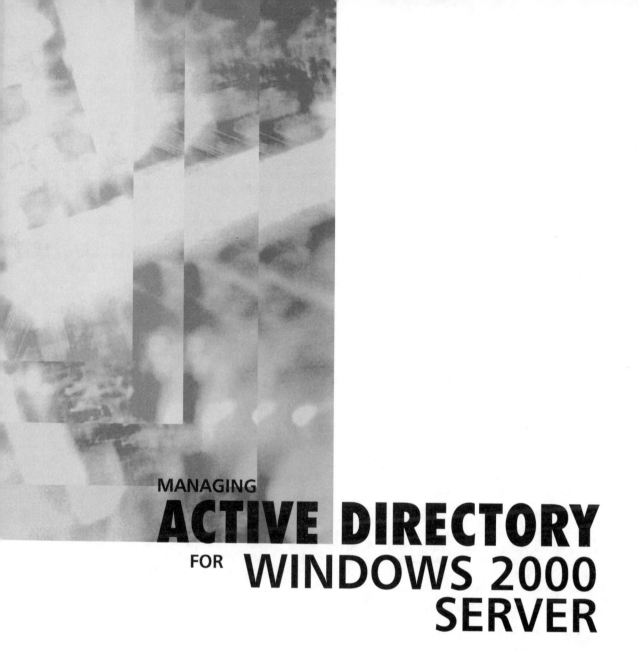

MANAGING
ACTIVE DIRECTORY
FOR **WINDOWS 2000**
SERVER

SYNGRESS®

KEY	SERIAL NUMBER
001	LMNP34RTN2
002	NWF36TK89Q
003	AKW58BXSL5
004	VG329ZX12T
005	Q256NVCR34
006	Y345NBVX12
007	C934KLVDFG
008	VPDX34KJ5D
009	Z23VPLM678

PUBLISHED BY
Syngress Media, Inc.
800 Hingham Street
Rockland, MA 02370

Managing Active Directory for Windows 2000 Server

Printed in the United States of America

1 2 3 4 5 6 7 8 9 0

ISBN: 1-928994-07-5

Copy Editor: Beth Roberts
Technical Editors: Gary Rosenfeld and
                   Stace Cunningham
Co-Publisher: Richard Kristof, Global Knowledge

Proofreader: Adrienne Rebello
Graphic Artists: Craig Enslin, Emily Eagar and
                 Vesna Williams
Indexer: Robert Saigh

Acknowledgments

We would like to acknowledge the following people for their kindness and support in making this book possible.

Richard Kristof, Duncan Anderson, Jennifer Gould, Robert Woodruff, Kevin Murray, Dale Leatherwood, Shelley Everett, Laurie Hedrick, Rhonda Harmon, Lisa Lavallee, and Robert Sanregret of Global Knowledge, for their generous access to the IT industry's best courses, instructors and training facilities.

Ralph Troupe and the team at Rt. 1 Solutions for their invaluable insight into the challenges of designing, deploying and supporting world-class enterprise networks.

Karen Cross, Kim Wylie, Harry Kirchner, John Hays, Bill Richter, Michael Ruggiero, Kevin Votel, Brittin Clark, Sarah Schaffer, Luke Kreinberg, Ellen Lafferty and Sarah MacLachlan of Publishers Group West for sharing their incredible marketing experience and expertise.

Peter Hoenigsberg, Mary Ging, Caroline Hird, Simon Beale, Julia Oldknow, Kelly Burrows, Jonathan Bunkell, Catherine Anderson, Peet Kruger, Pia Rasmussen, Denelise L'Ecluse, Rosanna Ramacciotti, Marek Lewinson, Marc Appels, Paul Chrystal, Femi Otesanya, and Tracey Alcock of Harcourt International for making certain that our vision remains world-wide in scope.

From Global Knowledge

At Global Knowledge we strive to support the multiplicity of learning styles required by our students to achieve success as technical professionals. As the world's largest IT training company, Global Knowledge is uniquely positioned to offer these books. The expertise gained each year from providing instructor-led training to hundreds of thousands of students worldwide has been captured in book form to enhance your learning experience. We hope that the quality of these books demonstrates our commitment to your lifelong learning success. Whether you choose to learn through the written word, computer based training, Web delivery, or instructor-led training, Global Knowledge is committed to providing you with the very best in each of these categories. For those of you who know Global Knowledge, or those of you who have just found us for the first time, our goal is to be your lifelong competency partner.

Thank your for the opportunity to serve you. We look forward to serving your needs again in the future.

Warmest regards,

Duncan Anderson
President and Chief Executive Officer,
Global Knowledge

About the Author

Melissa Craft (CCNA, MCSE, Network+, CNE-3, CNE-4, CNE-GW, MCNE, Citrix) worked with computers during high school, developing computer programs and testing hardware solutions as a summer job. During the 1980s and after graduating from college, Melissa designed business solutions for an insurance company using technology to automate processes, and using business process reengineering techniques. This position grew into engineering a wide area network, which subsequently turned into a career move permanently into engineering.

After making the jump to network engineering, Melissa threw herself at the task of truly understanding network engineering, gaining a myriad of technology certifications and, at the same time, deploying projects for clients. Over the years, Melissa has successfully designed, implemented, and integrated networks ranging in size from a few nodes to over 100,000 nodes. This consulting experience incorporated extensive project management, needs analysis, LAN and WAN design, deployment, and operational turnover.

In 1997, Melissa began writing magazine articles on networking and the technology industry. In 1998, Melissa contributed to *MCSE Windows 98 Study Guide (Exam 70-98)*, and since then Melissa has continued to write about various technology and certification subjects.

Currently, Melissa is a Senior Consulting Engineer for MicroAge Technology Services. MicroAge is a global systems integrator headquartered in Tempe, Arizona. MicroAge provides IT design, project management, and support for distributed computing systems. Melissa is a key contributor to the business development and implementation of professional services engagements. As such, she develops enterprise-wide technology solutions and methodologies focused on client organizations. These technology solutions touch every part of a system's lifecycle, from network design, testing, and implementation to operational management and strategic planning.

Melissa holds a bachelor's degree from the University of Michigan, and is a member of the IEEE, the Society of Women Engineers, and American MENSA, Ltd. Melissa currently resides in Glendale, Arizona with her family, Dan, Justine, and Taylor, her two Great Danes (a.k.a. Mobile Defense

Units), Marmaduke and Apollo, and her Golden Retriever (a.k.a. Mobile Alarm Unit), Pooka. Melissa can be contacted via e-mail at mmcraft@compuserve.com.

Technical Editors

Gary Rosenfeld (MCSE, MCP+I, CCNA) works as a Network Systems Consultant for Lucent Netcare in Philadelphia, Pennsylvania. Lucent Netcare is a global provider of network consulting and software solutions for the full lifecycle of a network, including planning and design, implementation, operations, and optimization. Gary is involved in designing and implementing complex Windows NT and Windows 2000 solutions for Fortune 1000 companies. He also dabbles in the internetworking realm when the opportunity arises. Gary lives in Flourtown, Pennsylvania with his beautiful wife, Jill, their wonderful son, Noah, and their lovable cat, Georgie.

Stace Cunningham (CCNA, MCSE, CLSE, COS/2E, CLSI, COS/2I, CLSA, MCPS, A+) is a systems engineer with SDC Consulting in Biloxi, Mississippi. SDC Consulting specializes in the design, engineering, and installation of networks.

Stace has participated as a Technical Contributor for the IIS 3.0 exam, SMS 1.2 exam, Proxy Server 1.0 exam, Exchange Server 5.0 exam, Exchange Server 5.5 exam, Proxy Server 2.0 exam, IIS 4.0 exam, IEAK exam, and the revised Windows 95 exam. He recently was an instrumental force in the design and engineering of a 1700-node Windows NT network that is located in more than 20 buildings at Keesler Air Force Base in Mississippi. Among his current projects is assisting in the design and implementation of a 10,000-node Windows NT network, also located at Keesler Air Force Base.

His wife Martha and daughter Marissa are very supportive of the time he spends on the computers located throughout his house.

Contents

Preface

Solutions in this chapter:

- Who Should Read This Book?
- Why Should You Read This Book?
- Why Did I Write the Book?
- Author's Acknowledgments

Introduction

Congratulations! You are about to embark on a grand computing adventure. Many people have been waiting for the next version of Windows NT, now rebranded as Windows 2000, before implementing it in their organizations. One of the main reasons some of them waited was to deploy the Active Directory—the subject of this book.

As you will discover, the Active Directory is a directory service similar to Banyan's StreetTalk or Novell's NDS (Novell Directory Services). For those who remember the early days of Novell NetWare 4.x with the first release of NDS, there are many similarities to the Active Directory release. The Active Directory, like the original NDS, has some room to grow. Microsoft learned from the successes and failures that other directory services experienced, and made the Active Directory architecture extensible to match the need for directory services growth. This technology is very compelling to IT managers because of its extensibility, scalability, and ease of management. To those who are looking to reduce time and effort in network administration with Active Directory implementation, exactly how much better the network functions, and how much they will actually save, will be determined by two factors:

- The initial network infrastructure and original (old) administrative process
- The Active Directory design and resultant (new) administrative processes

The majority of this book is dedicated to the planning of the Active Directory and the methods of its management. This will help you evaluate how Active Directory implementation will affect the costs involved in maintaining your network. There is even a chapter dedicated to disaster recovery, just in case something goes wrong.

Each chapter builds upon the knowledge learned in the last, with two exceptions: Chapter 2 "Migrating from NT 3.51 and NT 4 to Active Directory,"and Chapter 12, "Active Directory for Windows 2000 Fast Track." Chapter 2 discusses installation of the Active Directory and various migration scenarios. It is recommended that you have an Active Directory plan completed before you actually install it into a production environment. However, just to begin looking at the various Active Directory components, you will want to install it in a test environment or lab first.

Chapter 12 is an overview of the Active Directory. It gives a quick look at the Active Directory features and helps point you in the right direction for more information elsewhere in the book.

The scope of this book is limited even within the Windows 2000 product. It does not cover any Windows 2000 Server features that have absolutely nothing to do with the Active Directory.

Who Should Read This Book?

This book was written for the IT Manager, Advanced Systems Administrator, and Systems Engineer—otherwise known as my peers. Much of this book is highly technical and geared to familiarize the reader with using the Active Directory technology and understanding the underlying architecture. Although there is no requirement for you, the reader, to know either Windows NT or Windows 2000, it is expected that you will be able to install the operating system and work with it. It is not expected that you will know anything about the Active Directory . . . until after you have started reading this book.

Why Should You Read This Book?

If you are an IT Manager, this book will help you decide whether to deploy Active Directory in your environment. If you decide to implement it, this book will further help you decide which features to deploy, and in what manner.

If you are an Advanced Systems Administrator, this book will give you a deep understanding of how the Active Directory will affect your job if it is deployed in your environment. Once you have the Active Directory up and running, you will be able to manage your users and computers quickly and efficiently because of the knowledge you've gained.

If you are a Systems Engineer, you will probably spend much of the next couple of years planning for and deploying Windows 2000 in many different environments. Not only that, but your clients will look to you to bring best practices into their networks. This book will give you valuable planning information, and those best practices, too.

Why Did I Write the Book?

Because I think that the Active Directory is a difficult technology to understand, but once it is understood, it will help many people get their hands around their networks. I wanted to make the Active Directory easier for people.

Author's Acknowledgments

I would like to acknowledge the following people:

My family, Danny, Justine and Taylor—for giving me the time and space I needed to write this book, for walking the dogs, doing homework without being asked, cleaning the house, and for putting up with me while I was writing.

Christine Herfurth—for teaching me how to write, and for being a great mom.

John Trumble and Dean Tyree—for supporting my writing, giving me access to Microsoft resources, and for being absolutely cool to work with.

Amy Pedersen, Matt Pedersen, Andrew Williams, Chris Williams, and all the other great folks from Syngress—for being a wonderful publisher.

Gary Rosenfeld and Stace Cunningham—for endlessly reviewing the technical aspects of this book and keeping me honest.

Stuart Kwan, Microsoft—for giving me expert advice on Active Directory planning and DNS.

Ty Carlson and the RDP team from Microsoft—for answering my questions quickly and professionally.

Peter Houston, Microsoft—for explaining the VIA product in detail.

Joseph Dadzie, Microsoft—for all the data on Windows 2000 installations.

Grant Lawrence, FastLane—for making certain I met with the right FastLane folks and got all the information.

Ted Wong and Mark Kneuss, 3com—for giving me the information about DMTF and RIS.

Chapter 1

Introduction to Active Directory

Solutions in this chapter:

- Define a Directory Service
- Describe the Active Directory Service
- Define the Components of Active Directory
- Prepare for Active Directory Implementation

This is it—Active Directory Services. This is the beginning to a completely new way of looking at networks, networking, and Microsoft Windows 2000 Server. Microsoft created Windows 2000 to be the next generation of Windows NT. Windows 2000 has inherited a comprehensive networking platform, and the reliability and scalability of NT technology. However, Windows 2000 goes beyond the core NT technology and adds a new element with Active Directory Services (ADS).

In this book, you will go behind the curtains of the Active Directory and get a look at the real wizard driving the controls. You will learn about the Active Directory components and how they interact. You will explore the ways that you can use Active Directory to manage your Windows 2000 network. And when you have finished this book, you will be able to plan an Active Directory design and integrate it with legacy Windows NT domain architecture and various types of networking equipment.

It is time to get started and pull back the corner of the Active Directory curtain . . .

Introduction to Directory Services

Directory services have been available in networking as tools for organizing, locating, and managing network information for many years. Network directories are similar in concept to the telephone book Yellow Pages. The Yellow Pages are a listing of businesses and phone numbers that are indexed by the type of business and then alphabetized. Anyone can look up a business by type and name in order to get the correct phone number. On the network, a user could utilize a directory service to find all printing services, and then browse the listing of the one that is most appropriate.

The directory service is a concept that organizes all the pieces of a network together. It is available to each server that participates in the directory, and to each client that wants to access a server. DNS (Domain Name System) is one type of directory well known to Administrators. The DNS directory lists computers by their hostnames and associates them to their respective IP addresses. When a user needs to access a computer on the network and uses its hostname, the client computer contacts the DNS server to request an IP address.

For IT Professionals

Directory Enabled Networks

The Distributed Management Task Force (DMTF), whose Web site is www.dmtf.org, is currently developing a standard for Directory Enabled Networks (DEN). Even though many network operating systems support directory services of various types, most are vendor specific. This means that one server might be able to access a directory, but another will not simply because it is running a different vendor's network operating system. The result might be multiple directory services running on a single network, which poses problems for users who are faced with multiple logons (again) and for Administrators who must manage multiple directory structures.

Once vendors create DEN-compliant directories, multiple network operating systems will be able to participate in a single directory service. Don't worry! DEN compliance is a goal for Microsoft Active Directory services once the standard has been finalized.

A directory service such as the standard being developed for DEN will go beyond the simple organization of addresses and hostnames that DNS provides. Instead, the directory service will organize all the services and resources participating in a network, depicted in Figure 1.1.

Figure 1.1 Directory service structure.

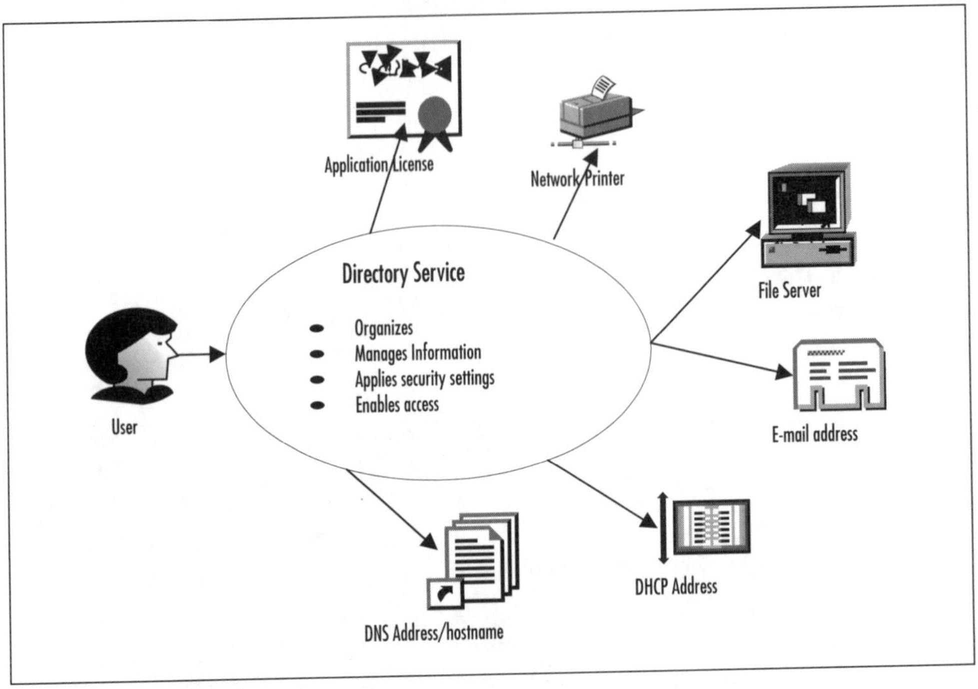

History of the Directory Service

Before directory services came about, networks were server-centric. Each server on a network had its own security system of user accounts. It would associate those user accounts to the files, directories, printers, and other services or resources that it had to offer. Sometimes the server would use the same system for this association as for the list of accounts, and sometimes it would use separate systems.

Many of the first networks began with a single server for the purpose of sharing its hard drive space at a time when hard drives were extremely expensive. Soon, these servers' hard drives would fill up, and at some point another server would be added to the network to allow further storage of shared files. It was with the additions of subsequent servers that administration became difficult. If a user needed to access more than one server, he or she needed to know how to access that specific server and needed a separate logon ID and password. It was difficult to keep the logon IDs and passwords synchronized since each server might have a different timing mechanism for password changes, and even a different Administrator creating logon IDs. The end result was a convoluted and difficult process for accessing resources on the network.

Microsoft Windows NT was released with a way to mitigate this confusing logon process when there were multiple servers. NT uses a domain architecture. The NT domain is a group of Windows NT servers that participate in a single security architecture. It consists of a primary domain controller (PDC), any number of backup domain controllers (BDCs), and any number of member servers and client computers. The PDC is the security manager of the domain. BDCs maintain a read-only copy of the security database, but the PDC is the single point of change control. Member servers and client computers contact a domain controller (DC) to access network resources. A domain is logically established in the structure shown in Figure 1.2.

Figure 1.2 The components of a single domain.

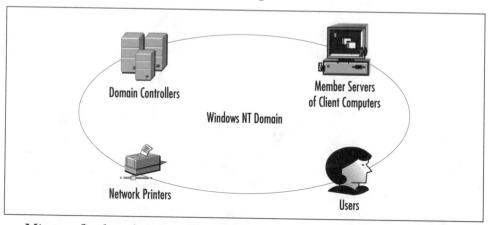

Microsoft also developed multiple domain structures to enable a distributed security structure. In order to enable users of Domain A to access the resources such as files and printers of domain B, then Domain B must trust Domain A. When drawn out, this trust relationship is shown as an arrow pointing from the trusting domain to the trusted domain. Microsoft defines various models for a multiple domain structure:

- **Master Domain model**: All resource domains trust a single Master Domain that contains all the user accounts. This is depicted in Figure 1.3.
- **Multiple Master Domain model**: All resource domains trust all Master Domains. Each Master Domain trusts all other Master Domains.
- **Complete Trust model**: All domains trust each other.

Figure 1.3 Legacy Windows NT Master Domain model.

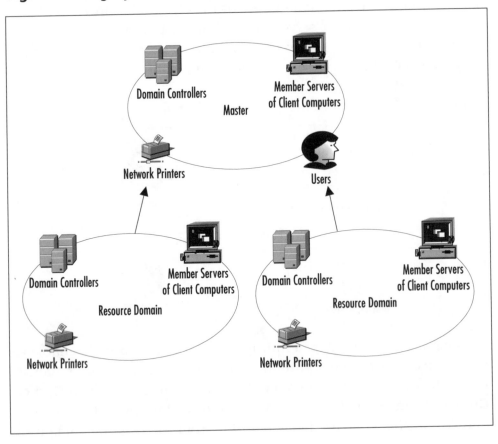

Although a domain is effective as a security model for a small or medium-sized organization, it does not have some of the features that a directory service offers. A domain structure is flat rather than hierarchical like most directory services, which means that security cannot be applied at different levels to different groups of computers. Since each domain is its own administrative area, the only way to implement a distributed administration system is to have multiple domains. Domains require a significant amount of traffic between clients and DCs. This traffic overhead is undesirable over wide area network (WAN) links that may have a limited amount of bandwidth available. Thus, multiple domains may be created to overcome WAN limitations. Trust relationships between multiple domains become cumbersome as more domains are added. As a result, trade-offs may be made between WAN performance or administrative needs and domain structures.

Directory services were developed as a way to overcome the single server and the domain architecture limitations. They are usually organized in a hierarchical fashion, encompass multiple servers and resources, and offer a fully distributed architectural model. Further, the directory services are normally established in an efficient database that is distributed throughout the network to prevent WAN overhead issues.

What Is in a Directory Service

A directory is a place to store information. A directory service includes both the entire directory and the method of storing it on the network so that it is available for any client or server. The type of information that is stored in a directory falls into three basic categories:

- Resources
- Services
- Accounts

For IT Professionals

About X.500

X.500 is a directory service standard ratified by the International Telecommunications Union (ITU-T) in 1988 and modified in 1993 and 1997. It was intended to provide a means to develop an easy-to-use electronic directory of people that would be available to all Internet users. The X.500 directory specifies a common root of a hierarchical tree. Contrary to its name, the root of the tree is at the top level, and all other containers are below it. The X.500 standard includes several types of containers with a specific naming convention for them. In this naming convention, each portion of a name is specified by the abbreviation of the object type or container it represents. A user has a CN= before the username to represent its "Common Name," a C= precedes a country, and an organization is heralded by an O=. When compared to IP domain names—for example, host.subdomain.domain—the X.500 version of CN=host/C=US/O=Org appears excessively complicated. Each X.500 local directory is considered a Directory System Agent (DSA). The DSA can represent either a single or multiple organizations. Each DSA connects to the others through a Directory Information Tree (DIT), which is a hierarchical naming scheme that provides the naming context for objects within the directory.

Although ADS is derived from the X.500 model, ADS does not implement all of the X.500 protocols because of the excess overhead involved or the lack of their general usage. These protocols include:

- Directory Access Protocol (DAP)
- Directory Information Shadowing Protocol (DISP)
- Directory Operational Binding Management Protocol (DOP)
- Directory System Protocol (DSP)

Continued

For IT Professionals Only

About X.500

ADS does implement the Lightweight Directory Access Protocol (LDAP), which affords an effective combination of DAP and DSP features, without involving any excess overhead.

Resources are the items attached to the network and made available to users. A resource can be a server's hard drive, an IP address, an application, a fax modem, a scanner, a printer, or any "thing" that can be used by a client workstation.

A service is a function on the network that makes the resources able to be shared. Most services are simply network applications. These two categories are typically related. For most services, there is an analogous resource, and for most resources, there is an analogous service (see Table 1.1). Sometimes, however, a resource or a service stands alone. The final category in a directory is an account. An account is usually a logon ID and associated password used for access to the network. It is used to grant the right to use a service or a resource.

Table 1.1 Examples of Resources and Analogous Services

Resource	Service that Supplies the Resource to Users
Server hard drive	File service
IP address	Dynamic Host Control Protocol (DHCP)
Application	Terminal server
Printer	Printing service

Each resource and service and account is stored as an object in the directory. In this way, there is a consistent way to name, organize, access, administer, and secure the network. A directory service, then, is a center of network operations for all servers providing services and resources, and for all client workstations requesting access to the services and resources. The information in the directory service manages how the services, resources, and accounts relate to each other.

There is a relationship within the directory between the various objects that represent resources, services, accounts, and their properties. For example, an account property might be the city in which the user resides, or a DNS hostname would have a property for the IP address, which that host has been assigned.

Another relationship between resources, services, and accounts is managed by Access Control Lists (ACLs). ACLs control whether an account has been granted the privilege to access any given service or resource located in the directory. An ACL can even grant the privilege to access other accounts and their properties for administration purposes.

The final relationship within the directory services is one of organization. A directory service can be organized into:

- A flat file, where all the elements are lumped together in a single group, and all rights and privileges must be granted explicitly.
- Multiple groups in a relationship with each other to provide a flow-through path for rights and privileges.
- A hierarchical tree structure, where rights and privileges can be inherited through nested Organizatinal Units (OUs).

The Directory Database

A directory is typically implemented in the form of a database. Databases have a specific organizational structure called a schema. A schema defines the types of objects that can exist in the directory.

The database that contains the directory is distributed throughout an internetwork. This enables the same information to be accessible to a person in Tokyo, Japan as it is to a person in London, England.

It would not be efficient if all people around the world were required to access a single server to find information. That situation would present serious bandwidth concerns, not to mention the fact that it presents a single point of failure if that one server went down. However, making copies, or replicas, of the entire database or pieces of that database and placing them on strategic servers throughout an enterprise network provides a method of access that does not overwhelm the network, as well as a method of fault tolerance.

When there are multiple replicas of a database, they need to be synchronized so that updates to the information are identical throughout the entire installed set. When updates are made, they are most effectively distributed via a transaction-oriented database update protocol, since only updates need to be changed throughout and not the entire database. When an object has a single property update, it is not necessary to copy the entire object with all its properties to each database replica. Instead, only the property that changed needs to be updated. For example, when a user is married, she may change her name. The Network Administrator would edit the Last Name property of the user account. The only information that is required to be changed on the database replicas is that last-name property. This update-based replication will minimize the synchronization traffic on the network, as well as the processing burden on the servers running the directory service.

There are two fundamental tactics when replicating databases:

- **Master-slave**: All changes to the directory must first be made to a designated master server and then propagated to all slave servers. Although effective from a change management perspective since there is a single point of administration, this method provides a single point of failure in the event the master server were to fail.

- **Multi-master**: Any changes made to the directory can be made to any directory server, which then propagates that change to the remaining directory servers. This method provides fault tolerance and distributed administration. However, the multi-master method does require a way to handle conflicting changes in the directory.

Directory Service Domino Effect

When a directory service consists of a distributed database using multi-master replication, and a hierarchical organization, it has a domino effect on the network's management:

- **Straightforward administration**: It collapses the management for users, applications, and network devices into a single point, but can be administered from anywhere in the network.
- **Centralized security**: It provides a single logon and consistent security mode throughout the network.
- **Extensible and interoperable**: It proffers a base of standards to all elements within the schema and enables the schema to be extended to include further objects and properties to allow other systems to interoperate.

As a result, more resources and services can take advantage of the directory service, making the entire network an open system. This model and its rewards are all representative of the Active Directory Service that is part of the Windows 2000 Server family.

Introduction to Active Directory

The Active Directory Service is the directory service provided with Windows 2000 server products. The Active Directory has the following characteristics:

- It is a database that is distributed across multiple servers.

- It uses a multi-master replication model to propagate updates throughout the network.

- It has an extensible schema, which represents user accounts, group accounts, resources, and services as objects.

- The database is organized in a hierarchical tree, which uses OUs to enable rights and privileges to be inherited.

Active Directory offers a nearly ideal set of directory characteristics so that a single directory and logon is available to all users, administration can be distributed, and the directory and its inherent security can be extended and scaled for small to large enterprises. Active Directory includes a few other features, too.

The Active Directory is an Extensible Storage Engine (ESE) database. ESE allocates a database of up to 17 terabytes and 10 million objects per domain. (One million objects is the recommended limit per domain.) ESE uses only the disk space necessary to hold the data for each object. If an object class has multiple attributes available for data, but an object of that class is created with values assigned to a couple of those attributes, then the ESE engine will only acquire the space necessary to store the values assigned.

Internet

ADS can be integrated into an Internet or intranet environment. Microsoft provides a software development kit (SDK) for Windows 2000 and Active Directory that contains the Application Programming Interfaces (APIs) that a web-based component can hook into. A web program can use these APIs so that it seamlessly accesses the Windows 2000 ADS. Since Web browsers are available on nearly every platform, this means that the Active Directory service is universally accessible via the Web.

Protocol Interoperability

ADS uses a naming organization that is similar to X.500, a standard for directory service namespaces. Although not exactly an X.500 directory, ADS uses LDAP, which was developed for use with X.500 directories and reduces the overhead that is associated with the X.500 system. Being able to use LDAP and supporting the X.500 naming model enables ADS to provide a general-purpose directory that can subsume and manage other, application-specific directories as needed. The future of ADS may bring about a single logon and password that can be synchronized throughout various systems in an internetwork, even though they might otherwise be incompatible, because of the use of standard protocols for communications.

ADS is dependent upon the TCP/IP protocol stack. In particular, it is dependent upon DNS. The TCP/IP protocol stack consists of multiple protocols; the main two are the Internet Protocol (IP) and Transport Control Protocol (TCP). The IP protocol assigns a logical address to each station on the network, so that they can be found. The 32-bit IP address has a format of four numbers from 0 to 255 separated by dots. This particular format is called the dotted decimal format, and an example looks like 10.155.3.253. This format is not easy for humans to remember. Hostnames were created to give user-friendly names to computers. A hosts file was placed on each computer to associate the hostname of a computer to its IP address. After some time, it became obvious that managing multiple hosts files was a difficult task. DNS was developed to provide a central, hierarchical directory for IP addresses that reduced the hostname to IP address management by reducing the number of machines that needed to be managed. ADS depends on DNS to locate DCs on the network.

Single Point of Administration

The Active Directory brings about the concept of *published resources*. A published resource is any file, network device, access sessions to mainframe and minicomputers, databases, Web services, and any other resource or service that is installed into the Active Directory and secured for user access. DNS is used by the Active Directory as a locator service for all participating servers and client machines to be able to access published resources. The resources are further organized in a hierarchy through the use of OUs. The OUs are contained within domains that are connected via name-spaces into domain trees, which are further organized into forest structures.

The domains no longer use a PDC or BDCs because they have changed to a multi-master architecture in which all copies of the Active Directory database are maintained on DCs that are peers of each other. This means that a single Active Directory database is the repository for multiple published resources and can be administered from the same application using any replica of the ADS database, updating other replicas through multi-master replication.

Scalability

ADS's architecture is akin to the Microsoft Exchange Server 5.5 directory structure and storage engine.

Multiple indexes of the directory provide swift information retrieval. The directory also supports sparse object storage. Sparse objects are those that have various properties but no values for all of them. The ADS structure can consist of one or more database stores that can contain a million objects in each.

Like the Microsoft Exchange directory, ADS can scale from small organizations with few published resources to large organizations that contain millions of published resource objects.

NOS Integration

Windows 2000 Server is the network operating system (NOS) that is seamlessly integrated with ADS. The Windows 2000 Server NOS is scalable at the server level, with three products—Windows 2000 Server, Windows 2000 Advanced Server, and Windows 2000 DataCenter Server—that support different sizes of server equipment, as shown in Table 1.2. ADS takes the scalability of the Windows 2000 Server family of products and raises it to the network level, since multiple Windows 2000 servers of varying types (whether Advanced or DataCenter or standard Server) can all participate in a single Active Directory.

Table 1.2 Scalability of Windows 2000

Component	Windows 2000 Server	Windows 2000 Advanced Server	Windows 2000 DataCenter Server
Number of processors	Four (4)	Eight (8)	Thirty-two (32)
RAM (Intel servers)	4GB	8GB using Physical Address Extensions (PAE)	64GB using Physical Address Extensions (PAE)
Network load balancing	Not supported	Up to 32 nodes supported	Up to 32 nodes supported
Clustering	Not supported	Up to 2 nodes in a failover group	Up to 4 nodes in a failover group
RAM (Alpha servers)	32GB	32GB	32GB

Where Active Directory Fits into the Overall Windows 2000 Architecture

Each time a Windows 2000 Server (any version) is installed with a new install, by default it becomes a member server. Upgrades are handled differently if a Windows NT PDC or BDC is being upgraded to Windows 2000. Member servers use an identical security architecture to the Windows 2000 Professional client workstations where they have flat file local databases. The flat file database allows local users and groups, as well as shared files and printers, in a server-centric model. Only when a member server or client workstation joins an Active Directory domain can it participate in the Active Directory. This does not remove the local database, and a user can still log on locally to the server or work station using it.

When the Windows 2000 Server joins an Active Directory domain, it can communicate with any DC for ADS security information. Domains are configured as top-level containers in a tree structure. Each domain is configured into a hierarchical structure using OUs. Domains sharing a contiguous namespace are organized into domain trees. There can be multiple domains in ADS, and multiple domains with different namespaces that participate in a single ADS are considered a *forest* of multiple domain trees, depicted in Figure 1.4.

Figure 1.4 Active Directory is a forest of trees.

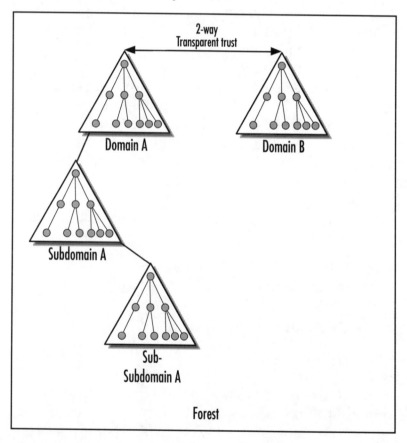

ADS provides domains and OUs to create a tree structure. Within the containers, whether they are a domain container or an

OU container within a domain, ADS supplies database objects that represent published resources such as users, groups, workstations, printers, et cetera. The result is a logical structure that can represent any enterprise of any size and organizational formation.

For IT Professionals

Multi-Master Replication

Multi-master replication occurs when each DC is a peer to all other DCs in a single domain. A change made to any replica of the Active Directory database on any DC is automatically updated on all the others.

Changes are replicated within the domain, but can also be replicated to other domains through what is best described as bridgehead servers. A bridgehead server is one in the network that is designated to send and receive replication traffic from other domain sites so that there is a management method to the traffic direction on the network. Using bridgehead servers enables the network designer to direct how replication traffic traverses the internetwork.

Active Directory can use two transports for this replication traffic:

- **SMTP**: Asynchronous replication via the Collaborative Data Objects (CDOv2) interface to Simple Mail Transfer Protocol (SMTP).

- **RPC**: Synchronous replication via Remote Procedure Calls (RPCs) over Transport Control Protocol/Internet Protocol (TCP/IP).

Keep in mind when designing your bridgehead servers that RPC communication is appropriate for most LAN and WAN connections between sites. However, SMTP communication is most effective for low-speed WAN connections, such as remote access connections over modems, between sites.

The hierarchical structure in ADS is the perfect basis for a flexible security service. ADS can secure objects using services such as Public Key Infrastructure (PKI) and can even extend to Kerberos and Smart Card technologies. Kerberos is the default authentication protocol in ADS. E-commerce support is provided through the use of LDAP over the Secure Sockets Layer (SSL), which extends ADS security into the Internet. These types of services integrate as objects, such as PKI certificates, in the authentication process using Smart Card technologies, and in extended properties of account objects so that they can support extra security requirements. The ADS architecture enables it to become the central authority for authentication and access control to the entire network and even the Internet.

Scope

The *scope* of an Active Directory is the portion of the internetwork that it covers. The scope includes:

- All the internetwork components that participate in the Active Directory
- All the LAN and WAN connections
- All domains that participate in the Active Directory forest
- All user accounts created in the various domain trees
- All resource and services provided by servers in the domains
- All computers that have joined any domain

In a lab environment, for example, an ADS scope is typically small, encompassing a few Windows 2000 servers and workstations and hardly any representative user and resource objects. It would not typically include any WAN connections. But ADS is scalable to a large enterprise internetwork that includes thousands of servers, millions of users and resource objects, and multiple WAN connections.

Namespace

A *namespace* is any dataset in which a name can be looked up and resolved. This broad definition includes all directory services, from DNS to ADS. Name resolution is the process of looking up a name and finding its properties, or looking up its properties and finding a name. In DNS, a name of a computer, called a hostname, is resolved to the computer's IP address. In ADS, the name of any object (whether it is a user account, resource, or service) is resolved to that object itself. Once a user or even an application resolves the name to the object, the user or application can browse the object's property values, if permitted to do so. If that user or application has security access, it can even manipulate the values of those objects.

The ADS namespace is directly related to DNS. Each domain is granted a DNS domain name. They may be a nested set of domains, where the top level is domain.com, the next lower levels are subdomain1.domain.com and subdomain2.domain.com, and a tertiary level is subsub.subdomain1.domain.com. This nested set of domain names is the ADS namespace. An Active Directory forest can have one or more namespaces.

TIP

Whenever defining a namespace in the Active Directory for an internal, private network, make sure it is not the same namespace that is used on the Internet, or that it is a subdomain in the Internet namespace. This will avoid name resolution problems when users are connected to both the private network and the public Internet network. For example: If your namespace on the Internet is company.com, then the namespace on the private network could be either mycompany.com or corp.company.com to satisfy this design requirement.

Name

Each object has a name that represents it in the ADS tree. The name for a server would be its DNS name, such as server.company.com. The name for a user account would be the simple logon name. For example, in a company with a naming convention for users that specifies the first letter of the first name concatenated with the first five letters of the last name, the name of a user object representing Benjamin Johnson would be BJOHNS. This type of name should be unique within any single domain.

Distinguished Name

In accordance with the X.500 model, each ADS object possesses a distinguished name (DN). The DN identifies the object by its name, and includes the trace of all of the containers above it with their respective names, until the top of the tree is reached. Each DN is unique within a forest, even if multiple objects have the same name in different domains. For example, Benjamin Johnson with the name BJOHNS can exist in the Panther domain, while Beverly Johnston with the name BJOHNS can exist in the Cheetah domain, as shown in Figure 1.5. They may appear to have identical names, but in the Active Directory their DNs are different because they include the domain name as part of the DN:

    /O=MicroAge/DC=Cheetah/CN=Users/CN=BJOHNS
    /O=MicroAge/DC=Panther/CN=Users/CN=BJOHNS

Relative Distinguished Name

The *relative distinguished name* (RDN) of any object is the part of the DN that represents the object. In the example for Beverly Johnston in the Cheetah domain, her DN is /O=MicroAge/DC=Cheetah/CN=Users/CN=BJOHNS, and her RDN is CN=BJOHNS. The RDN is typically the simple name of the object.

Figure 1.5 Tracing DNs through the Active Directory tree.

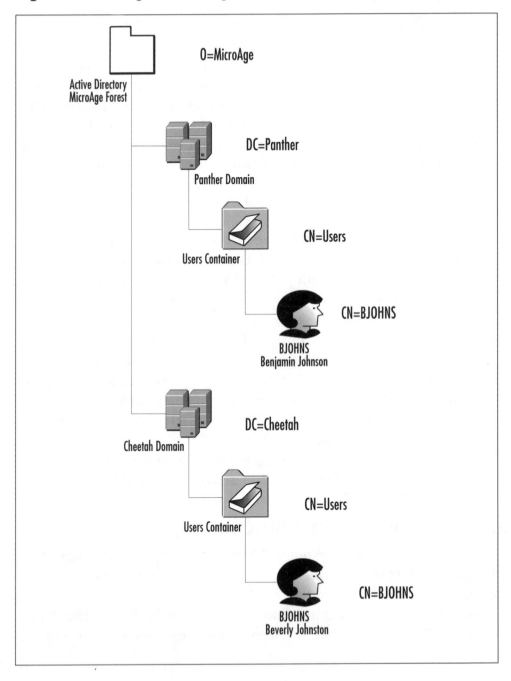

User Principle Name

The *User Principle Name* (UPN) is a naming format that uses a domain name as part of the username. It is a new concept for usernames. Since DNS is provided in ADS as the locator service, incorporating the domain name as part of the username means that user objects are easily located and authenticated. This can facilitate the logon process for users who roam from site to site. Additionally, the UPN format—user@subdomain.domain.com—can be identical to the e-mail address for that user, making it easier for that user to remember. The use of UPNs for logon is optional. The traditional logon format where the user logon name, password, and domain must be entered in separate textboxes is still available in Windows 2000. UPN usage requires that each user account name is unique within the Active Directory. If both Beverly Johnston and Benjamin Johnson had user account names of BJOHNS because of the naming convention, they would have a name conflict with the UPN format, because they both would be known as bjohns@microage.com.

Naming Contexts and Partitions

A *naming context* is also known as a *partition* because it is the part of the Active Directory database that is replicated. There are three types of naming contexts:

- Schema
- Configuration
- Domain

The schema is the description of the types of objects and properties that are available throughout the ADS database. The schema must be identical on all DCs so that objects and their properties can be recognized from any point in the internetwork. The configuration of the Active Directory is principally the method of replication and any ADS database descriptor information. The method of replication must be known throughout the internetwork so that DCs know where to send updates within domains, and when to send updates outside of the domains. Descriptor information includes information about the shape of the Active Directory itself, such as which domains are connected to which other domains through what bridgehead servers. Finally, subtree information is a contiguous set of database objects. Subtrees are typically separated at the domain level. This information must be replicated in order for authentication and access control to function properly.

Global Catalog

The *Global Catalog* (GC) is a listing of the objects within the Active Directory. It contains enough information to locate a replica of the ADS partition, which contains the object without the querying user or application needing to know the location of that object within the ADS hierarchy. The user or application will need to know one or more attributes of the desired object to perform the query.

Object

So far, the term *object* has been used to describe how the Active Directory works. What an object is, though, is a representation of a user, resource, or service within the ADS database. Each object is described by a set of properties, or attributes. Each property has a corresponding value. Table 1.3 lists examples of various objects and their analogous properties and values.

Table 1.3 Relationship Between an Object, Its Properties, and Values

Object	Property	Value
User	E-mail address	myname@mycompany.com
User	First name	George
Server	Name	SERVER01
Server	DNS name	Server01.mycompany.com
Printer	Type	HP Laserjet 5si

Container

A *container* is an object in the directory that simply contains other objects. Containers are similar to folders in a filesystem. Container objects can contain other containers in the same way that a filesystem folder can contain other folders. A container does not represent any user, service, or resource, but it does have its own attributes and values. Instead, a container is what shapes the Active Directory into a tree structure. Both domains and OUs are examples of containers.

Tree

A *tree* is a hierarchical organization of containers and objects. The tree is similar to the entire filesystem on a computer's hard drive. The tree has multiple branches created with nested containers. Nested containers are similar to folders in the filesystem. The ends of each branch are objects that represent users, services, and resources. These objects are analogous to the files inside folders.

Domains

The *domain* is a group of Windows 2000 computers that participate in the same security subtree.

The Active Directory consists of one or more domains. Each domain can span both LAN and WAN links, depending on the network design and subsequent domain implementation. Multiple domains can exist on the same LAN. When there are multiple domains using different namespaces in the Active Directory, it is considered to be a forest of domain trees. This forest must enclose domains that share a common schema and configuration. They produce a GC of users, services, and resources.

Domain Trees

The *domain tree* is a group of contiguous domains that share a common schema and configuration, and are united by trust relationships to create a single namespace. ADS can contain one or more trees, which can be depicted via their trust relationships or via their namespace.

Viewing Trust Relationships

Trust relationships are the connecting points in a domain tree. To show this relationship, there is a logical structure of each domain with arrows showing the explicit trust relationships between domains, and any implicit trust relationships that result from them.

NOTE

Transitive trusts are new to Windows 2000. The legacy Windows NT trust relationships were nontransitive. In the legacy Windows NT domain architecture, for example, the Tabby domain can trust the Calico domain and the Calico domain can trust the Persian domain, *but* the Tabby domain does not automatically trust the Persian domain. However, in the Windows 2000 architecture, trust relationships are transitive. In this architecture, and using the Tabby -> Calico->Persian trust relationships, there is a new *transitive trust relationship* in which the Tabby domain trusts the Persian domain.

ADS uses the Kerberos security protocol to establish trust relationships between domains. The Kerberos trusts are transitive and hierarchical. The hierarchical trust relationship in Kerberos is such that those domains that use the same namespace as others are automatically trusted by their subdomains. Transitive trusts are those that flow between multiple domains where A trusts B, B trusts C, and it is implied that A trusts C. A sample trust relationship set is shown in Figure 1.6.

Figure 1.6 Viewing implicit and explicit trust relationships.

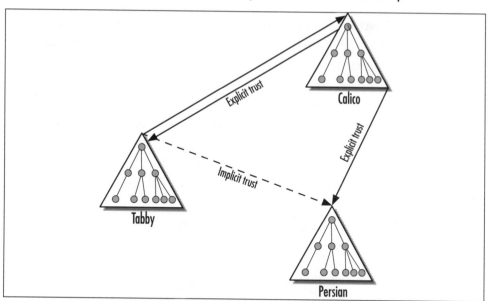

Viewing the Namespace

The namespace is a logical representation of the domain tree using its domain name hierarchy. This method is related to DNS, which is deeply infused in ADS as a locator service. The namespace method traces the domain names in a contiguous hierarchy. Figure 1.7 shows how a namespace can be depicted.

Figure 1.7 Viewing the namespace.

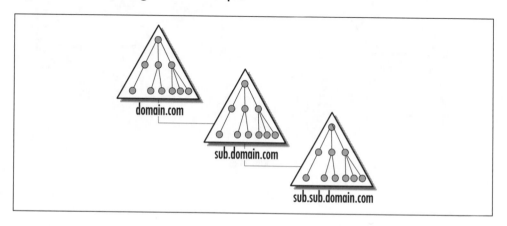

Forests

As mentioned earlier, a *forest* is a set of domain trees that share a common schema, configuration, and GC. However, a forest has one more requirement: it can have two or more namespaces among the participating domain trees.

The forest uses the name of its root domain, which is the first domain installed in the forest. It exists as a set of domain trees that trust each other via transitive and hierarchical trust relationships using the default Kerberos security trust model that is implemented by ADS. Figure 1.8 depicts a forest.

Figure 1.8 Multiple namespaces in a forest.

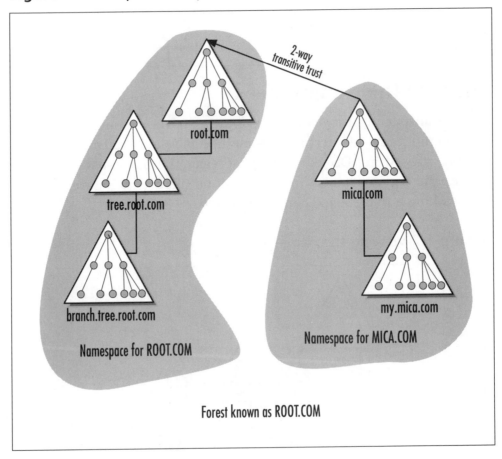

Sites

Think of a *site* as a geographically based location for servers. The official definition for a site is one or more IP subnets that share a fast and reliable connection. It is recommended that a site consist of links with greater than 512 Kbps of available bandwidth. Available bandwidth is the amount of bandwidth that is not being used by other network traffic. If a link exists for a T-1 line of 1.544 Mbps, it would appear that it has more than enough bandwidth to meet this recommendation. However, if that T-1 line was saturated with network traffic, it would not be sufficient.

The site definition is vague enough to allow a site to encompass high-speed WAN links; however, a site is best configured as one that only contains LAN connections that are less likely to become saturated with network traffic. IP subnets of a single IP network typically are designed to share LAN connectivity.

The servers that are in a single site are automatically configured for replication to each other. If those servers are only connected with high-speed reliable links, then the replication traffic can take advantage of the physical network.

Authentication traffic also takes advantage of site configuration. When a user logs on to the Active Directory, the workstation will try to locate servers in the same site as the user first, then try other servers in other sites next. The local site is determined by the IP subnet in which the workstation exists. It looks up a server that is in a site that contains that IP subnet in order to log on. Taking advantage of a physically close server, and a fast connection, makes the user perceive a higher performance from the network.

Architecture

Architecture implies structure and building of something. So how do you construct an Active Directory? The way answer to that question is *any way that will fit your organization.* You see, the way that Microsoft developed the Active Directory provides a flexible model that can incorporate any type of physical internetwork and any type of logical organization. The network impacts the Active Directory Service design in four ways:

- Data model
- Schema
- Security model
- Administration model

Data Model

The data model for Active Directory is derived from X.500; however, it is not identical to X.500. When X.500 was first implemented, it was discovered to have some significant overhead issues in its use of OSI protocols encapsulated in TCP/IP. Later, LDAP was developed to access an X.500 directory and avoid the overhead, which is why its name begins with the word "lightweight." Active Directory uses a similar data model and the LDAP protocol to gain the best of the X.500 directory standard and avoid the worst.

The ADS data model provides for a hierarchical directory that uses objects to represent services, resources, and users. It further enables attributes to describe the objects. This hierarchy, however, can be created for any type of enterprise, and can be developed to encompass both a physical structure and a logical organization of the users and groups within the enterprise.

Schema

The *schema* defines what types of objects can be stored in a specific Active Directory. For example, an extremely simple schema might define three object classes as a server, an OU, and a user. Each of these object classes would have attributes such as the server IP address, the OU name, and the user e-mail address. When an actual server, OU, and user object are created, those attributes are given values. The value for the server IP address attribute might be

10.10.10.5, the value for the OU name attribute might be HQ, and the value for the user e-mail address attribute might be user@mail.corp.com. This is summarized in Table 1.4.

Table 1.4 Schema Objects, Attributes, and Values

Object Class	Object	Attribute	Value
Server	Server.domain.com	IP address	10.10.10.5
Organizational unit	CN=HQ	Name	HQ
User	USER	E-mail address	user@mail.corp.com

The Active Directory schema can be extended to include additional objects. For example, a backup program that is written to take advantage of the Active Directory could add an object class for the backup service and add an attribute to the server object class to enable it as a backup service provider or a backup service requester. The schema must be updated across all the DCs that contain a replica of the Active Directory in order for those objects and properties to be recognized and administered from any point in the internetwork.

The ADS schema is stored within the directory itself. This reduces the overhead involved with users or applications that run queries on the Active Directory. It also allows the schema to be extended dynamically, with immediate access to the new object classes and attributes. The ability to perform schema extensions is protected by ACLs so that only authorized users can extend the schema.

TIP

When an application that extends the schema is installed on the network, the application will require the name and password of a user that has the capability of extending the schema. Otherwise, the installation will fail.

Security Model

When a Windows 2000 server joins a domain or becomes a DC, it automatically begins participating in the Active Directory. The Active Directory uses the Kerberos security model. The ADS uses Kerberos version 5.0, an authentication protocol that was developed by MIT and is published by the IETF in RFCs 1510 and 1964. Using Kerberos, the ADS can verify the identity of any user, service, or resource on a network that without this verification would otherwise be unprotected from public use. Kerberos does not rely on the NOS to authenticate and does not trust specific IP addresses, which are both common security methods in use today. Instead, Kerberos uses credentials to verify identities.

Once an identity is authorized to access the directory, the security within ADS takes over. In the Active Directory itself, ACLs are defined by the Administrator to allow (or deny) any user, resource, or service to access any other user, resource, or service. The ACLs are flexible enough to enable access to use a service or resource, or even to change the values of their attributes.

Administration Model

The Active Directory allows an Administrator to delegate authority to other users over segments of a domain. In the legacy domain model for Windows NT, the Administrator delegation level was set for the entire domain, regardless of the groups and organizations that participated in the domain. Now, with the ability to segment a domain into a hierarchical tree structure using nested OUs, the administration model can be set to whichever level best suits the enterprise. The result is that an Administrator is granted an appropriate area of control.

Gathering Information for an Implementation of Active Directory

The first activity for an enterprise to engage in when developing an Active Directory Service plan is to gather information about the enterprise. This information will reflect both the network's physical structure and the enterprise's logical organization. The following list represents the types of documents that are recommended to discover the network's physical structure. Note that the documentation of your network may be structured differently and will not map directly to this list.

- Topology maps detailing the WAN links of the internetwork
- Topology maps detailing the LANs that make up the internetwork
- Lists of servers, including current NOS version, service pack updates, and services that are provided to the network (file, print, RAS, SQL, e-mail, etc.)
- Lists of printers and location
- DNS structure
- Lists of other network resources and their locations
- Traffic flow and network baseline performance
- Inventory of the client workstations

Aside from the physical structure of the network, you will also need information on the logical organization of the enterprise. This information is typically documented in:

- Organizational charts
- Lists of users and their location
- Lists of groups and their purpose
- Workflow between groups
- Information regarding future growth plans

Organizational Characteristics for an Implementation of Active Directory

The ADS architecture consists of three main logical organizing concepts:

- **Forest**: A set of namespaces representing multiple domain trees.
- **Domain tree**: A set of domains that are hierarchically named to participate in a single namespace.
- **Organizational unit**: A container within a single domain that organizes the domains users, resources, and services.

A forest is global, which means that it can include any or all users, resources, domains, and physical LAN and WAN connections on the internetwork. The domain is based on the DNS domain name. The OU is a logical container that can organize the resources, services, and users within a domain in a nested hierarchical tree structure.

Objects and OUs

Objects are the items that are organized in the Active Directory. The objects can be anything that the schema allows, such as users, groups, printers, servers, and so on.

The objects are stored in OUs, which then become an administrative tool for grouping objects in a hierarchical system similar to a filesystem on a hard drive. The interesting concept about OUs is that they are themselves a type of object. A user can be granted access rights to an OU for administration purposes, while another user would not have administrative access to that OU even though that other user has administrative rights elsewhere within the same domain.

Organizational and Network Infrastructures

An Active Directory should be designed to take advantage of the network infrastructure and work seamlessly with the enterprise organization. When designing an Active Directory, keep in mind the following issues:

A forest can be anywhere and everywhere. It does not matter what the network infrastructure is like, or what the logical organization of the enterprise is. A single forest consists of multiple namespaces representing domain trees that trust each other and share a common schema, configuration name context, and GC. There can be multiple forests in a single internetwork. Multiple forests do not need to be created for administrative purposes or security purposes, but may be desirable to separate test network information from production network information.

Domains have the same characteristics traffic-wise as they did in the legacy Windows NT system. Domains have more replication, query, and authentication traffic within their confines than they do between them. As a result, domains should be designed to encompass high-speed and reliable LAN and WAN connections, but should probably not encompass low-speed and unreliable WAN connections.

OUs can be designed to match the administrative delegation within the enterprise. If an existing Windows NT domain structure had two domains in order to separate the administrative duties, now they can be combined into a single domain with two OUs to provide the same administrative delegation. Nesting an OU within another OU is also appropriate to further delegate administrative duties.

Nesting OUs has an impact on authentication traffic over the network. Group policies can be applied to each OU in a nested system. As each group policy is processed down nested OUs in the tree, the authentication traffic increases. However, this is not an issue if there are no group policies, which are inherited by their contained objects, applied to those OUs.

Microsoft has created a flexible, scalable, and hierarchical architecture for the Active Directory. It can function on any internetwork, and meet the security and administrative requirements of any enterprise organization. The Active Directory can take networks into the next millennium with Windows 2000.

Summary

There are all sorts of directory services available on networks. These range from vendor-specific directories to directory service standards, and can include flat files and hierarchical tree structures. A directory service, however, is simply a repository that is available for network participants to look up information about users, services, or resources on the network. Exchange Server, Novell Directory Services, Domain Name System, and Banyan Vines are all examples of different types of directory services.

The Active Directory Service (ADS) was developed by Microsoft to provide a best-in-class directory service solution to the new Windows 2000 Server family. ADS is implemented as a distributed database using multi-master replication. It provides a hierarchical tree structure that supports delegated administration and can scale from small networks to enterprise internetworks.

ADS consists of the following components:

- **Namespace**: A DNS name structure of *subdomain.domain.com* whose root domain name can be shared by domains through subdivision by subdomains.

- **Domain**: A set of computers and users and other resources that participate in a single domain namespace, and share a single schema, configuration, and global catalog (GC).

- **Domain tree**: A set of domains that share the same root domain namespace, but differ by the use of subdomains, and have the same schema, configuration, and GC.

- **Forest**: A set of multiple domains that have multiple namespaces among them, but share the same schema, configuration, and GC.

- **Organizational unit**: A container for objects within a domain.

- **Object**: A user account, service, or resource that is represented within the Active Directory. Objects have attributes that are assigned values to describe each one specifically.

- **Schema**: The set of objects and their attributes that can possibly exist within the Active Directory.

- **Site**: A set of IP subnets that define a physical location for servers.

The Active Directory Service encompasses both the physical structure of the internetwork and the logical structure of the enterprise organization. In order to prepare for an Active Directory implementation, both of these areas must be fully documented and understood.

Once this information has been gathered, it should then be reviewed for the impact it may have on the Active Directory design. In this way, the optimal design for ADS can begin to take shape. See Chapter 3, "Active Directory Naming Strategies," for more on design.

FAQs

Q: What is the difference between the legacy NT PDC and BDC and the Windows 2000 DC?

A: The legacy PDC is a single master of the domain database. The legacy BDC is a slave to the master in its own domain. All changes must be made at the PDC, which makes it a single point of failure. If the PDC goes down, any BDCs on the network are available with a read-only copy of the security database. If changes must be made to the security database, one of those BDCs must be promoted to the PDC, or the PDC must be brought back online. In Windows 2000, each domain controller (DC) holds a read-write copy of the Active Directory. The architecture uses multi-master replication between all DCs. Changes can be made to any DC and then replicated throughout the internetwork.

Q: I have a test network and a production network. I want to make sure that users do not see my test lab users when they query the Global Catalog (GC). Should I put my lab servers in the same forest as the production servers?

A: Not if you want them to have a different GC. Since a forest shares the same schema, configuration, and GC, the test network should not be part of the same forest as the production network. If testing a new application that extends the schema, using a different forest will prevent extra objects and attributes from being added to the production schema. The configuration can be changed for the test forest without impact on the production network by using separate forests. Finally, a separate test forest will prevent test users from showing up in the GC.

Q: Our company has an Internet site called company.com, and we are planning to add an intranet site. We want the intranet to use the Active Directory security mechanisms. Can we use the same namespace for the intranet?

A: It is not recommended to use the same namespace for internal resources (the intranet) as for external resources (the Internet site). It can cause problems with Active Directory since it uses DNS for its locator service. There are two options: Either use a subdomain (sub.company.com), or use a different namespace altogether (mycompany.com).

Chapter 2

Migrating from NT 3.51 and NT 4 to Active Directory

Solutions in this chapter:

- Active Directory Service Installation
- Windows 2000 Migration Strategies
- Delegating Administrative Authority
- Adding to Multi-Master Replication
- Migrating Users and Groups
- Migrating from Novell NetWare

Upgrading a server, which everyone is used to using, causes more problems than installing an entirely new network from the ground up. An upgrade requires a significant investment in preparing for the migration. The migration typically must take place over a weekend and during evenings so it will not interrupt users during business hours. And the migration team must develop a contingency plan—just in case th emigration fails or there is some form of data loss. New installs do not have these issues, although it is usually preferred that they take place during evenings and weekends to avoid business interruptions.

Introduction

There is a whole slew of prep work to complete in order to migrate any operating system successfully. When migrating to a new directory service, the prep work is increased even more by all the planning that is needed. A migration project consists of the following basic phases:

1. **Envisioning.** The migration team is assembled, and the members of the team determine the business requirements and vision for the Active Directory and Windows 2000.

2. **Planning.** The technical requirements for the Active Directory and Windows 2000 are defined, the tasks to complete them are determined, the resources for the project are gathered, and team members are assigned tasks and given dates and milestones.

3. **Developing.** A lab or test system is created where the migration team can test the proposed technical configuration and ensure that it meets the business requirements defined in the Envisioning phase; the team may develop an automated installation process and a quality assurance process, and will deploy a pilot group of users to ensure success.

4. **Deploying.** Windows 2000 and Active Directory are installed across the production network, clients are granted access to the Active Directory, the system is assured to be stable through quality assurance, and the systems are turned over to the operations support staff.

Your migration project will probably encompass more planning and development issues than are described here. Each enterprise has its own business requirements and usually an existing internetwork with its own technical requirements. The project must take into account these factors when planning things such as the Active Directory security strategy or Domain Name System (DNS) requirements.

TIP

Before beginning your migration, make sure to have your Active Directory sites, forest, domain, and organizational unit (OU) structure documented, as well as your DNS strategy and your security strategy. For more information on these subjects, review Chapters 3, 4, and 7.

Server Migration Strategies

To determine the strategy for migrating servers, the first task to complete is to examine the existing domain structure and network environment. In addition, standard Active Directory planning tasks, which are discussed in Chapter 3, "Active Directory Naming Strategies," should be undertaken.

1. Develop a DNS namespace and domain plan.
2. Create a forest plan.
3. Devise the OU hierarchy.
4. Create the Site topology plan

The planning tasks will involve documentation of the existing network. Most organizations have some documentation already existing for their networks. This documentation should be gathered, and if not current, updated to represent the present network. The documentation will validate the design plans and must include the information listed in Table 2.1.

Table 2.1 Analysis Requirements

Documented Item	Purpose	Example Usage
Network server hardware	To determine compatibility, and if not compatible, an upgrade strategy.	Refer to the Microsoft Windows 2000 Hardware Compatability List (HCL) or to www.hardware-update.com
Applications running on the servers	To determine compatibility, and if not compatible, an upgrade or replacement strategy.	Refer to application vendor's site or Microsoft Application Compatibility List at www.microsoft.com/ windows/server/deploy/ compatible/default.asp.
Network infrastructure	To determine the bandwidth available to new network traffic, assist in the domain and site designs; if not sufficient, to determine an upgrade strategy, to assist with protocol requirements.	Review large DNS zone transfers, replication traffic, and other traffic design needs.
Server locations and functions	To deΩtermine which servers are best as domain controllers (DCs) and DNS servers, to determine site locations.	Dedicated file or Web servers, PDCs or BDCs. Review functions and needs by users.
Security policies	To assist in the design of domains and group policies, to determine which security components to include in the Active Directory.	Account policies in User Manager for Domains. Review functions and needs for network.

Once the network documentation has been gathered and the design completed, the migration strategy must be planned. Although there are many methods of doing this, the following is a solid approach. First, look at the forest plan. If there is a single forest, then selecting a forest is easy. If there are multiple forests, the optimal selection is to migrate the forest that is least likely to have an impact on production if the migration fails for any reason.

For example, The Honey Bee Corporation has three namespaces: honeybeeswax.com, honeybee.com, and workerbee.com. The worker-bee.com namespace is dedicated to a lab network, and the other two namespaces are on the production network. The Honey Bee Corporation decided to have two forests, one for the lab network and the other for the production network. For their migration strategy, then, the forest least likely to cause problems when it is migrated is the lab network forest, of which the root is the workerbee.com DNS namespace. Figure 2.1 illustrates the Honey Bee Corporation forest plan including subdomains.

Figure 2.1 Honey Bee forest plan.

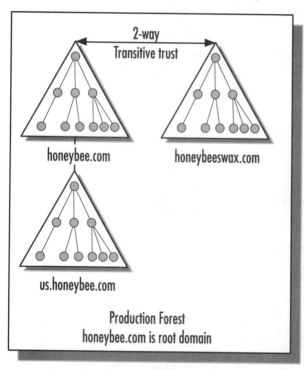
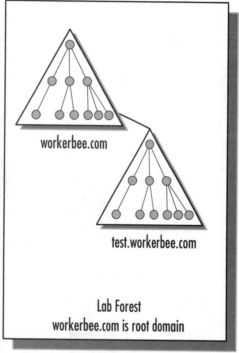

There are two options for migrating each domain when migrating a legacy Windows NT domain structure. There will be a domain upgrade, or there will be a domain restructuring. A domain upgrade is simply migrating each domain to a Windows 2000 domain. This method begins with the upgrade of the primary domain controller (PDC), followed by the backup domain controllers (BDCs), and finally the member servers. A domain restructuring is a complete redesign of the domain structure either prior to or after the upgrade to Windows 2000. Because of the Active Directory capabilities for delegation of administration and site-centric traffic management, many organizations may consolidate their domain structure into a simpler design that still satisfies business requirements.

Deciding whether to upgrade or restructure is a matter of reviewing the optimal plans that the Active Directory can offer. Although a legacy Windows NT domain structure may satisfy many business requirements, simply upgrading it to the Active Directory may not be the optimal Active Directory design. Take a company that has two business units, Payroll and Service, that each have separate administration. A legacy domain structure would be two separate domains, even though the two business units may share the same facilities, as illustrated in Figure 2.2.

Figure 2.2 Legacy domains can cross physical boundaries.

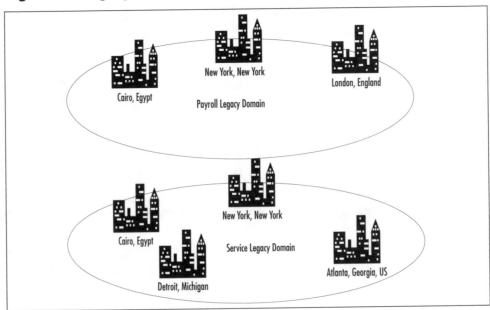

If this company simply upgraded the existing domains from NT to Windows 2000 Active Directory domains, the network would experience more traffic than necessary. Network traffic within a domain is higher than that between domains. When the traffic from two separate domains travels across the same links, it is not optimal for the network because there is higher bandwidth utilization. In Figure 2.2, there would be more traffic in the links between Cairo, Egypt or New York, New York and every other site because of the two domains having domain controllers (DCs) in those sites.

However, if the company with these two legacy domains restructured into a single larger domain under Active Directory, it would not experience the higher bandwidth utilization. The company could easily create OUs to delegate administration in the restructured domain. It would use sites within the domain to centralize traffic at each of the locations.

An organization can best evaluate whether to upgrade or restructure by starting with a blank page. If there were no domain structure in place, what would be the optimal Active Directory domain for the organization? If that domain structure matches the existing domain structure, an upgrade path is best. Otherwise, the organization should consider a restructuring process.

TIP

If you plan a new domain structure and realize that there are more domains in the Active Directory than there were in the legacy structure, you will want to revisit your plans. The Active Directory can be optimized in a simple structure. The more simple the structure, the easier it is to manage the Active Directory.

The first domain that is created in a forest is the root domain. This means that the first set of DCs that must be installed and/or migrated must belong to the root domain. Take the Honey Bee Corporation, for example. In the lab network, there is a single DNS namespace with the root domain of workerbee.com. As its first task, Honey Bee Corporation simply migrates an existing lab server acting as a PDC over to the workerbee.com domain as a DC. The remaining servers designated for that domain are then migrated, starting with the BDCs and ending with the member servers. After migrating the root domain, Honey Bee Corporation follows the namespace down to the subdomain test.workerbee.com and begins by migrating servers. Honey Bee Corporation does not have another domain in the lab to migrate, so it migrates member servers and then promotes some of them to DCs using the Active Directory Wizard to create the new domain.

Figure 2.3 Migration strategy for a single domain.

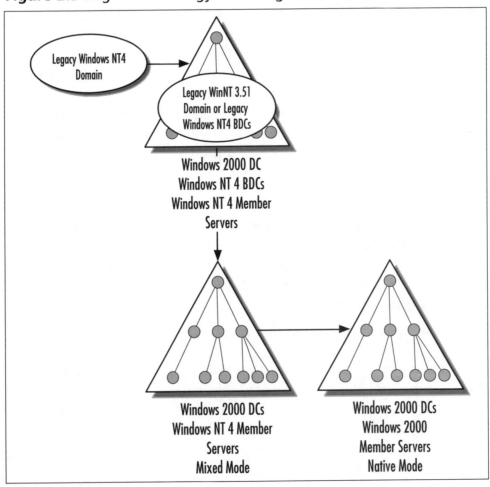

The following are high-level overviews of the migration process. If you have vertigo, be careful—we are more than 1,000 feet up from the tactical steps of actually deploying.

If there are multiple forests, one must be selected for the first migration. As stated previously, the first forest migrated should be the one with the least impact on the daily production network. Once the forest has been selected, the forest migration strategy is as follows:

1. Migrate the root domain first. If creating a new root domain instead of migrating an existing domain, then create the root domain first. Figure 2.3 illustrates the process of migrating a single domain to Windows 2000.

2. Completely migrate the root domain before starting the next domain. When migrating from an existing Windows NT domain to an Active Directory domain, there will probably be a period of time during which the domain works in *mixed mode*. A mixed-mode domain has at least one Windows 2000 Server DC and one or more legacy Windows NT BDCs. Transitive trusts are only supported in *native mode*. A native-mode domain just has Windows 2000 DCs. For this reason, each domain should be migrated in its entirety before migrating the next domain in the Active Directory forest. A migrated domain will remain in mixed mode even after all the DCs have been upgraded to Windows 2000 until the Network Administrator switches it to native mode.

3. Follow the DNS namespace for each domain thereafter so that each domain tree is migrated completely before migrating the next domain tree. For example, if migrating the root.com first, the second domain to be migrated is trunk.root.com, and the third is leaf.trunk.root.com.

4. When migrating the next domain tree, start at the root of its namespace and work through each domain to the end of the domains. For example, after migrating the root.com domain tree, migrate the nextdomaintree.com and its subdomains trunk.nextdomaintree.com and leaf.trunk.nextdomaintree.com in that respective order.

Within the forest, each domain must be migrated completely before starting the next. The domain servers have their own migration strategy.

1. Complete all preparation work of cleaning users, groups, and applications. Perform a full backup of the PDC before migrating.

2. When migrating, begin with the PDC first. Even if you intend to have newly installed Windows 2000 servers installed as DCs, you must migrate the PDC before installing the new Windows 2000 servers. If you attempt to install an Active Directory DC into an existing Windows NT 4.0 domain with an existing PDC, it will fail. An Active Directory DC cannot exist in the same domain with a legacy PDC.

3. Perform a full backup of each BDC before migrating it.

4. After the PDC has been migrated, the BDCs should be migrated next.

5. Perform a full backup of each member server before migrating.

6. After all DCs have been migrated, the member servers should be migrated to Windows 2000.

7. The last step in the domain migration is to perform a quality assurance check to verify the printers, clients, users, and other resources that were migrated.

Domain restructuring is the migration strategy for merging two or more domains into a single Active Directory domain. This may be necessary if the domain and DNS plan collapses domains in favor of using sites to manage the physical network traffic and using OUs for delegating administration. The destination domain is the one in which all the users, computers, and resources will reside when migrated to the Active Directory (see Figure 2.4).

1. Begin by migrating legacy NT domains to the destination domain first, or create a new domain for destination by installing at least two Active Directory DCs. By installing more than one DC, additional copies of the Active Directory exist for fault tolerance.

2. Move user and group accounts into the destination domain from the other domains.

3. Move computers and member servers into the destination domain from the other domains.

4. Back up data on merging DCs from the other domains and run fresh installation into the Active Directory domain as DCs, or as member servers if they are no longer needed as DCs.

5. Reinstall applications on the newly installed servers.

6. Restore backup data to the newly installed servers.

7. Upgrade member servers into the Active Directory domain as members.

8. Verify resources, users, groups, and computers as a final quality assurance check.

Figure 2.4 Domain restructure: collapsing domains into a single Active Directory domain.

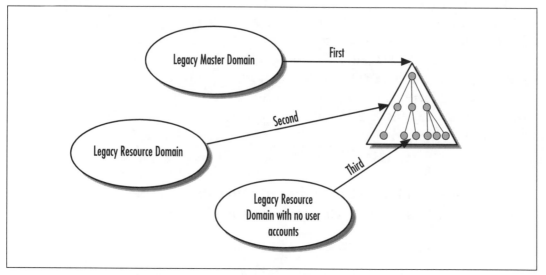

Primary Domain Controllers (PDCs)

Some preparation should be completed prior to migrating a PDC. The first effort is in streamlining the domain. Before starting this, a complete backup should be executed in case some account was

For IT Professionals

Cleaning Up the Legacy Domain

Migrations tend to be more of a problem than fresh installations because they pull along all the old problems that were sitting in the legacy domain. The domain upgrade migration takes the entire legacy NT domain Security Accounts Manager (SAM) and translates it to the corresponding Active Directory components. If there is an empty NT global group, it will be migrated. If user accounts still exist for people who have left the organization, they will be migrated. If there is a right to access a resource that may have been granted in error to a local group, it will be migrated. If there are permissions granted to resources that have since been moved or deleted, they will be migrated.

Not only do these objects cause a security risk, but the additional objects will increase the time it takes to upgrade the SAM to the Active Directory. This is additional time that is completely unnecessary, because after being migrated, cleaning up those objects would still require the same amount of time as before. Cleaning up the legacy domain is a vital step in the migration process!

deleted that should have been retained. After that, the Network Administrator has the following tasks to complete:

1. Delete old user accounts.

2. Delete the home directories associated with the old user accounts.

3. Remove empty groups.

4. Consolidate groups and simplify the group structure.

5. Remove computer accounts from the domain if they are no longer used.

6. Verify that the domain security policies are correct.

7. Simplify protocols so that only TCP/IP (if possible) is used.

8. Verify and validate the DNS, DHCP, and WINS configurations.

9. Make sure that existing DNS systems support Service Locator Resource Records (SRV) and, preferably, also support dynamic updates.

10. Update Windows NT and any applications with the latest service packs.

11. Convert the filesystem to NT File System (NTFS) on all DCs.

12. Verify that the server hardware is compatible with Windows 2000.

13. Make sure that any NT v4.0 clients are upgraded with the latest service pack.

14. Uninstall third-party backup programs and virus detection programs. These applications have been proven to cause failures during Windows 2000 upgrades.

15. Run WINNT32 /CHECKUPGRADEONLY from the Windows 2000 setup files to ensure that the server can be upgraded.

Before migrating any servers, a test should be conducted. This pilot migration should verify not only that the migration will work, but that a contingency plan to back out of the Windows 2000 migration will also work. One way to do this is by creating a backout BDC. The tasks involved in creating a backout BDC are as follows:

1. Use legacy Windows NT servers with hardware comparable to that available on the production network.

2. Back up each pilot server.

3. Create a synchronized BDC for the domain.

4. Remove the synchronized BDC from the domain.

5. Execute the migration with the PDC first.

6. Recover the domain with the BDC.

7. Repeat the process, but recover the domain using the backup tape.

Changes Required When Upgrading a Domain Controller

When legacy NT 4.0 DCs are upgraded to Windows 2000, two components on the network must typically be upgraded as well.

- DNS
- NTFS

Active Directory requires DNS in order to function. The DNS server must support SRV because they are used to locate Windows 2000 DCs. Another feature that can facilitate DNS administration is dynamic update protocol. If upgrading an existing Windows NT 4.0 DC that is also a DNS server, these capabilities are automatically upgraded with the new Windows 2000 DNS. If a DNS server does not support these features, it must be upgraded.

Active Directory DCs must have NTFS in order for Active Directory to be installed. If the server is already running NTFS v4.0, it will be upgraded to NTFS v5.0. If the server is not running NTFS, the file system must be converted to NTFS in order for the Active Directory to be installed.

Backup Domain Controllers (BDCs)

Before upgrading the domain, one recovery method is to prepare a recovery BDC. This BDC is useful if there is a need to roll back changes if something goes wrong. The first thing to do is make sure that the legacy Windows NT domain has a BDC. If it does not, a BDC should be installed.

The BDC should have a copy of each of the services that are running on the PDC. For example, if the PDC is also a DNS server, DNS should be installed and configured on the BDC. Other services that should be copied are DHCP, WINS, and any business-critical messaging, print, and file services. A backup copy of the data used by each of these services should be placed on the BDC. There is no need to start any of these services unless there is a failure.

The BDC should be synchronized with the PDC so that it has the most current security account data in it. This can be done through the Server Manager utility, shown in Figure 2.5. The steps you take to synchronize the entire domain, including the recovery BDC, are to click the Computer menu and then click Synchronize Entire Domain.

Figure 2.5 Synchronizing a legacy domain.

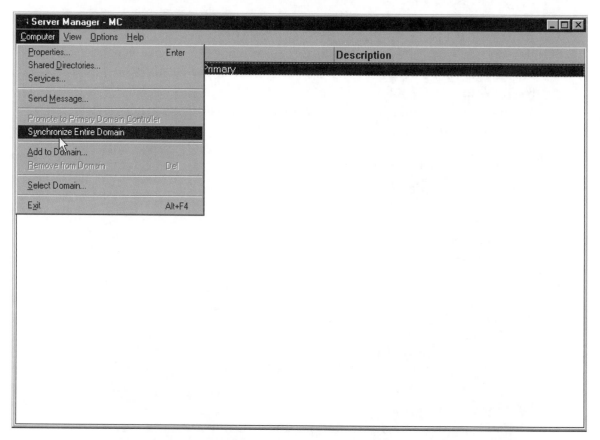

After synchronizing, the BDC should be taken offline. An interim step can be taken before taking the BDC offline to ensure that the network is recoverable. This process is to promote the BDC to a PDC and verify that each service will work. If that is successful, then promote the former PDC back to the PDC, which automatically demotes the recovery machine to a BDC. After verifying data integrity, simply shut the recovery BDC down and take it off the network.

For IT Professionals

About Windows NT 3.51

Migrating computers from one operating system to another can be a dilemma. There are issues with application compatibility and hardware compatibility—especially when th operating systems have great differences. It is more likely for a successful migration.

ify that each service will work. If that is succe from Windows NT 4.0 to Windows 2000 than it is for a migration from Windows NT 3.51 to Windows 2000.

The Windows NT 3.51 operating system is ancient in terms of software age. When it was developed, computers in the workplace tended to be 486s. The Windows 2000 operating system does not support most of the computers that were around when Windows NT 3.51 was developed.

Even if the hardware is compatible, the applications may not work. Applications that were developed to be installed into either Windows NT 3.5x or Windows NT 4.0 tended to create different registry keys for each operating system at the time of installation. Migrating the more similar Windows NT 4.0 may work, but migrating from Windows NT 3.51 probably will have errors and issues.

To solve these issues, an incremental upgrade strategy may succeed better than a direct upgrade. For instance, the Windows NT 3.51 computers can first be upgraded to Windows NT 4.0. After that is completed, the computers can be upgraded to Windows 2000.

Two known issues regarding using Windows NT 3.51 in a Windows 2000 environment involve authentication and SIDHistory. Authentication problems occur when a user from a Windows 2000 account domain attempts to access a resource on a Windows NT 3.51 server in a resource domain. The Windows NT 3.51 domain does not construct tokens including any groups except those from the account domain that the user is logging in

Continued

For IT Professionals

About Windows NT 3.51

from. This is unlike the behavior of both Windows NT 4.0 and Windows 2000 and may result in a denial of access to a resource, or access to a resource that should be denied.

Member Servers

Member servers are designated as resources in both the legacy Windows NT domains and the Active Directory domains. A member server does not have a copy of the domain security accounts or active directory. Instead, member servers provide services to users such as file and print services, Web services, databases, messaging, remote access, and so on.

A user can gain access to the member server either by authenticating through the domain in which the member server is a part, or authenticating to a domain that trusts the member server's domain, or authenticating to the member server's local accounts database. The local accounts database, which is the local SAM on legacy Windows NT servers, stores a set of local users and local groups. The SAM participates in the registry.

Promoting Member Servers with Dcpromo

Even though a server was a member server in a legacy Windows NT domain, it can easily be promoted to an Active Directory DC after it is upgraded to Windows 2000 Server. This is a change from legacy Windows NT where DCs had to be specified during installation only. The legacy NT server's role could not be changed afterward. Now, the server can be promoted to a DC and demoted to a member server whenever deemed necessary.

Windows 2000 Server provides a tool with which to promote a member server to a DC: the Active Directory Wizard, or DCPRO-MO.EXE. As a member server, the Windows 2000 Server uses DNS

to contact a DC and check to make sure that requesting users actually have the correct rights to use whatever resource they are
requesting. When a member server is promoted to a DC, the server
copies the Active Directory locally. As a DC, the server simply uses
its local database to ensure that there are appropriate permissions.
The Active Directory Users and Computers Management Console
enables a Network Administrator to manage the database for user
permissions from any DC.

Another change that occurs when a member server is promoted
to a DC is that it can now make changes to the Active Directory on
its locally stored database. The server then participates in the replication topology, which increases the traffic between it and its peer
DCs on the network.

Upgrading with the Windows 2000 Setup Wizard

The final step before upgrading a legacy Windows NT server to
Windows 2000 is to run the WINNT32 setup file with the /CHECK-
UPGRADEONLY switch. This action will be a final verification that
the server can be upgraded.

If upgrading directly from the CD-ROM, after inserting it, the
dialog box shown in Figure 2.6 will appear. If upgrading from a network share, this prompt does not appear.

Figure 2.6 Upgrading from the CD-ROM.

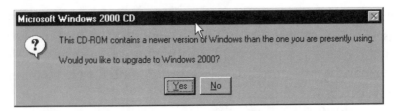

The installation wizard begins with the screen shown in Figure 2.7. This dialog lets the installer select between an upgrade of the existing server, or a new installation of Windows 2000 in a different directory. The second option creates a dual boot machine.

Figure 2.7 Selecting between an upgrade and a new install.

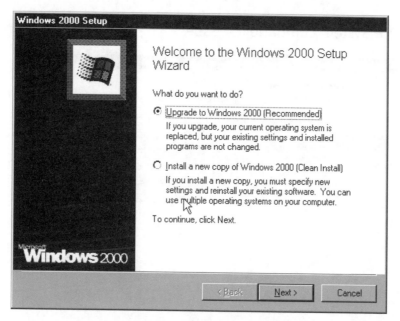

The second wizard screen is a standard license agreement dialog. After selecting the agreement option and clicking NEXT, the third screen appears as shown in Figure 2.8. This screen is significant because it will show any running services or programs that are known to be incompatible with Windows 2000 Server. If any of these services or programs are vital to the production network, the following steps should be taken:

1. Click DETAILS and investigate the compatibility issue.

2. If the answers are not satisfactory that the installation can continue, click CANCEL and bail out of the setup program.

3. Further investigate the compatibility by checking Microsoft's Web site at www.microsoft.com and the vendor's Web site.

4. Create a strategy for removing, replacing, or upgrading the application.

5. Upgrade or replace the application, or uninstall it.

6. Begin setting up Windows 2000 Server again.

Figure 2.8 System compatibility issues.

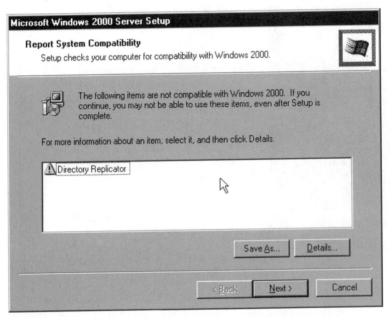

After clicking NEXT in the System Compatibility dialog, the rest of the installation continues without user input. Files are copied. The system reboots automatically and enters the Windows 2000 text mode setup portion. This completes without user interaction and automatically reboots. The Windows 2000 Server graphical setup completes without need for user input. After a final reboot, the server starts for the first time as a Windows 2000 Server. If the upgraded server was a PDC or BDC on a legacy NT domain, the Active Directory Wizard begins automatically.

Installing Active Directory Services

The Active Directory Wizard installs Active Directory Services. This wizard is available from the Windows 2000 Configure Your Server screen, or can be prompted with the DCPROMO.EXE command.

The Active Directory Wizard branches out at each screen to enable you to install the right configuration. Table 2.2 lists the steps you need to take to reach the configuration you desire.

Table 2.2 Active Directory Installation Scenarios

Prior Server Role	Action	Resulting Role	Resulting Domain and Forest	Steps in Active Directory Wizard
Domain controller (DC)	Demote	Member server	N/A	1. Click NEXT for first screen. 2. If this server is also a Global Catalog Server (GCS), a warning message will pop up. Click OK to confirm. 3. If this is the last DC in the domain, check the box. Click NEXT. 4. Provide the Administrator name and password that is authorized to remove this DC. Click NEXT. 5. Provide a password for the new local Administrator account. Click NEXT. 6. Click NEXT on the Summary, then click FINISH.
Member server	Promote	First domain controller in new domain	Root domain in new forest	1. Click NEXT for first screen. 2. Select "Domain controller in new domain." 3. Select "Create a New Domain tree." 4. Select "Create a New Forest." 5. Either select to configure the DNS client on the server or install and configure DNS

Continued

Prior Server Role	Action	Resulting Role	Resulting Domain and Forest	Steps in Active Directory Wizard
				on this server. 6. Give the new domain a DNS name. 7. Give the new domain a NetBIOS name. 8. Select a location for Active Directory files. 9. Select a location for the system volume. 10. Select whether users will access this domain via NT4 RAS servers. 11. Provide the password to be used for Active Directory restore.
Member server	Promote	Additional domain controller in existing domain	Any domain in any forest	1. Click NEXT for first screen. 2. Select "Additional domain controller in existing domain." 3. If the DNS client is not configured on this server, this will need to be done prior to continuing through Active Directory setup. 4. Select a location for Active Directory files. 5. Select a location for the system volume. 6. Provide a password to restore Active Directory.
Member server	Promote	First domain controller in new domain	Subdomain in existing domain tree	1. Click NEXT for first screen. 2. Select "Domain controller in new domain." 3. Select "Create a new child domain in an existing tree." 4. Either select to configure the DNS client or install and configure DNS on this server. 5. Give the new domain a DNS name.

Continued

Prior Server Role	Action	Resulting Role	Resulting Domain and Forest	Steps in Active Directory Wizard
				6. Give the new domain a NetBIOS name. 7. Select a location for Active Directory files. 8. Select a location for the system volume. 9. Select whether this domain will have NT4 RAS servers. 10. Provide a password to restore Active Directory.
Member server	Promote	First domain controller in new domain	New domain tree in existing forest	1. Click NEXT for first screen. 2. Select "Domain controller in new domain." 3. Select "Create a New Domain tree." 4. Select "Place this new domain tree in an existing forest." 5. Either select to configure the DNS client on this server or install and configure DNS on this server. 6. Give the new domain a DNS name. 7. Give the new domain a NetBIOS name. 8. Select a location for Active Directory files. 9. Select a location for the system volume. 10. Select whether this domain will have NT4 RAS servers. 11. Provide a password to restore Active Directory.

Interim Mixed Domains

A mixed-mode domain is one that includes both Windows NT 4.0 BDCs and Windows 2000 DCs. This should not be confused with *native mode*, which is discussed in this section. There are some benefits to having mixed domains:

- Multi-master replication can occur for the Windows 2000 DC that acts as a PDC.

- The Network Administrator can retain Windows NT 4 BDCs for as long as needed and still be able to use Windows 2000 Server features.

There are drawbacks to using the mixed-mode domains:

- The domain size is constrained by Windows NT 4 requirements for maximum number of 40,000 objects.

- The Network Administrator cannot implement new Active Directory security groups, such as Universal Groups.

- Other features for the Active Directory are not completely implemented until the domain is changed to native mode. These features are listed in Table 2.3.

For IT Professionals

What Happened to NetBIOS?

NetBIOS does not go away in Windows 2000; instead, it is present as a backward compatibility feature for legacy Windows NT. You may not see the word "NetBIOS," but the "Down-level name" that appears in various dialog boxes and installation screens is the NetBIOS name.

Mixed Mode

After migrating the PDC and while running in mixed mode, the new Windows 2000 DC will act as a PDC Emulator in the domain. There is only one PDC Emulator in the domain, regardless of the number of Windows 2000 DCs. The PDC Emulator acts as a PDC for nonmigrated BDCs and clients. It will handle password changes for clients and BDCs, act as a Windows NT Master Browser, and provide the replication source for BDCs.

Table 2.3 Active Directory Features and Mode Compatibility

Active Directory Features	Native Mode Function	Mixed-Mode Function
Kerberos transitive trusts	Available	Available
Kerberos authentication	Available	Available only on Windows 2000 DCs and utilized by Win2k clients and other Kerberos clients
Organizational units (OUs)	Available	Available but only can be administered using Windows 2000 tools
Active Directory scalability	Available	Available only when no DCs are running NT4
Active Directory security groups (nested groups)	Available	Not available; can only use legacy Local and Global groups
Multi-master replication	Available	Only available on Windows 2000 DCs
Group Policy	Available	Only available on Windows 2000 Servers
Netlogon Replication	Not available; replaced by the File Replication System (FRS).	Available as a backwards compatibility feature for NT 4 BDCs.

Native Mode

Native mode domains are those that only have Windows 2000 DCs and have been manually changed to native mode. After upgrading the PDC, the BDCs should be upgraded as soon as possible. This will enable the domain to be switched to native mode, at which point clients and servers alike will be able to participate in the Active Directory advanced features. Once a domain is in native mode, it cannot be switched back.

For example, in mixed mode, the domain will be limited to a total number of 40,000 objects, whereas in native mode this number can be at least 1 million. To switch a domain to native mode, start the Active Directory Users and Computers console by clicking Start | Programs | Administrative Tools, and then selecting Active Directory Users and Computers. In the left pane, click on the domain that will be changed to native mode. From the Action menu, choose the Properties option. When the properties dialog appears, on the General tab that is shown in Figure 2.9, click CHANGE MODE.

Figure 2.9 Switching to native mode.

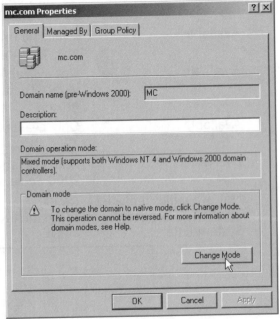

Migrating Components

When performing a domain upgrade, the domain components, such as users and groups, are migrated automatically. However, restructuring domains into a single Active Directory domain will require components to be migrated. The scenarios listed in Table 2.4 will apply to a domain restructure that requires migration of components.

Table 2.4 Restructuring Scenarios

Restructure	Process
New forest migration	Create a new forest of Windows 2000 servers and migrate components from existing legacy Windows NT domains. Take existing domains offline and remove. The process for a new forest migration is illustrated in Figure 2.10.
Merge domains	Perform domain upgrade of those legacy domains that will participate in the new forest, then migrate components from the remaining legacy Windows NT domains. Take legacy Windows NT domains offline and remove.
Split domains	Create a new domain and migrate components from the legacy NT domain. Delete the components from the legacy NT domain that remain within the Active Directory. Either create a new domain and migrate the remaining components, or perform a domain upgrade.

Using Organizational Units (OUs) to Create a Hierarchical Structure

Even when upgrading a domain, the OUs will need to be established and users moved into the correct container OUs. When restructuring domains, one of the first steps is to create a hierarchical structure for each domain with OUs before migrating the components.

OUs are created in the Active Directory Users and Computers Management Console. They should be planned out prior to being created, and typically provide one of four functions:

Figure 2.10 Domain migration.

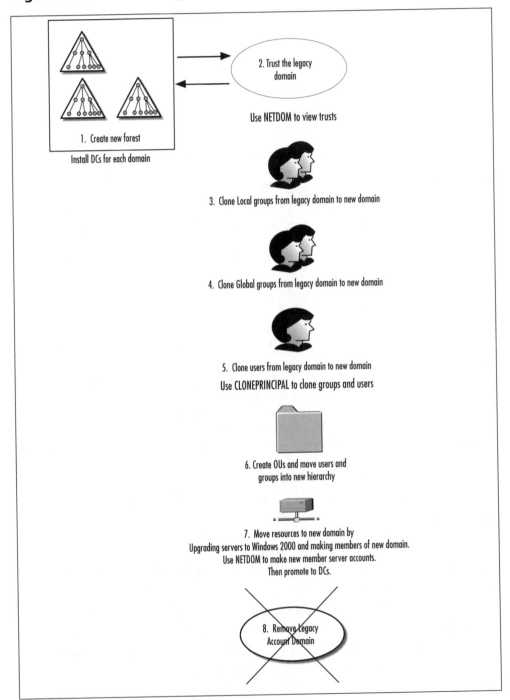

- Delegating administration
- Hiding objects
- Applying group policy
- Organizing objects logically

The OUs designated for delegating administration will typically be the top-level OUs in the hierarchy because that will simplify the administrative structure. Administrators may be separated by geography or by business unit. There may also be levels of administrative authority, such that some Administrators have more control over more objects or properties than others. When delegating administration, the highest level of administrative authority should be granted at the top, and then lesser authority in OUs further down the tree. Below those top levels, the OUs for hiding objects and applying group policy will further organize objects.

User Accounts

Network Administrators usually want the users migrated along with their rights to network resources. The only way to accomplish this feat is to make sure that when a user is migrated from one domain to another, and that user account belongs to one or more Global groups, the Global groups are moved as well. Some Global groups associate users with network resources via ACLs. In order to maintain users access to those resources, both the users and the group must be migrated at the same time.

One utility used for migrating user accounts is called ClonePrincipal. The name is derived from the fact that it can clone a security principal. Security principals are users and groups. ClonePrincipal uses customizable Visual Basic scripts for migrating objects incrementally to the Active Directory from a legacy Windows NT domain. The migration of Global groups is discussed later in this chapter.

Another utility that can migrate user accounts is the Active Directory Migration Tool (ADMT), described in Chapter 11, "Plugging Into The Active Directory."

How to Hide Objects

Sometimes Administrators do not want some objects to be seen in the tree, even when users do not have the authority to view their attributes. One use of OUs is to place one or more objects into OUs and limit the ability of users to see the objects in the entire OU by removing the List Contents for those OUs. To hide objects in this way:

1. Open the Active Directory Users and Computers Management Console.
2. Navigate to the OU where you will place the hidden objects.
3. Right-click on the OU and select Properties.
4. Click on the Security property page.
5. Revoke all permissions by removing them from the Security property page.
6. Click Advanced.
7. Uncheck the box for Inherit Permissions from Parent, and click Ok to return to the Security property page.
8. Add the groups that need to have rights to this OU on the Security property page with the appropriate rights.
9. Add any objects into the OU that you want hidden from users' view.

Machine Accounts

Machine accounts are comprised of both Windows for Workgroups, Windows NT and Windows 2000 computers. Some of those machine accounts can be clients, and others can be servers and DCs.

Each legacy Windows NT computer has its own local SAM. Each SAM contains Local groups. In the legacy system, users became members of domain Global groups, and domain Global groups became members of computer Local groups. Then the Local groups were granted access to resources on the local machine. When migrating machine accounts, all the Local groups should be migrated as well.

Member servers and client computers can join new domains at the computer. From the Network Properties, there is a button enabling domain membership that can be changed to an Active Directory domain. However, the computer account must be available within the new domain, or the user making the change must have a name and password to an account with the proper administrative rights for joining a domain.

NETDOM is a command-line utility that can manage computer accounts, domains, and trust relationships. The NETDOM utility can perform the following functions:

- Add, remove, and query machine accounts in a domain, even specifying the OUs.
- Join Windows 2000 computers to a domain.
- Establish and manage a domain's trust relationships.

Nested Groups

Windows 2000 has four types of groups: Local, Domain Local, Domain Global, and Universal. A Local group is limited to resources within a single computer, but can have members from any trusted domains. Domain Local Groups are limited to resources within a single domain, but can have members from any trusted domains. Domain Global groups are capable of being granted access to any trusted domain, but can have members only from the local domain. Universal groups can be granted access to any trusted domain running in native mode, and can have members of both users and computers from within the local forest.

Nested groups are a method of reducing the numbers of members in an Active Directory group. Group memberships are limited to 5000 or fewer members. The limitation is placed on the group because an update to the group membership requires that the entire group's membership list be replicated.

Nested groups not only help reduce the number of members in a group, but also facilitate administration by enabling a master security group that can have multiple logical groups of users that share work functions.

The ability to nest the groups is available when the domain is in native mode, and nesting configurations are listed in Table 2.5. The reason for this is that legacy NT domains do not support nested groups. For backward compatibility, local groups can contain Global groups, which then contain user accounts.

Table 2.5 Nesting Groups in Native Mode

Container Group	Group Members	Other Members	Member Source
Universal group	Universal groups Global groups	User accounts Computer accounts	Any domain, same forest, or trusted
Global group	Global groups	User accounts	Same domain
Domain Local group	Universal groups Global groups	User accounts	Any domain, same forest, or explicitly trusted
Domain Local group	Domain Local group		Same domain

Global Groups

Since Global groups are security principals, migrating Global groups can be performed with the ClonePrincipal utility. To ensure that the correct users can access the correct resources through the migration of the Global group, the user accounts must be migrated at the same time.

Another method of moving a Global group is to recreate the group in the Active Directory and then add the correct members to it. The Global group is traditionally a holder of users and less likely to be granted access to resources directly. Instead, it was usually granted rights to resources by being made a member of Local groups that had those rights. So, in order to grant permissions to resources, the Global group must be made a member of other Local groups in the Active Directory that have those rights until the domain is switched out of mixed mode and into native mode. Once the domain is in native mode, the Global group can be changed to a Universal group or become a member of other Global, Universal, or Domain Local groups.

Delegating Administrative Authority

One reason for merging legacy NT domains that were used for ensuring separation of administration is to take advantage of Windows 2000 Active Directory for the delegation of administration. In the Active Directory, responsibility is delegated by the OU, but can be inherited by lower, nested OUs. This directly affects how OUs are designed, since the simplest design would place the highest level of administrative capabilities at the highest level of OUs. The migration strategy is to map out which users should have the highest level of administrative control, which should have partial control, and which may have the object- and attribute-level control. After completing that, delegate authority to those users at the top of the OU hierarchy for the full control, mid-level for partial control, and closest to the users for per-object and attribute control, as illustrated in Figure 2.11.

To start the Delegation of Control Wizard, in the Active Directory Users and Computers Management Console, right-click on an OU and select Delegate Control. As you follow the wizard through the steps needed for delegating control in the Active Directory, you will find that there are predefined roles. A Network Administrator should not limit himself to this predefined set, and should investigate the variety of permissions allowed by selecting the "Do customized delegation" instead of a predefined role. The Network Administrator can use the customized delegation to grant control over certain object types, such as only user accounts or only computer objects. To find out more about delegating control, see Chapter 4, "Designing a Domain Structure."

Figure 2.11 Delegation of administration design.

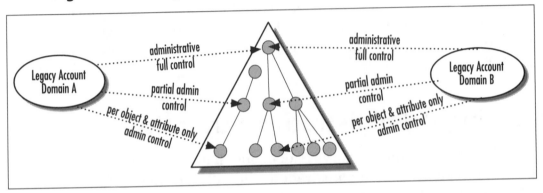

Insert into the Replication Topology

When there is a single DC in the Active Directory, there is no need to establish replication. Replication only concerns the DC computers in the Active Directory, because they hold the copies of the Active Directory databases. When there is a single DC, there is no other DC to replicate changes to or receive updates from.

The issues arise as soon as the second DC is installed. Now, there is a need to replicate something depending on whether the second DC is in the same site or a different site. Same site, or intra-site, replication occurs automatically. Each DC runs a service called a Knowledge Consistency Checker (KCC). The KCC generates an intrasite topology running over RPC (Remote Procedure Calls) whenever a new DC is installed into a site.

When a DC is installed into a different site, the Network Administrator has the option to let the KCC automatically generate the intersite replication topology, or to manually establish it. When the Network Administrator manually establishes the connections for replication, there is the opportunity to create bridgehead servers that direct the replication traffic over certain network links. To find out more about the replication system, see Chapter 8, "Planning and Implementing Sites."

Migrating from Novell Directory Services

Soon after Windows 2000's release, Services for NetWare will be provided as a new product to assist with NetWare migration. This product includes MSDSS. Many organizations have invested time and effort in creating a directory services tree (NDS) for Novell NetWare and then educating their users on navigating its specific OUs. The NDS model they used can be migrated to the Active Directory so that users have a familiar navigational structure to use. There is a Directory Services Migration tool used specifically for this process.

1. The Directory Services Migration tool must run on Windows 2000.

2. Network traffic is reduced if the Directory Services Migration tool runs on a DC.

3. The tool can be used for multiple migrations of NDS trees as well as legacy NetWare server binderies.

4. Each migration is established as an individual project within the tool. A migration can consist of a portion of an NDS tree or the entire tree itself. This enables an incremental migration.

5. Before beginning a migration, the Network Administrator should have complete documentation of the NDS design, administration, and groups. Additionally, the Administrator should have full documentation about the Active Directory design, administration, and groups.

6. The Active Directory should be readied to receive the new resources by having the domains, DCs, OUs, and groups already designed and implemented.

7. Each migration project begins with the selection of the Novell NetWare resources that will be imported offline. The Network Administrator has the option to change some of the resource properties to fit the Active Directory model. Then the offline project can be exported to the Active Directory. Additionally, files can be moved from NetWare servers to the Windows 2000 servers for any NetWare servers that will be taken offline through the tool. The project should end with a quality assurance check to ensure that the migration was successful.

Installing the Directory Service Migration tool is a matter of starting the Windows 2000 Configure Your Server from the Administrative Tools menu, then selecting the Add/Remove Windows Components selection. The Directory Service Migration tool can be found within the Management and Monitoring Tools Details section of components. Selecting this tool will automatically install Gateway Services for NetWare if it has not already been installed. The new Directory Service Migration tool can be found in the Administrative Tools menu.

After starting the Directory Service Migration tool, a new project must be created. To create a new project, click the Action menu and select New Project. After creating the project, the first item is finding what NetWare resources are available on the network. Creating a new view will start the Discover wizard and do just that. To create the view, right-click on the new project, select New and then View from NetWare. This step allows you to select the source users, groups, and containers that will be used for that project.

The objects are stored in an offline project database. The next step is to make any necessary changes to the objects, whether to conform to a new naming convention, establish new passwords, or move them into different containers.

The project data can be exported into the Active Directory next. This is done by right-clicking an object in the Directory Service Migration tool project, selecting Task from the popup menu, and then selecting Configure Object to NTDS. The Configure Objects to NTDS wizard will prompt for the Active Directory destination OU, and after clicking FINISH, the object will be exported. Migrating files is performed by right-clicking NDS volume objects in the project and selecting File Migrate from the popup menu.

Upgrade Clients to Windows 2000 Professional

Whether to upgrade a client workstation or not is a concern for many organizations. Some organizations have legacy applications that are not compatible with Windows 2000 Professional, although many will find comparable applications that are Windows 2000 compatible. Some will be faced with extra costs required to upgrade hardware to be compatible with Windows 2000 Professional, although many have planned for this change since the announcement of Windows 2000's release. All organizations will need to plan for user support and training. Even though the usability features of Windows 2000 can make end users more productive in the long run, there is a learning curve at first. These organizations must weigh these concerns against the overall benefits that Windows 2000 Professional can bring them:

- **Enhanced security**: Support for Smart Cards and the Public Key Infrastructure.

- **Enhanced reliability**: More reliable than previous versions of NT, fewer reboots when changing configuration of the workstation.

- **Enhanced usability**: Proven graphical user interface with improvements geared toward the way people work.

- **Enhanced performance**: Snappier performance.

- **Enhanced manageability**: Plugs right into the Active Directory and takes advantage of all the Active Directory management features.

Once a decision has been made to upgrade to Windows 2000 Professional at the desktop, there is a secondary decision about whether to upgrade the servers or the clients first. If an organization plans to roll out Windows 2000 Professional by using the Remote Installation Service (RIS) of Windows 2000 Server, the îwhich firstî decision is fairly obvious—Windows 2000 Server first. This decision is in line with long-standing networking best practices when deploying new netoworks:

1. Establish the network infrastructure first.
2. Security and servers next.
3. Workstations last.

NOTE

RIS is a new feature of Windows 2000 that enables the operating system to remotely install software from a central distribution point. It requires either a BIOS or chip on the Network Interface Card (NIC) that will enable it to be managed remotely. These chips are called PXE ("pixie"), which stands for Pre-eXecution Environment. PXE is part of the Wired for Management protocol set. Although these are not the only manufacturers with WfM technology, Phoenix BIOS produces a BIOS that is PXE capable, and 3Com produces NICs that are PXE capable.

Additionally, when installing the Windows 2000 Server first, there is only a single, Active Directory-enabled Windows 2000 Professional image that must be created and maintained. However, when installing the Windows 2000 Professional workstations first, they will probably need to be updated immediately after the Windows 2000 Servers are installed in order to be able to access resources that are migrated to a new area in the new Active Directory. A second image must be created for all new workstations deployed after the Windows 2000 Servers are installed. This translates into additional work and affects the bottom line of a deployment project's budget.

When an organization has Windows 95 or Windows 98 clients, it will need to provide access to the Active Directory in order for the clients to function on the network. An interim solution is found in the DS (Directory Services) Client. The DS Client enables Windows 95 and Windows 98 computers to work in the Active Directory in the same way as a native Windows 2000 Professional computer would. This includes the ability to:

- Query the Active Directory for users and resources
- Install Active Directory printers

For more about the DS Client, see Chapter 11, "Plugging into Active Directory."

Summary

Migrating to Windows 2000 from legacy Windows NT domains can take the form of one of two types of migrations:

- Domain upgrade
- Domain restructure

The type of migration depends entirely on the plans for the Active Directory for the Forests, Domains, and Domain Name System (DNS) namespace, Organizational Units (OUs), and Site topology, and how they fit with the existing domain structure. A domain upgrade occurs if the legacy domains will remain intact as Active Directory domains after migration. A domain restructure is when the domains are merged or split into different configurations. The first place to start when migrating is with the forest:

1. Migrate root domain first.
2. Migrate each domain completely before starting the next.
3. Follow the DNS namespace to the next subdomain to migrate each domain tree before starting the next.
4. Completely migrate each domain tree before starting the next forest.

Drilling down further into the migration strategy, the method of migrating each individual domain is next.

1. Complete all preparation work and back up the PDC.
2. Migrate the PDC.
3. Perform a full backup of each BDC before migrating it.
4. Migrate each of the BDCs next.
5. Perform a full backup of each member server before migrating.
6. Migrate each member server next.
7. Verify the working condition of printers, clients, users, and other migrated resources.

When restructuring a domain, there are additional steps that require individual components to be migrated from source legacy domains to the target Active Directory domain(s). For example, the process to merge domains is as follows:

1. Migrate the destination domain or create a new Active Directory destination domain.
2. Move user and group accounts into the destination domain from the other domains.
3. Move computers and member servers into the destination domain from the other domains.
4. Back up data and install DCs from the merging domains into the Active Directory domain.
5. Reinstall applications.
6. Restore backups of data.
7. Upgrade member servers with Windows 2000.
8. Verify resources, users, groups, and computers.

When Windows 2000 Server is installed on a new computer, it will automatically install as a member server. However, when upgrading a PDC or BDC, Windows 2000 Server will automatically begin the process to install the Active Directory by starting the

Active Directory Installation Wizard as soon as the Windows 2000 Server installation is complete.

An Active Directory domain has two modes, mixed mode and native mode. When running in mixed mode, the Active Directory will act as a PDC for any legacy NT BDCs. This enables backwards compatibility, as well as an incremental upgrade strategy such that each server can be migrated and verified before beginning the next. Native mode is required for using Active Directory features such as nested groups. Native mode cannot be used until all BDCs are upgraded, and the domain cannot be returned to mixed mode after switching.

Two utilities are critical components for moving users, groups, and computers: CLONEPRINCIPAL and NETDOM. CLONEPRINCIPAL is a customizable scripting program that can copy a security principal (e.g., user or group) from one domain to another. NETDOM is a command-line utility that can manage domain trusts, machine accounts, and domain memberships.

After components have been migrated, the Administrator may want to delegate control over some of them. Delegation of administration is necessary when merging two legacy NT domains and using the OU structure to separate the administrative duties. The Delegation of Control Wizard is available in the Active Directory Users and Computers Management Console.

Inserting into the replication topology is an automatic function within a site. The Knowledge Consistency Checker (KCC) will generate the replication topology whenever a new domain controller is added. Only domain controllers are involved in the replication topology. New sites require that connection objects are created to establish replication between sites.

Migrating from NDS is a process that many organizations will be required to undergo. This process is simplified by the Directory Services Migration tool. The tool allows the import of objects from NDS into an offline project database that can be remodeled to fit the new Active Directory structure. The objects can be exported incrementally to the Active Directory thereafter.

FAQs

Q: I want to migrate our network by starting with the member servers, then follow that with the BDCs, and finally by migrating the PDC so that we can have a working copy of the NT domain SAM constantly updated until we are ready to cut over. Can this migration strategy work?

A: No. Active Directory domain controllers cannot exist in the same domain as a Windows NT PDC. The strategy should be changed to start with the PDC and follow with the remaining BDCs and then member servers.

Q: When I tried to upgrade a Windows NT 3.51 member server to Windows 2000, it failed. What should I do?

A: After reverifying that the hardware and applications are compatible, and that the users, groups, and registry are cleaned up of any unnecessary entries, you should try to upgrade the Windows NT 3.51 server to Windows NT 4.0 first. After a successful upgrade to Windows NT 4.0, try upgrading to Windows 2000 Server.

Q: What types of applications will cause the worst problems with upgrades?

A: The two types of applications that cause the worst problems are virus detection applications and tape backup applications. Not only do these applications have very specific registry entries that are difficult for the upgrade to process, but their nature is one that prevents the operating system from being changed. Take a virus detection program: It looks for changes to the boot files and has different methods of preventing them from being changed, whereas the upgrade process makes necessary changes to those same critical files. The conflict causes errors and issues. The backup application is necessary for restoration of the server files if there is a problem, so completely removing it is probably not the best tactic. The best thing to do is to uninstall all virus detection programs and turn the backup application service off. If, after upgrading, the backup application does not work, it can be reinstalled over the old one.

Chapter 3

Active Directory Naming Strategies

Solutions in this chapter:

- **Understanding DNS Usage with Active Directory**

- **Determining the DNS Strategy**

- **Defining Naming Conventions for DNS and ADS**

Planning the Active Directory naming strategy is the launch point for deploying Windows 2000. This may seem a tedious task, but it is critical to the performance and usability of your network. In order to determine the naming strategy, you will need to gather information about the enterprise. This information includes the existing Domain Name System (DNS) configuration, the existing NT Domain configuration and the current naming conventions used on the network.

Introduction

Before deploying Windows 2000, the project team should fully understand the components of the Active Directory namespace plan. The namespace plan incorporates the naming strategy for DNS, since it is so tightly integrated in the Active Directory. It also describes the domains and their structure for all of the Windows 2000 domains, and the standards that the team will adhere to when creating objects and published resources in the Active Directory tree.

Do not make the mistake of discounting the importance of a solid namespace design. The namespace plan impacts all sorts of network mechanisms, including:

- Administrative efficiency
- Change management
- Network usability
- Bandwidth overhead issues
- Network availability and fault tolerance

As this list shows, this is a critical stop on your way to an Active Directory enabled network.

What Is DNS?

DNS is a general purpose data query service for the TCP/IP protocol suite. The data that are typically queried are hostnames (a.k.a. the name of the computer), and the responses are typically the hosts' IP addresses. DNS grew out of a legacy system whereby each UNIX computer was required to maintain a mapped list of hostnames and IP addresses in a text file named *hosts*. Eventually, these hosts files became unwieldy and difficult to synchronize across networks.

DNS was developed to solve the administrative problems associated with using hosts files. It provides a hierarchical tree system of DNS organizations that are hosted by DNS servers, each of which maintains its own mapped lists of hostnames and IP addresses. Not only does the organization maintain this list, but it also has authority over a partition of the DNS namespace. If an address is not found when a query is made by a client, the DNS servers are capable of passing the request up the organizational tree to a server that may have the mapping or know of a server that does.

DNS requires a name format that fits its hierarchical nature. A fully qualified domain name (FQDN) is the name of a host that includes the names of each level of the hierarchy from the host to the root of the DNS tree with each separated by dots (.). For example, the FQDN of the Dot server in the Dot domain under the Commercial (.com) domain would be DOT.DOT.COM. DNS names are treated in a case-insensitive manner, so that a host named seven.nine.borg.com would require that there are no hosts named Seven.nine.borg.com or any other capitalization permutation. Although these domains are well-known, Table 3.1 lists some that you may encounter when on the Internet. These, and others, are discussed in RFCs 1034 and 1035.

Table 3.1 Top-Level Domain Names and Types of Organizations that Use Them

Domain Name	Use
.com	Commercial
.edu	Educational
.net	Network operations
.gov	United States government
.mil	United States military
.us	United States
.uk	United Kingdom
.au	Australia

DNS uses a hierarchically structured namespace, a portion of which is illustrated in Figure 3.1, and can associate more data than just an IP address with the hostname. This information is known as a resource record, or RR. Clients issue queries to DNS servers to look for services that meet their specific needs. For example, an Internet mail server uses a Mail Exchange (MX) RR. Most data in DNS databases today represent some type of RR. A simple hostname to IP address association is known as an Address (A) RR.

DNS requires name servers that maintain the information about the domain tree structure. These servers will maintain a subset of the domain information and are considered an *authority* for that subset of the tree. That subset of the domain, consisting only of the authoritative information, can be organized into *zones*, which are then automatically distributed to redundant DNS name servers. Clients use an application called a *resolver* to query their DNS server. DNS servers also have an application called a *resolver* that extracts data from the DNS database in order to respond to a client request. When the resolver cannot extract data from that particular name server, it can pursue the query through referrals to other name servers via recursive process to resolve the names for which they are not authoritative. The referral process is shown in Figure 3.2.

Figure 3.1 Hierarchical nature of DNS.

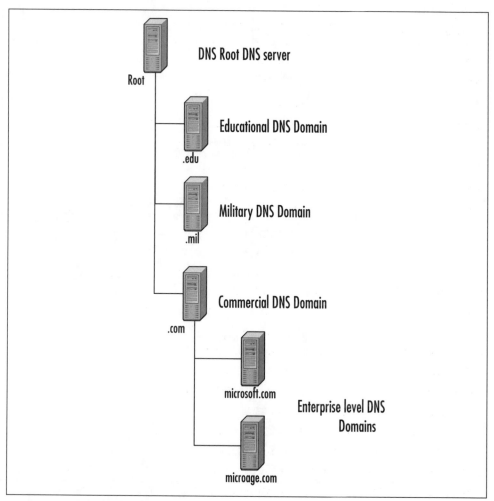

How DNS Zones Function

Primary DNS name servers maintain local files for the zone. Any changes to the zone must be made to the primary name server. Secondary DNS name servers obtain their information from any server that has authority for the zone in a *zone transfer*. A master name server is one that a secondary name server contacts in order to initiate the zone transfer.

Figure 3.2 How the DNS referral process works.

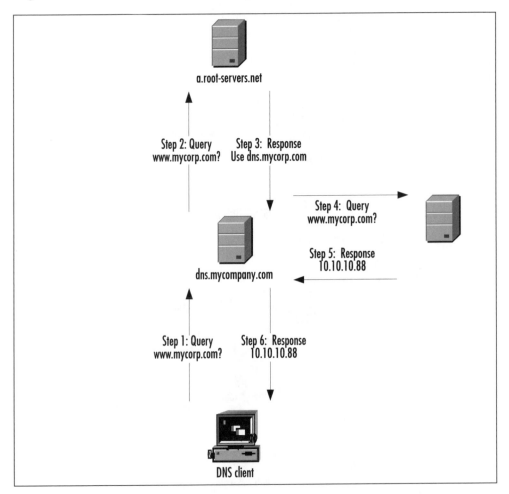

Zones are part of the DNS namespace for which a specific server, or redundant servers, is responsible. The zone represents a single database of records containing information about a specific part of the domain namespace. A DNS name server can then be a primary name server for one zone, as well as a secondary name server for another zone. The zone does not need to hold all the subdomain information beneath the root domain of the zone. Zones are aware of the subdomains for which they are not authoritative through the use of name server (NS) records for the subdomain authoritative DNS servers, as illustrated in Figure 3.3.

Figure 3.3 DNS authoritative zones.

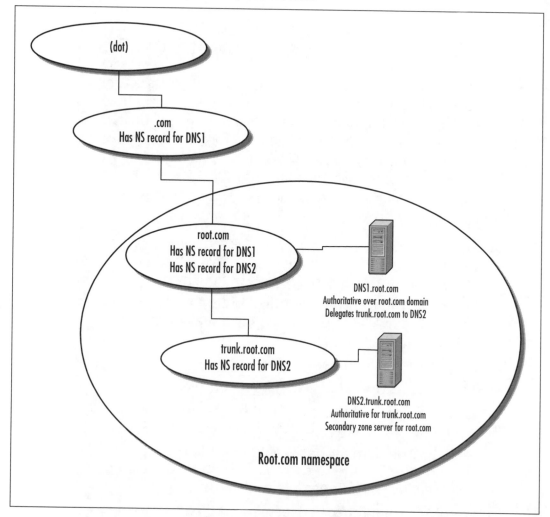

Active Directory's Integration with DNS

Active Directory Services (ADS) are so tightly integrated with DNS that it is amazing that Microsoft did not name it Active DNS instead! DNS is required on the network for Active Directory to be installed and to function. This is a major change for those who are migrating from non-TCP/IP networks. There are two impacts on the DNS service when employing Active Directory Services.

For IT Professionals   About SRV RRs

SRV (service locator) RRs are used to locate Active Directory domain controllers (DCs). This type of RR enables multiple servers that provide the same type of service to be located with a single DNS query. Under Active Directory, the SRV RR is the means by which clients locate DCs using LDAP (lightweight directory access protocol) via TCP port 389.

SRV RR fields consist of *service.protocol.name ttl class SRV preference weight port target*:

- **Service:** A name for the service. RFC1700 defines the names used for well-known services. Otherwise, the Administrator can specify his own name.

- **Protocol:** The transport protocol used. RFC 1700 defines the available protocols, but usually this is TCP or UDP.

- **Name:** The DNS domain name.

- **TTL:** Time to Live. This field can be left blank.

- **Class:** One of four classes. IN is the most common and represents the Internet. This field can be left blank.

- **Priority:** The number between 0 and 65,535 representing whether the target host should be contacted first. The lowest number has priority over others.

- **Weight:** The number between 1 and 65,535 used to load balance when two or more target hosts have the same priority. Usually set to 0 when load balancing is not used.

- **Port:** The transport protocol port represented by a number between 0 and 65,535. Well-known services use ports that are listed in RFC 1700.

- **Target:** The host's DNS domain name that is providing the service.

Continued

For IT Professionals

About SRV RRs

An example of an SRV RR that will look for a service from one of two different servers is:
ldap.tcp.name SRV 0 0 389 dns1.root.com
SRV 1 0 389 dns2.branch.root.com

1. In order for clients to log on to Active Directory, DNS is required to locate the DCs. The Net Logon service requires a DNS server that supports the SRV RRs because SRV RRs both register and identify the DCs in the DNS namespace.

2. The Active Directory can stow DNS zone information and replicate it throughout the enterprise.

The requirement of being able to contact a compatible DNS server by Active Directory DCs is absolute. When a Windows 2000 Server is promoted to a DC, it must have a DNS server available to it. If no DNS server is discovered on the network, the DNS service is installed by default on the new DC. The Active Directory Installation Wizard screen for DNS installation is depicted in Figure 3.4.

DNS is not only required by Active Directory, but also can interact with WINS, the Windows Internet Naming System. WINS provides NetBIOS computer name mappings to IP addresses. DNS can provide name resolution for any names that it learns from WINS.

After Active Directory is installed, there are two ways to store and replicate DNS zones.

- Standard text-based file storage for the zone
- Active Directory integrated storage for the zone

Text files that store zones have a .DNS extension and are stored in the %SystemRoot%\System32\DNS directory on each Windows 2000 server acting as a DNS server. The first part of the name is the name of the zone; for example, the ARABLE zone will be stored in the ARABLE.DNS file.

Figure 3.4 DNS is required for Active Directory installation.

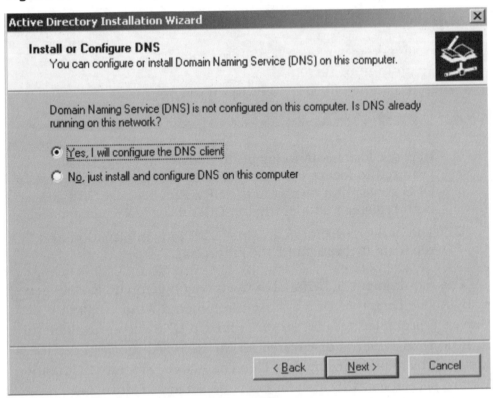

How Active Directory Uses DNS

Windows 2000 DCs register SRVs so that Administrators can use several servers for a single domain and move services among the DCs. Every DC that has a registered SRV RR, also registers an A RR, so that its individual host address can be found. For example, when looking for the address http://www.mycorp.com, the lookup is for http.tcp.www.mycorp.com. The www, in this case, refers to a service that is shared by multiple individual servers. The query retrieves a Web document from any of the available servers.

The main impact that SRV records have on the internetwork is that the DNS servers must support them, and preferably would support dynamic updates as well. SRV records are described in RFC 2052, and dynamic updates are discussed in RFC 2136. These requirements limit the versions of DNS that can be used. The following are supported:

- Microsoft's Windows 2000 DNS, which supports SRV records and dynamic updates for DNS (of course!)
- UNIX BIND version 4.9.7, which supports SRV records
- UNIX BIND version 8.2.1, which also supports Dynamic DNS updates, and incremental zone transfers.

TIP

The only option that you have if your DNS does not support SRV records or dynamic DNS updates is to upgrade or migrate to a DNS version that does for the zone that supports the Active Directory DCs.

DNS has its own Microsoft Management Console (MMC) snap-in utility. All management for DNS can be executed from this utility, which is displayed in Figure 3.5. If you are tied to the command line, Microsoft also provides a command-line tool for DNS called DNSCMD.

When DNS is integrated into the Active Directory, the DNS zone benefits from multi-master replication. An update is received for a zone by any DC. The DC writes the update to the Active Directory, which is then replicated to all other DCs. Any DNS server that queries the Active Directory anywhere in the internetwork will receive the updated information. When you use the Microsoft Windows 2000 DNS integrated with Active Directory, there is no need to implement any other type of replication for DNS other than that already configured for Active Directory. The way that this works is shown in Figure 3.6.

Figure 3.5 Microsoft Management Console utility for DNS.

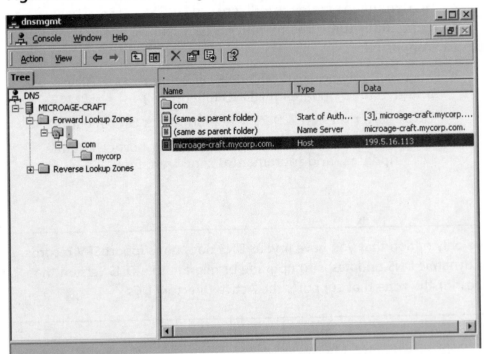

Dynamic updates are helpful for reducing the administration needed for DNS. However, a primary DNS server can be the single point of failure when it becomes unavailable. Since the primary server holds the only DNS database that can be updated, a dynamic update will fail when that server is down.

There is always the chance for conflicts when multi-master replication exists. When Microsoft's DNS is integrated with Active Directory, name-change conflicts are handled on a first-come, first-served basis. If two DNS servers create the same name or make changes to an RR, the first one to write it to the Active Directory wins.

Dynamic updates allow computers to register themselves in the DNS system. Windows 2000 computers and its DNS service all support this, as well as the Windows 2000 DHCP service. The Windows 2000 DHCP service will remove any records that it registered upon the DHCP lease's expiration. In order to use the benefits of dynamic updates, the DNS server must support RFC 2136.

Figure 3.6 Multi-master replication for DNS.

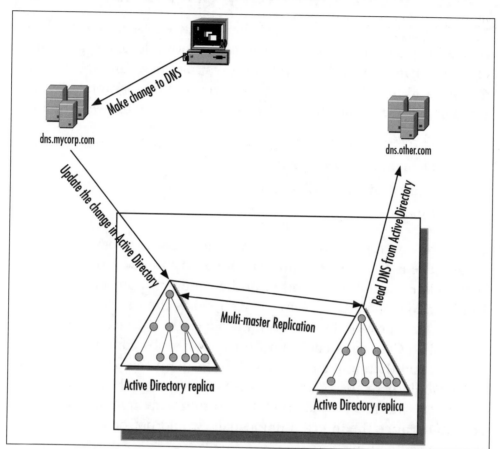

Active Directory has an additional benefit for keeping the DNS records up to date. Active Directory timestamps each RR. RRs are refreshed periodically. When an RR does not refresh for a number of intervals, it is considered stale and is then scavenged from the database. In order to enable the aging and scavenging of Active Directory-enabled DNS:

1. RRs must be timestamped.
2. Zones must have a refresh interval and a no-refresh interval set.
3. Scavenging must be enabled for each zone and name server.
4. The name server must have a scavenging period established.

Planning Active Directory and DNS

There are four areas to document for an Active Directory and DNS namespace design. These will encompass both a logical organization of your network, including joint ventures, business units, and workgroups, and the physical network, including the geographic distribution of the users and the network topology. The four areas include:

- Forest plan
- Domain and DNS strategy
- Organizational Units (OUs)
- Site topology

Unless you register a private DNS name, using a local DNS namespace is easier said than done if you try to use a namespace that ends in ".com" or any other of the common Internet domains. However, Microsoft Active Directory supports the use of the ".local" domain for a private, local DNS namespace. In this scenario, a company called Cyberlabs could implement cyberlabs.com on the Internet and then implement cyberlabs.local on the private network. There would be a clear distinction between local and Internet resources, and there is no need to maintain near-mirrored DNS servers because the internal namespace would not be exposed to the Internet.

For IT Professionals

Designing Active Directory on a Network Connected to the Internet

When you select your Active Directory domain names and you are planning to be connected to the Internet, you can do one of the following:

For IT Professionals

Designing Active Directory on a Network Connected to the Internet

- Select a brand new, unique DNS name (or names) that you must register with InterNIC.

- Use an existing DNS namespace that has already been registered with InterNIC and is running on the Internet providing Web services.

- Use a subdomain of an existing DNS namespace that has already been registered with InterNIC but is NOT running on the Internet providing Web services.

- Use a local DNS name that is completely outside the Internet.

You can have a separate DNS zone for a new DNS namespace, for a subdomain of an Internet-used DNS namespace, or for a local DNS namespace. However, you will have the most problems when you use an existing DNS namespace and share it with Internet Web servers.

Sharing a DNS namespace with Internet Web servers provides a way for unintended persons to access your network simply by having the names of your Windows 2000 servers available in the DNS server that services the Internet. A person can run nslookup and check out the entries against your DNS server. The way to get around this is to establish two DNS servers with primary zone authority for the same namespace. Place one of the DNS servers inside your firewall and include all the Active Directory servers in that zone, as well as the Internet servers required for users to access the Internet. Place the second DNS server outside the firewall and make certain to exclude all the Active Directory servers. While this setup is confusing and requires extra management, it does provide a way to use the same namespace and maintain a measure of security.

Forest Plan

The forest plan document for most enterprises will be a short document because of the nature of forests. A forest is a collection of multiple domain trees with multiple namespaces that not only trust each other, but share a common configuration, schema, and global catalog (GC). The trust relationships within a forest are transitive, and configured automatically. A forest is a logical formation that does not significantly impact, nor is impacted by, the network's topology. The structure within a forest is transparent to users. The GC shields them from domains and OUs. A forest should encompass most of the computers in any enterprise network, if not all of them. The forest plan should document the namespaces and trust relationships expected between domains. A pictorial representation of a forest is shown in Figure 3.7.

There are causes for having two or three forests, however. Since the forest shares:

- A common schema (collection of objects and attributes allowed in the Active Directory database)
- A common configuration (globally available configuration for replication and interdomain activity)
- A common GC (actual user accounts and published resources in the tree)

the production network will benefit by being separated from any domains and forests that are connected to the Internet. This also applies to lab networks, since testing a different configuration or adding to the schema should be kept outside the production network until deployment. A separate lab forest or Internet forest keeps test users and public user accounts out of the GC.

The final reason that a network may implement more than one forest is for administrative separation. This is a common situation in companies that interconnect for joint ventures, or for those that have subsidiaries. The forest is the absolute separation of administrative authority. Two forests allow Administrators to have the authority

Figure 3.7 Multiple namespaces exist in a single forest.

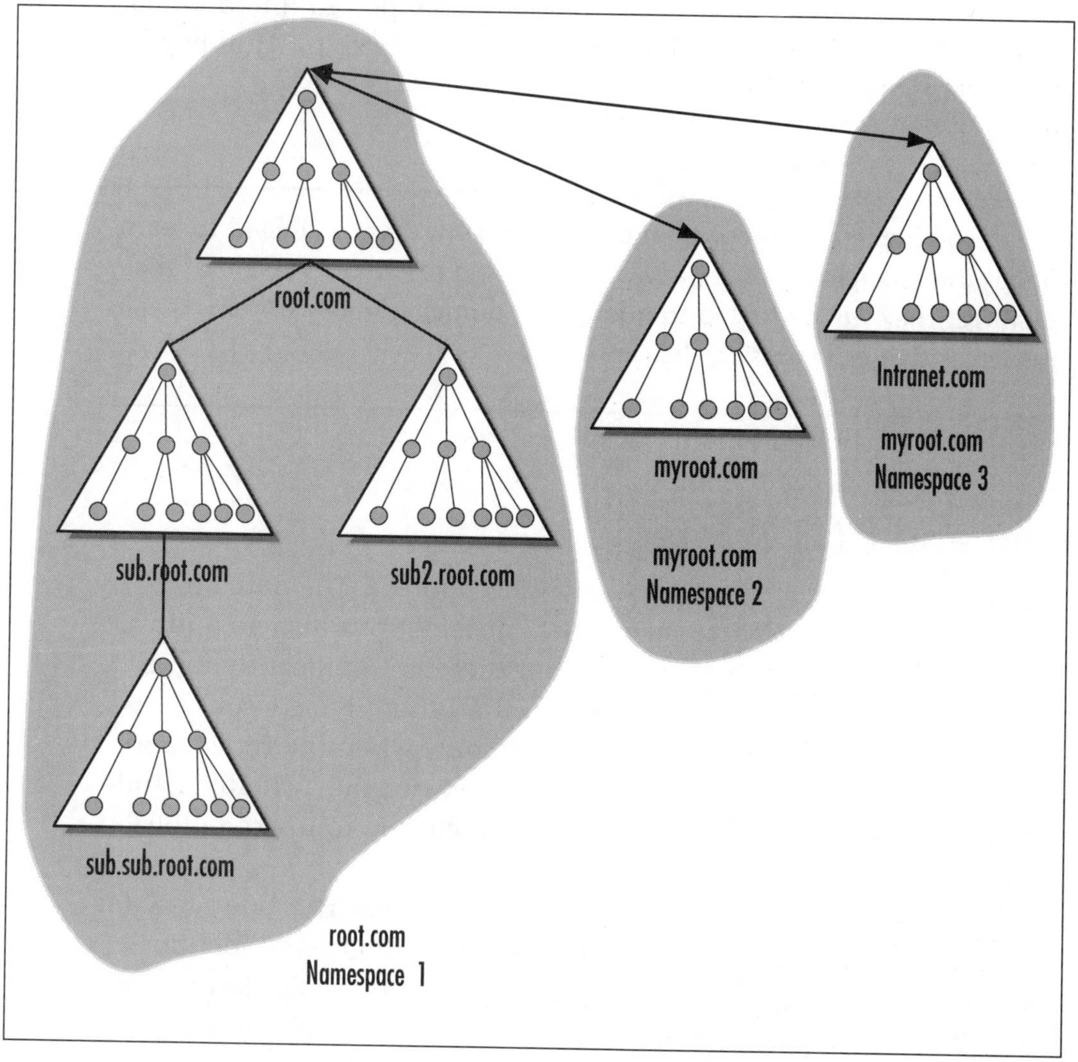

over the configuration, the schema, the GC, and security completely separated from another Administrator's sphere of control.

Once a domain is created, it joins a forest. That domain cannot be moved between forests; it is a permanent member of the original forest. Furthermore, a forest cannot be split or merged (yet), but there is a tool provided for importing and exporting Active Directory objects, LDIFDE.EXE, which is found in the WINNT\SYSTEM32 directory. LDIFDE stands for LDAP Directory Import File Directory

Export, and uses the LDAP protocol to access the forest's GC, and export the objects into a text file that can be imported into another forest. More about LDIFDE can be found in Chapter 6, "Building Trees and Forests."

TIP

When you implement more than one forest, your users will need to learn about their namespace if they will be accessing resources outside of their own GC. They will be forced to query each domain directly for all resources that exist outside their forest.

Domain and DNS Strategy

Domains are the top-level division within a forest. The domain should not only be treated as a logical division, but also as a physical division. The reason for this is that there is significantly more traffic within the confines of a domain than there is between domains. New domains should be added only when the replication, query, and authentication traffic will overwhelm the available bandwidth of a slow network link and it is not feasible to upgrade the link.

The domain is an administrative division, offering a boundary for security policies. All objects within a domain are granted identical security policies, which can be accessed through the Security Settings Microsoft Management Console (MMC) utility found in the Administrative Tools menu. These include:

- Password policy
- Account lockout policy
- Kerberos ticket policies

Since the domain is the division for policies, it is also the division for authentication. In this case, a user authenticates for logon

For Managers

Legacy NT Domain Planning Issues No Longer Apply

Windows NT domain planning had several issues that are now obsolete in the domain planning process for Windows 2000 Active Directory.

- There is no longer a need to delegate administration by separating domains. Instead, legacy NT domains can be combined and OUs can be used for administrative delegation.

- Since the Active Directory is scalable to millions of objects, there is no longer a 40,000 user limit for the SAM, or Security Account Manager.

- The Active Directory uses multi-master replication, so there is no need to plan for a PDC or BDC. Instead, only DCs (Domain Controllers) must be planned.

and access to resources to any of the DCs that belong to the user's domain. The user cannot authenticate to any other domain even if it is in the same namespace or forest.

Root Domain

The first domain installed for the forest is the root domain. This domain will be the first domain created in the forest, and since it contains the management information for the schema of the entire forest, it should contain servers that are distributed to all physical sites (if feasibly possible). The Domain Admins group of the forest root domain is, by default, the schema administrator group for the entire forest. In view of this requirement, there are two ways to design the root domain:

- As a standard domain that contains user accounts and published resources

- As an empty domain that has no purpose other than to publish the schema and make it available to all other domains

The advantages of dedicating a root domain as in the second option is that there are no Domain Administrator conflicts and the domain never becomes obsolete. The first option has the advantage, especially when there is only a single domain, of being able to distribute more than just the schema to multiple sites.

About Domains

The main recommendation for planning domains and DNS is simply to delegate a separate DNS zone for each Active Directory domain. You should ensure that there are at least two DNS servers running on DCs, or available to those same DCs, in the Active Directory domain.

When planning domains, there are a few rules to consider that may impact the decisions you make for your network:

- A domain's name cannot be changed.

- Two domains cannot be merged.

- A single domain cannot be split into two.

You can, however, still use the import/export tool called LDIFDE.EXE to move objects outside both the domain and the forest. To move objects within the forest, but to a different domain tree, use the MOVETREE tool from the Windows 2000 Resource kit. Both LDIFDE and the MOVETREE tool are described in Chapter 6.

DNS Servers

Active Directory requires DNS servers to be available at all times. While it is convenient to use Active Directory DCs to provide the DNS services, this may not always be feasible. In order to ensure that DNS is always available for Active Directory, the recommendation is to provide, at a minimum, one primary and one secondary name server per domain. This will enable:

- Load balancing between the name servers
- Faster access, especially when placing the secondary name server across a WAN link
- Redundancy, in case of failure of one of the name servers

If at all possible, it is recommended that there is at least one DC running the DNS service in each Site. This will enable much faster access and ensure that DCs are not cut off from DNS if a WAN link goes down. These servers can be secondary servers for the zone, rather than primary.

The minimum hardware requirements for a Windows 2000 DC running the DNS service on an Intel processor server are 100 bytes of RAM per RR on top of the RAM required for the server operating system, and at least a Pentium II 400 MHz processor.

NOTE

All of the client computers on the internetwork should be configured to query both a primary DNS server and a secondary DNS server. Clients will use the DNS service to locate a DC in their local site in order to log on to the network, as well as queries for services.

Organizational Units (OUs)

OUs are the container objects that sit within domains. They are a logical arrangement of objects, that can be nested, and have no impact on the network traffic. Two items will impact the OU design:

- Group Policy
- Administration

In both of these cases, the OU is the boundary. Different group policies can be applied to different OUs. Different Administrators can be granted administrative access to different OUs, without concern for conflicts over administrative control.

How you create the OU hierarchy can reflect the company org chart, or some other tree structure that seems sensible. The Microsoft utilities do not require users to navigate the hierarchy of OUs, although some tools do expose them, so there is no true need to create OUs that serve no purpose other than the reflection of an org chart. Instead, focus on the purpose that the OU will serve, whether to provide group policy, administrative area, hide objects, or to group a set of users logically together.

OUs are the most flexible container objects in the Active Directory. Unlike forests and domains, OUs can be created, moved, added, or deleted whenever needed. These changes have no impact on the network. Objects within OUs can also be easily moved, created, added, and deleted. When these changes are made, the major considerations are simply about how the group policy and administration issues will change.

Group policies will affect the time that it takes for a user to log on. The more group policies there are, the longer it takes. If an Administrator applies multiple group policies to a single OU, the user's logon time will suffer. If the user is located three nested groups down, and the Administrator has applied a single group policy at one of the levels, that user will log on faster than the user with multiple group policies applied to a single OU. Group policies are the reason for logon times being increased. The problem, however, with OU design is that when there are multiple nested OUs, Administrators are more likely to apply group policies to each OU in the hierarchy than apply multiple group policies to a single OU. When planning the OU structure, make sure to state where group policies will be applied, and whether multiple group policies will be acceptable.

Site Topology

The Site topology is a representation of the physical network. It consists of Sites that are connected by Site links. (Note that this is very similar to Exchange Server's directory in which Sites are connected by Site connectors.) The Site is a physical division of the network. When users authenticate to the network, their authentication traffic will be directed to a DC within their own site. Additionally, sites will maintain more query and replication traffic within them.

Sites, as well as their Active Directory names, should represent the physical network, and should have a DC, DNS Server and Global Catalog within each. The site should consist of networks that are connected by fast and reliable links. They can be LAN or extremely high-speed WAN links. A Site should not span a medium- or low-speed WAN link (e.g., less than 10 Mbps), except in certain cases.

Unlike domains, Sites are easily added, moved, changed, or deleted. This is one of the methods that makes Active Directory scalable with the internetwork's growth. In order to manage Sites, you can use the Active Directory Sites and Services MMC utility. This can be located by clicking Start | Programs | Administrative Tools | Active Directory Sites and Services.

Naming Conventions

The key to a solid namespace design is simplification. The simpler the namespace design, the easier it is to manage and add to later on.

The namespace should fit the ideal network for the enterprise, even if the ideal network is not quite what exists currently. After designing the ideal network's namespace, make adjustments only for the anomalous network devices. Eventually, the network will adjust toward the ideal by taking this approach.

Finally, the namespace design should be enabled for change management. Most enterprises are not static entities. People are promoted to new positions, move to different departments, start new business units in another city or country, leave the company, and so on. The PCs that they use either move with them, or change hands and are reconfigured. New PCs, servers, and printers are added to the network and old ones are retired. All organizations experience these changes, just in various percentages. If the Active Directory namespace does not support changes, it will not be a success. Instead, it should support changes so that it is easy to move objects around the tree. One way to enable the Active Directory for change management is to standardize unique names throughout the tree. This simple standard will ensure that no conflicts from moves, adds, or changes will ensue.

Defining DNS Names

The rules regarding DNS names are simple:

- Domain names should be less than or equal to 64 characters.
- Each host in the DNS database is allowed to have a name of up to 63 characters in length, and many allow names up to 255 characters.
- All hosts must have unique names. For example, a host named george.microage.com and a host named george.eng.microage.com are each considered unique.
- All subdomains must have unique names within their parent domain.

DNS names for each domain should be defined when creating the domain plan. Each domain should be assigned a name that follows the format of root.com. Domains that will share the same namespace as the forest root domain will have a subdomain name format of parent.root.com. Any domains beneath them in the domain tree hierarchy will have the sub-subdomain name format of child.parent.root.com. Further subdomains are allowed, but not recommended because of the complexity added to the internetwork. Trust relationships will follow the tree structure.

For Managers

Naming Conventions

Naming conventions for user accounts are sometimes the keys to the internetwork for hackers. Many organizations use a standard of the first letter of the first name and the first five to seven letters of the last name as a standard for user names. Hackers find it effortless to discover a user's name. The only other piece of information is the user's password, which is sometimes written on a Post-It note and pasted on the PC itself, or sometimes given by an unsuspecting user to a call from "IT Support" (a.k.a. the hacker).

The other thing that organizations typically do is to leave the default administrator name for the network. In Windows 2000, this is a domain administrator named "Administrator." Again, hackers have half the key to the network when an organization leaves this account with its original name intact.

Finally, organizations that are on the Internet already have a widely published domain name for their Internet presence. Many of them use that same name, or a subdomain of it for their private, internal network. Again, there is no guessing involved in locating servers on the private network for a hacker using as lookup.

So what does an IT Manager do to secure the network through naming conventions?

- Do not use the user's name, or permutations of it, as the user's logon id unless you add numbers or other data to the logon id to disguise it.

- Do not be tempted to use a United States social security number for a user's id, either. A social security number not only places a user's personal information at risk, but companies with international sites will have users who do not have social security numbers.

Continued

Naming Conventions

- Rename the Administrator account. Remember, however, some applications are written to look for the ìAdministratorî account in order to be installed, although most allow you to input a different name.

- Create Administrator accounts with randomly generated names using both upper and lowercase letters and numbers. Who is to know that the Administrator's name is X3460GzwGm?

- Always remember to enforce a strict password policy, especially if the organization is connected in any way to the Internet.

- Register a new domain name with InterNIC for your internal network that is completely different from the one used on the Internet.

Aside from DNS naming conventions, there are other interoperability issues with names for most internetworks because of legacy systems. The following rules will help evade many trials and tribulations when connecting to legacy systems.

- Always create unique names for users, computers, printers, and other resources.

- Avoid the following characters when creating user or computer names since many computers will translate these as encoding characters or will not understand them: !@#$%^&*()_?<>'î;:[]{}\|/.,

- Keep object names for logon ids to eight characters or less. Many legacy systems stop after eight characters.

- Keep object names for computers to eight characters or less. Many legacy systems stop after eight characters.

Continued

For Managers

Naming Conventions

- Do not depend on the letter case (upper and lower) to create unique names. Many computers translate both Frank and fRANK to equate to FRANK, so they would no longer be unique.

- Do not depend on a distinguished name to create unique names. Legacy systems may not understand context-sensitive names and will translate /CN=M1craft3/CN=USERS/DC=Panther/DC=MicroAge/DC=com to simply be M1craft3. So if there is another M1craft3 in the Active Directory, but in a different tree location or domain, the name will not be unique.

Each DNS root domain namespace should be registered with InterNIC. This will avoid conflicts if there is another one being used on a connected network or the Internet.

The DNS name for a domain in the Windows 2000 is defined when the first DC for that domain is installed with Active Directory. The Active Directory Service is installed with the Active Directory Installation Wizard, as shown in Figure 3.8.

Figure 3.8 Naming a new domain in the Active Directory.

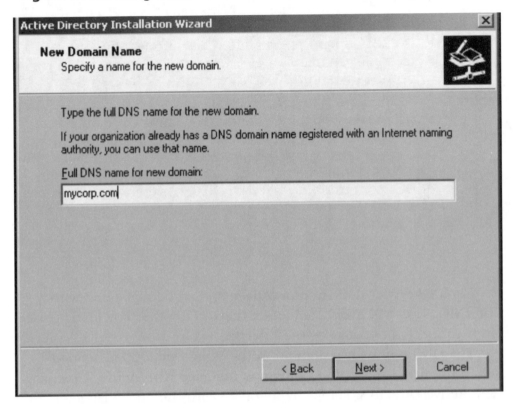

Defining DNS Zones

All DNS zones and RRs are managed in the DNS Management Console. To add a zone, follow these steps:

1. Click Start.
2. Select Programs.
3. Select Administrative Tools.
4. Choose DNS. The DNS Microsoft Management Console utility will start.

For IT Professionals

Naming Convention Rules

Microsoft's DNS service that comes with Windows 2000 is more forgiving when it comes to naming conventions than the DNS applications from other vendors. Even if you are using Microsoft's version of DNS, you may, at some point in time, connect to a network that uses a different vendor's DNS. When that happens, the naming conventions that you are using will need to be compatible with both DNS versions. Otherwise, you will encounter a few problems.

Standard DNS naming rules, which are understood by all DNS versions, are as follows:

- Use a registered DNS name. You can register DNS names with InterNIC.

- Use the standard character set of A through Z, a through z, and 0 through 9 and the dash (-) character. Note that the Windows 2000 DNS will support both the underscore (_) and Unicode characters.

- When in doubt, verify your naming strategy with RFC 1123, which is available on the Internet at http://freesoft.org/CIE/RFC/1123/index.htm.

5. Select either Forward Lookup Zones or Reverse Lookup Zones below the server that will be managing the zone, depending on which type of zone you are adding.

6. Click the Action menu.

7. Select Create a New Zone. The Add New Zone Wizard will begin.

8. Select the zone type.

9. Assign a name and complete the wizard. The new zone will appear in the DNS utility.

Adding an RR also occurs in the DNS Microsoft Management Console utility.

Naming Conventions for Active Directory

Active Directory is an open directory service in that it supports a wide range of protocols, objects, and application programming interfaces (APIs). These are the mechanisms that define the availability of the Active Directory to various types of clients.

As a result of Active Directory's support for diverse protocols, Active Directory supports many different name formats:

- Internet e-mail addresses, as described in RFC 822— name@mycorp.com

- Uniform Resource Locators (URLs) for HyperText Transfer Protocol (HTTP)—http://www.mycorp.com

- Lightweight Directory Access Protocol (LDAP) names— LDAP://myserver.mycorp.com/CN=myname,OU=Users, O=Mycorp,C=US

- Universal Naming Convention (UNC) names— \\myserver.com\myvolume\file.ext

Such diversity in naming format support enables companies to select nearly any names that are appropriate for their company. The major influence on a naming convention will be the connectivity to external systems on the internetwork. Windows 2000 Active Directory is more forgiving than other systems for names in that it supports a wider variety of characters and character sets, and even lengthier names.

Migrating an Existing Exchange Server Design

The Active Directory inherited many of its characteristics from Exchange Server's directory system. Additionally, the design premises are nearly identical. If an organization already has a highly performing Exchange Server directory with basically the same scope of sites, users, computers, and servers, then it can mirror the design of the Active Directory and expect good results.

Migrating an Existing Novell Directory Services Design

Many organizations have invested a significant amount of time and effort in a Novell Directory Services design. This design is generally a geographical division at the top of the tree and an organizational division lower down. If the Novell Directory Services design follows this scheme *and* it has the same scope, it is easy to translate it into an Active Directory design. Instead of each top-level OU, replace it with an appropriate domain. Then retain the hierarchy of OUs that exist within that top level and place them within the domain.

You will find a handy wizard for migrating Novell Directory Services information into the Active Directory in the Administrative Tools menu.

Virtual Containers

The Active Directory can incorporate information from other directory services through a *virtual container*. The other directory service must be LDAP compliant for this to work. The Active Directory implements a virtual container in what amounts to a pointer to the foreign directory service. The foreign directory server's DNS name is contained as part of the virtual container's properties. When a client performs a query on the virtual container, DNS locates the foreign directory and passes an LDAP query to it. The response to that query is returned to Active Directory, which then presents it to the client.

Summary

DNS (Domain Name System) is tightly integrated with Windows 2000 Active Directory Services. Active Directory uses DNS for its locator service for the NetLogon service. The DNS must support SRV resource records (RRs), and preferably will support dynamic updates as well. This integration runs in both directions. Not only does Active Directory use DNS as its locator service, but the Active Directory can manage and maintain the DNS information within itself as well.

When Active Directory manages the DNS information, there are many benefits:

- Multi-master replication
- Scavenging of stale RRs
- Support for dynamic updates

Because of DNS integration, the entire Active Directory planning is involved in the DNS namespace design. There are four planning areas:

- Forest
- Domain
- Organizational Unit (OU)
- Sites

The Forest plan describes the number of forests that will exist on the internetwork. The Domain plan discusses the DNS namespaces, their hierarchy, and their corresponding Active Directory domains. The domains should denote a physical structure as well as a logical structure because of the amount of traffic that occurs within a domain. The Organizational Unit plan represents the logical hierarchy within the domain. It has little impact on the network, but provides an easy unit for administrative delegation. Sites are a physical representation of the network. When there are multiple Sites, the Active Directory uses Site links to direct traffic between them.

Naming conventions should be defined for the user accounts and published resources within the Active Directory. The naming conventions should support the Active Directory and any legacy systems to which users or computers may connect. Legacy systems tend to have stricter naming requirements than the Active Directory.

The DNS domain name is applied to a domain at the installation of the first domain controller (DC) in that domain. If using the

Microsoft DNS service, DNS can be managed through the Microsoft Management Console DNS utility found in the Administrative Tools menu. The Active Directory also uses DNS to locate and connect to foreign directory services, and treat them as virtual containers.

FAQs

Q: Our company uses a DNS server that does not support SRV resource records (RRs). Can we use it when we implement Active Directory?

A: No. The Active Directory relies on SRV RRs in order to locate domain controllers (DCs). All DNS servers for the namespaces that the Active Directory encompasses must also support the SRV RRs.

Q: Our company uses a DNS server that supports SRV RRs but does not support dynamic updates. Can we still use it when we implement Active Directory?

A: Yes. However, dynamic updates are preferred when using the Windows 2000 DHCP service, which can dynamically register IP addresses and hostnames for clients, and can remove them from the DNS database once the DHCP lease has expired.

Q: We are planning to create two forests on the internetwork. We will use one forest as a testing area and the other for production. We plan on developing the domains and their DCs on the test forest and then move them to the production forest later on. Is this a viable plan?

A: No. Although the use of a separate test forest and a production forest is recommended, domains do not have the ability to be moved from one forest to another. In this case, domains cannot be moved from the test forest to the production forest.

Q: The manufacturing department has a policy of changing passwords once every six months, while the HR department has a policy of changing passwords once every three weeks. Can these policies be implemented with OUs in the same domain?

A: No. Security policies, including the password policy, Kerberos tickets, and the account lockout policy, are applied to an entire domain. If there are two different security policies, they must be implemented in two different domains.

Q: We have installed two domains into our forest, and we want to install a third domain that will be the forest root. How do we go about doing this?

A: This is an impossible scenario. The first domain installed into a forest is the forest root. It is the home of the schema for the entire forest. There is no way to change the forest root domain.

Chapter 4

Designing a Domain Structure

Solutions in this chapter:

- Designing a Forest

- Designing a Domain Tree

- Designing an Organizational Unit Structure

- Designing a Site Topology

- Using OUs for Delegating Administration

The enterprise's business requirements will guide the Active Directory domain design. The design will depend not only on business requirements, but also on the network that already exists and the way that the enterprise is organized.

Introduction

Each company, organization, or government office is different and has its own requirements for technology. Windows 2000 Server with Active Directory Services is flexible enough to meet most business requirement sets, but its implementation will vary widely.

In this chapter, you will follow the actions and decisions that a consultant might make when designing a network. Rules regarding network designs are never hard and fast; some network designs simply result in a more optimal performance than others. However, performance is not necessarily the top business driver for an organization. Here are two different organizations to demonstrate how to design a domain structure for Active Directory with the business in mind.

The first is Tekkietech.com. Tekkietech.com is a new Internet company that provides technical services around the globe. It prides itself on having the latest technology on its production network. The Tekkietech.com sales division demonstrates that new technology on the production network to customers. Tekkietech.com has large offices with over 1000 users in each in eight major cities all over the world, and small branch offices with less than 50 users each in various test markets. There is a European base of operations in Germany, several United States bases, two Australian offices, a large office in South Africa, and an office in Japan. Each continent competes against the offices in other continents, in a friendly way. Tekkietech.com is involved in a joint venture with a German Internet Web development company. The joint venture uses a Domain Name System (DNS) namespace of Deutek.de. Tekkietech.com has the following business requirements:

- Must be able to support widely varying technologies.

- Performance of the network is the highest priority.

- Availability of the network is the next highest priority.

- Internet connectivity is required for all sites both incoming and outgoing.

- The Internet portion of the network is publicly available, while the private portion of the network must sit behind a firewall and be secured from the public.

Tekkietech.com network consists of eight major sites and 72 branch offices. Each office, regardless of size, is connected via high-speed WAN links with redundant failover connections to a major office in the same country. Most of the WAN connections are ATM, although some connections use OC-48 and T-3 lines. Half the users have laptops, the rest have desktops. There are at least four servers in each office. Some of them use Windows NT, some use NetWare, and others use various versions of UNIX. All of the offices have a remote access server and an Internet Web server. The intranet Web servers (for internal use only) are all located in the United States in a single office and are managed by a single intranet Webmaster group. Other than the intranet Webmaster group, infrastructure support has several groups located in major sites. Most of the Web servers provide Internet pages, but the Web servers at the main sites provide additional Internet services such as FTP, and media services such as video presentations. Tekkietech.com has four registered DNS names: Tekkietech.com, tekkies.au, tekkies.de, and mytekkies.com. The mytekkies.com namespace is used for the intranet, while the others are used for the Internet.

Tekkietech.com's business units are organized as shown in Figure 4.1.

The second sample organization is Insurance, Inc. Insurance, Inc. sells insurance through 3000 independent agencies all over the United States. It has a single, central office with 250 employees. This office manages all aspects of the insurance sales, service, legal, and marketing for the entire company. The agencies are not

Figure 4.1 The org chart for Tekkietech.com.

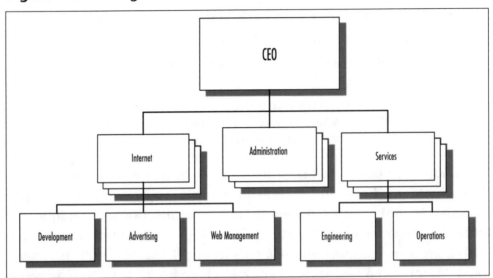

employed by Insurance, Inc., but are considered contractors who are paid commissions only on business sold. Insurance, Inc. has a single computer connected to the Internet, located in the legal department and used for verifying insurance laws and regulations on a subscription legal repository Internet Web site. The business requirements are as follows:

- Insurance, Inc. is extremely concerned about the network's security (as shown by their meager Internet configuration).

- Budget is their next priority.

- Performance is the least of their worries.

- The new network should allow remote access by agents and employees, because Insurance Inc. believes it will increase productivity.

- No applications should be allowed to run on a remote machine, only on a networked machine.

- The new network must be Y2K compliant.

- All executives will be assigned new laptops. The marketing department and managers may be given laptops or desktops.

- Insurance, Inc. wants a centralized and easy-to-manage network.

Insurance, Inc. has a legacy Novell NetWare 3.11 network, and all workstations are desktops running Windows 3.1 or Windows 95. Most of these workstations are 386 and 486 processor machines. Insurance, Inc. expects that all computers on the network will be replaced. The accounting department is running Token Ring, while the rest of the office is running Ethernet over thick coaxial cable. Insurance, Inc. is planning to have the office rewired with Category 5 copper unshielded twisted pair wiring before rolling out Windows 2000. The IT department does not run a lab and is not considering building one. The network only runs IPX.

Insurance, Inc.'s org chart is shown in Figure 4.2.

Figure 4.2 Org chart for Insurance, Inc.

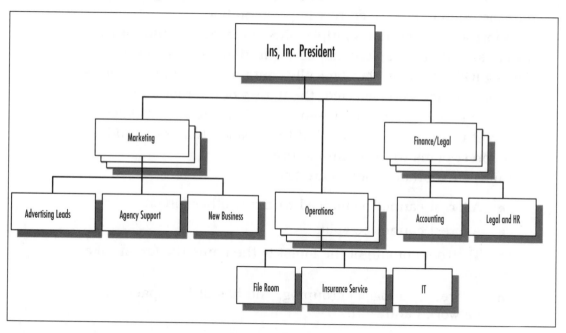

Designing Active Directory

Both Tekkietech.com and Insurance, Inc. will require the same four documents:

- Forest Plan
- Domain/DNS Strategy
- Organizational Unit (OU) Structure
- Site Topology

The differences in the companies, however, will create very dissimilar contents. Here is how the consultant will walk through each of these documents for each of the two companies.

Forest Plan

The first thing the consultant will do is review what a forest is, what belongs in a forest plan, and the rules surrounding forests. This is a refresher step to ensure correct implementation.

A forest is a group of multiple DNS namespaces (and multiple domains) that share a common configuration, schema, and Global Catalog (GC). A forest plan typically contains the number of forests, the reasons they were selected, the names of the root forest domain, and an optional pictorial representation. This consultant likes to draw pictures because clients find them easier to understand, so these forest plans will contain pictures.

Rules surrounding forests are few:

- A forest cannot be merged with any other forest.
- A forest cannot be split.
- The root domain of the forest is the name the forest takes on.
- A forest is a logical grouping, and has little impact on network bandwidth.

Tekkietech.com

Several namespaces already exist for Tekkietech.com. The Mytekkies.com namespace is used for the private intranet, and the remaining namespaces are used for the public Internet. The Deutek.de namespace is set aside for a joint venture. Another namespace that Tekkietech.com may possibly want to add is a lab name-space. The lab namespace would support Tekkietech.com's need to use networking technology for demonstration purposes. Separating these namespaces into separate forests would keep them from shar-ing the schema, configuration, and GCs.

For Tekkietech.com, the consultant would design four forests. They would be selected for the following reasons, and are shown in Figure 4.3:

Figure 4.3 Tekkietech.com's forest plan.

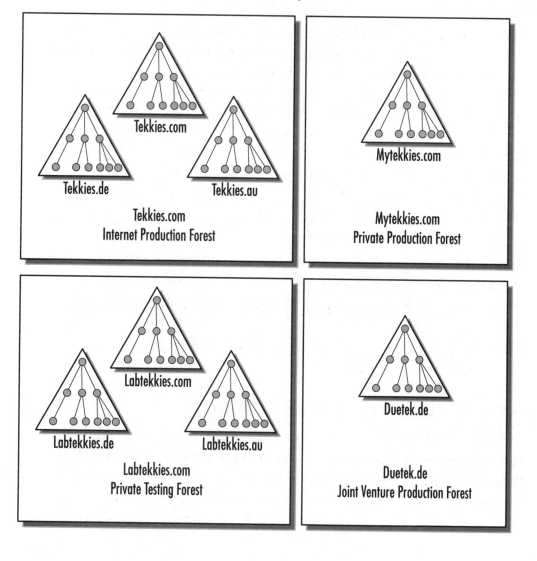

- Tekkietech.com, Tekkies.de, and Tekkies.au would all become part of the Tekkietech.com production forest used on the Internet since each of these domains participates in the Internet.

- Mytekkies.com would become the root of the internal, private forest also used for the intranet because it is not used on the Internet, providing a secure division.

- Deutek.com would be the root of the joint venture's forest, since it is the DNS namespace used by the joint venture.

- A new namespace would be registered for InterNIC to be used for a lab namespace because a new forest was designated for lab usage. In order to mirror the production forest, there would be three namespaces for this forest. Assuming that the consultant registers three namespaces for the lab—labtekkies.com, labtekkies.de, and labtekkies.au—they would comprise the fourth forest.

Insurance, Inc.

The consultant does not have any namespace for Insurance, Inc. Active Directory cannot be implemented without a namespace. The consultant must register at least one domain name with InterNIC on behalf of Insurance, Inc. Since there is no lab, and the security requirements specify that no Internet connectivity will take place with the production network (at least for the foreseeable future), there is no need for more than a single forest. Assuming that the consultant is able to register Insurinc.com with InterNIC, that will be the namespace for the root domain of the forest. Figure 4.4 shows Insurance, Inc.'s forest plan.

Domain Plan Including DNS Strategy

The consultant will begin the domain planning session with the same step as in the forest planning, with a review of domains, DNS, and the rules surrounding them.

Figure 4.4 The Insurance Inc. forest plan.

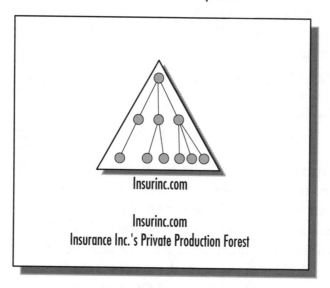

Insurinc.com

Insurinc.com
Insurance Inc.'s Private Production Forest

A domain is the top-level division within a forest. There is significantly more traffic within the confines of a domain than there is between domains. The traffic between domains is mainly replication of schema, configuration, and GC data. The traffic within a domain includes query, authentication, and further replication of the domain objects in the Active Directory. Sites centralize this traffic somewhat by formalizing the paths for replication traffic. (More about sites and replication traffic in Chapter 8, "Planning and Implementing Sites.") There is a preference to send query and authentication traffic to domain controllers (DCs) within the same site as the user making the request. New domains should be added only when the total of the replication, query, and authentication traffic will overwhelm the available bandwidth of a slow network link and it is not feasible to upgrade the link. With the capability of domains and sites to be able to cross each other's boundaries, determining the traffic needs becomes somewhat of an art. The following traffic guidelines are not absolute, but look for minimum bandwidth of:

- 512 Kbps available bandwidth within a site, whether or not it spans multiple domains.

- 256 Kbps available bandwidth within a domain that spans multiple sites, where no sites span it and other domains.

- 56 to 128 Kbps available bandwidth where a domain and site share a boundary—larger for those GCs with more than half a million objects.

- If using a single domain model, these issues do not apply.

Aside from traffic issues, a domain should be added when the domain-level security policy for passwords and account lockouts must be different for two separate sets of users.

DNS provides mapping between IP addresses and hostnames. It can also map to further information such as service resource records (SRV RRs). DNS is used by the Active Directory as a locator service for logon, for locating DCs, and GC servers.

Rules surrounding domains and DNS are as follows:

- A domain's name cannot be changed if it is a root domain, or easily changed otherwise. Note that the domain's globally unique identifier cannot be changed, but display names for nonroot domains can be renamed in the Active Directory.

- Two domains cannot be merged.

- A single domain cannot be split into two.

- DNS must support SRV RRs.

- DNS must be available for DCs at all times.

- At a minimum, there should be one DC and one DNS server in each site.

- A DC is allowed to also be the DNS server running Microsoft's DNS service.

- One recommendation is to have a single root domain hold the schema, and lower-level domains contain the resources and users in the tree.

- Domains are an administrative and security boundary, so plan domains accordingly.

- DNS names should be registered with InterNIC. InterNIC does not require subdomains to be registered, simply the parent domain level.

Tekkietech.com

Tekkietech.com has four forests. The domains in the production Internet and joint venture forests are concentrated in geographic areas. They decide that they will have the DNS namespace represent single domains without subdomains for all the forests except the private, production intranet forest. For this forest, Tekkietech.com asks the consultant to create a plan that will enable a flexible and growth-oriented domain strategy for subdomains.

The consultant looks at Tekkietech.com network. Since Tekkietech.com wants flexibility, the consultant recommends that the root domain be dedicated to the schema and also contain all the DNS servers, which means that the consultant will be able to distribute the DNS servers wherever the schema needs to be. The consultant realizes that there will be at least one subdomain for mytekkies.com.

Additionally, the consultant looks at the WAN links, in which all the sites are linked by high-speed network links and most have redundant, failover links. The availability of the bandwidth is very high on every link. There is no need to separate any domains to prevent replication from spanning a slow WAN link.

Then the consultant looks at the logical configuration of Tekkietech.com. The offices exist in Germany, the United States, Australia, South Africa, and Japan. The consultant knows that there are some security issues with international offices. For one thing, software containing 128-bit encryption cannot be shipped outside the United States. Additionally, there are some business politics that separate each office group by its continent. The consultant recommends that the level of domains below the root domain for mytekkies.com consists of the following:

- **Us.mytekkies.com:** Represents the United States. It uses 128-bit encryption exclusively from all other same-level domains.

- **Australia.mytekkies.com:** Represents Australia. It is separated from the other same-level domains for business politics.

- **Europe.mytekkies.com:** Represents Europe. It is separate from the other same-level domains for business politics.

- **Asia.mytekkies.com:** Represents Asia. It is separate from the other same-level domains for business politics.

- **Africa.mytekkies.com:** Represents Africa. It is separate from the other same-level domains for business politics.

The consultant looks further into the organization and network, and sees that all of the intranet servers are running in the United States and are managed by a single Webmaster group. This group wants to have complete control over the intranet. Therefore, below the Us.mytekkies.com, the consultant recommends that there are two subdomains, one dedicated to the intranet and the other dedicated to the private network. These are designated as:

- Intranet.us.mytekkies.com
- Net.us.mytekkies.com

The final domain plan for the mytekkies.com forest is depicted in Figure 4.5.

Insurance, Inc.

The consultant has a single forest in Insurance, Inc. with a root domain of Insurinc.com. The consultant considers that Insurance, Inc. is a relatively small company with a single physical location, but with remote access services likely providing Terminal Services to several thousand agents. The consultant knows that Insurance, Inc. is not growth oriented. It does not implement technology unless there is a business requirement for it. Insurance, Inc. does not have

Figure 4.5 Domain plan for mytekkies.com.

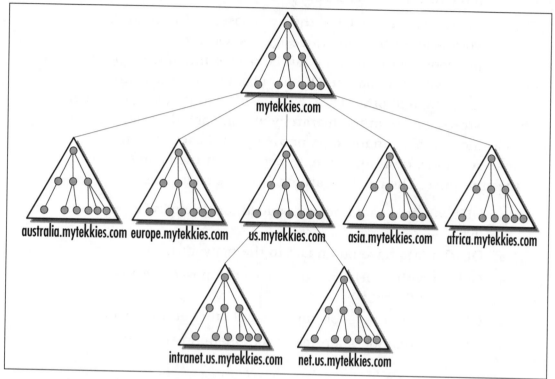

a large IT department, does not connect to the Internet because of strict security reasons, and does not have a technology lab. There is no reason to implement more than a single domain with a single DNS name, Insurinc.com, as shown in Figure 4.6.

Figure 4.6 Insurance, Inc.'s domain strategy.

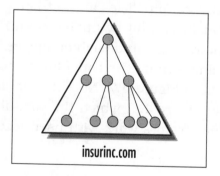

Organizational Unit Strategy

The consultant will review OUs, their purpose, and uses in the internetwork before beginning to design the OU strategy.

OUs are container units that can be nested into a tree structure, or hierarchy, within a domain. OUs can contain user accounts, resource objects, and other OUs. OUs reside within a single domain. The OU strategy is an initial hierarchy within each domain. OUs are flexible enough to be changed as needed, so this strategy may change over time, or at any time, to better meet the changing needs of the enterprise. The rules regarding OUs are as follows:

- OUs can be created, moved, added, or deleted whenever needed.
- OU changes have no impact to the network traffic.
- Objects within OUs can also be easily moved, created, added, and deleted.
- OUs are containers for implementation of group policy.
- OUs are containers for delegation of administration.

Tekkietech.com

The consultant decides to simplify the OU structure within each of the domains for mytekkies.com forest by making them identical. Since the domains are used to separate most of the political and administrative units, there is no need to create OUs for the delegation of administration. Group policies are not likely to be implemented except on a business unit by business unit basis. The company is exceptionally large, and each employee is easily identified by his or her business unit. The consultant decides to create the OU strategy shown in Figure 4.7. Note the similarity of this figure to the org chart in Figure 4.1, which the consultant duplicated to help Network Administrators work with user accounts.

Figure 4.7 OU strategy for mytekkies.com subdomains.

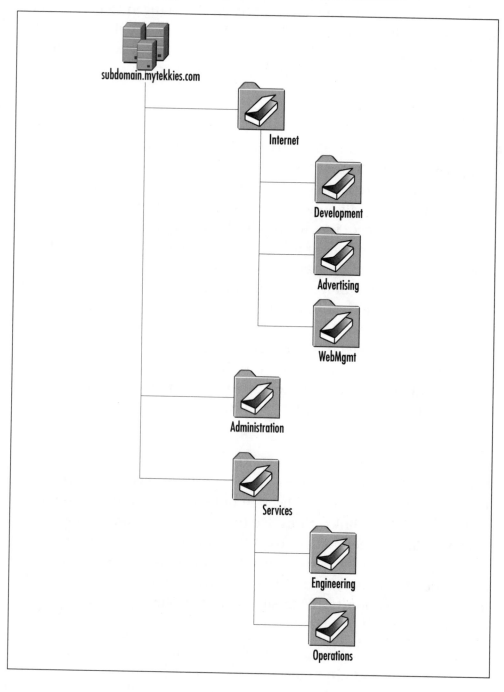

Although the original OU strategy is identical for each of the mytekkies.com subdomains, it can be easily changed to better meet business requirements later. The OU strategy, although important, is the simplest to design because there are no impacts to the network or problems with changing it after the fact.

Insurance, Inc.

Insurance, Inc. has a logical structure of associates, but this is complicated by the numerous agencies that work independently for the company. There is no need for delegation of administration, and the IT department will only implement group policy for the accounting group. Insurance, Inc. must add these users into the domain in order to grant them access to the network, but they do not fit into the org chart. The consultant divides the top-level OUs into corporate and agency containers. Within the corporate container, the consultant reflects the Insurance, Inc. org chart. There are so many agents that the consultant does not want to lump them into the same container. Instead, the consultant places each state (since Insurance, Inc. only sells within the United States) beneath the agency container, and then the agencies within each state. This structure is represented in Figure 4.8.

Site Topology

For the final design component, the consultant reviews Active Directory sites. A site is a collection of IP subnets that are connected by fast, reliable links. Sites are typically LANs, and do not contain WAN links except where the WAN link is very fast and reliable. The site is used to create physical divisions of the network. It directs authentication and query traffic for users within a site to a DC within a site. Replication traffic is similarly controlled. The following design rules apply to sites:

- The site topology should reflect the network's topology.
- Each site should have a dedicated DC.

Figure 4.8 Insurance, Inc.'s OU strategy.

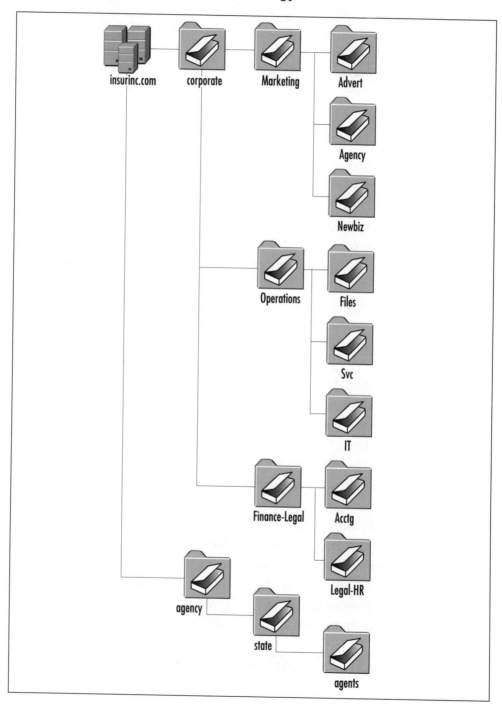

- No site should span a slow or unreliable network connection, especially WAN connections.

- Sites do not need to be created for clients that connect via remote access.

- Sites are easily added, moved, changed, and deleted.

Tekkietech.com

When the consultant looks at the Tekkietech.com network for the mytekkies.com forest site topology, it appears extremely large and complex. The network is interconnected by extremely fast and reliable network links. It also has the design separation already established between the offices in the five continents at the domain level. The consultant could very easily establish a single site within each domain to represent the offices within the continent. The consultant could also establish a site for each physical office, whether it is one of the eight major offices or one of the 72 test market offices, which would create 80 sites for the network.

Considering that Tekkietech.com has enough DCs, both the designs are feasible. The consultant must thoroughly examine the way that the WAN connections are established. It is discovered that each major office is a central hub for WAN connections to the nearest test market offices. This creates a network that consists of eight areas of concentrated WAN/LAN traffic.

With this in mind, and knowing how easy it is to change the site topology at any point in time, the consultant decides to establish a site for each major office. If there are problems for any particular office that warrant it having its own site, then it can be added at that point in time. The consultant creates a site link system and places all site links within site link bridges, that directs traffic in a serial fashion throughout the sites shown in Figure 4.9. This places the traffic on links between sites that are nearest each other. The consultant has rejected the hub and spoke system, which would place a single site as the main hub for the sites and all other sites would link to it because the serial system actually reflects the network connections available.

The consultant does follow the rules and places the following servers in each site:

- A DC for the root domain of mytekkies.com.

- A DC for the domain in which the site actually resides; for example a DC for Japan.mytekkies.com would reside at the Tokyo site.

- A DNS server.

Figure 4.9 Site topology for mytekkies.com forest.

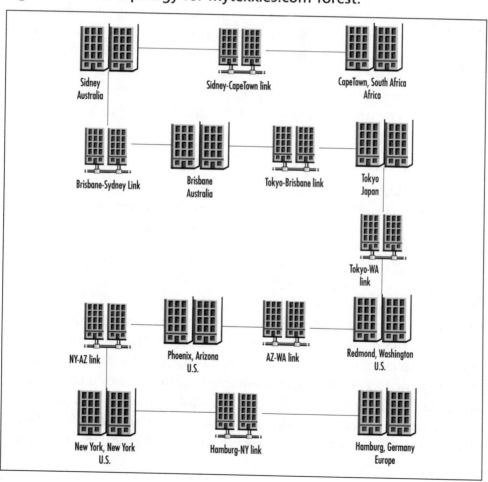

Insurance, Inc.

The consultant has a very simple job when designing the Insurance, Inc. site topology. Since the Insurance, Inc. network is located in a single site, and no sites need to be created for remote access, there need only be a single site for Insurinc.com with no site links required.

Organizational Unit Structure

OUs are containers within a domain that can nest within each other to develop a hierarchy. They are not used for user account policy, but are used for group policy and for the delegation of administrative authority. An Active Directory user does not always have to navigate the OU hierarchy to locate services and information, so the optimal structure for OUs should reflect the boundaries needed for applying group policy or for delegating authority. It is a good rule of thumb to keep the OU names short enough to remember.

OU Objects in the Active Directory

OUs are container objects within the Active Directory. They contain other objects, but they also have attributes and values applicable to them. Policies can be applied to OUs, and those policies can be inherited by sub-OUs. This facilitates administration for group policy.

Group Policy and OUs

Group policies settings are applied to users and computers in order to manage the desktop configuration. A specific policy is applied to a site, domain and/or an OU as needed. The group policy can be filtered to control access. Group policies will affect users' login time when they are in a nested OU that has multiple group policies. Longer names for OUs will also affect processing at login time. See Chapter 9, "Group Policies and Security," for information on how to apply group policies.

For IT Professionals

Designs

There is more than one right way to design a network. Optimal designs take into account the business requirements, current network environment, and potential growth of a company. The designs for forests, domains, OUs, and sites could be completely different for two companies and still be considered "correct" or "good." This reflects the flexibility of Active Directory more than it does the benefits of a good design.

In the cases here, the selections the consultant made were based on the business requirements for the company and its existing environment. Would it have made sense to have two domains for the Insurance, Inc. network? Perhaps it would be nice to separate the agencies from the corporate culture, or maybe separate the operations folks from the marketing and legal departments. Would it add any benefits to the network to create that separation? Probably not. In this case, simplicity of design is the best option. Performance was not a high requirement; centralization and ease of administration were. Here are some design tips:

- Do not be afraid to create a design that seems aberrant from standard models, if it supports business requirements.

- Try to keep your designs as simple as possible.

- Pay strict attention to the design of items that cannot change or be moved, merged, or split, such as forests and domains.

- Play with a couple of design scenarios before you select a final design. Make sure it supports each of your business objectives, and you can justify that design above the others.

Continued

For IT Professionals	Designs

- Make sure that whatever design you specify, you will have enough servers to support its creation.
- Always register your DNS names with InterNIC.
- Wear caffeine-tolerant clothing during your design process—you will probably spend long hours on this part of the job. <grin>

Delegating Administration

The Legacy NT delegation of administration did not offer much in the way of flexibility.

- Administrators were forced to use built-in local groups on the servers for administrative authority.
- They had to adjust predefined rights, if they were not sufficient or too lax.
- Their administrative design typically resulted in oodles of Domain Administrators so that everyone could access what they needed to.
- They created resource domains just to delegate administration, which then resulted in too many domains and complex trust relationships.

Delegating administration is more powerful and flexible in Windows 2000 than it was in earlier versions of NT. Using the flexibility of the Active Directory, delegation of administrative responsibility can be applied at the OU level. The Administrator can assign administrative rights for each object's attribute and whether that control can be inherited. The result is that the appropriate Administrators are granted the appropriate control of their assigned users and published resources. If an Administrator delegates "Full Control" to another user, then that user is able to delegate administrative authority to others. Otherwise, the delegation of administration is completed by selecting the authority level over each object class and the ability to modify specific attributes. The process is fairly simple:

1. Create a group.
2. Grant the group specific access.
3. Populate the group with users.

Windows 2000 even supplies a Delegation of Control Wizard in the Active Directory Users and Computers Microsoft Management Console (MMC) utility (which can be found in the Administrative Tools folder under Programs in the Start menu). This makes the process even easier to execute. The following steps must be taken to use the Delegation of Control Wizard in order to delegate Full Control to another Administrator for a single OU (the OU is also called a folder in the wizard). (See Figure 4.10.)

1. Click Start | Programs | Administrative Tools on any DC.
2. Select Active Directory Users and Computers.
3. After the window opens, in the left pane of the window, navigate to the OU to which you will be delegating administrative rights.
4. Right-click on the OU and select Delegate Control from the popup menu.
5. The wizard box will start with a Welcome dialog. Click Next.
6. The next screen will show the path of the folder. Click Next.
7. The Group or User Selection screen will appear. Click Add.
8. Select the group to which you will be giving administrative access.
9. The group's name will appear in the window. Verify it is correct, and click Next.
10. In the Predefined Delegations window, select "Do customized delegation," and click Next.

Figure 4.10 Customized delegation.

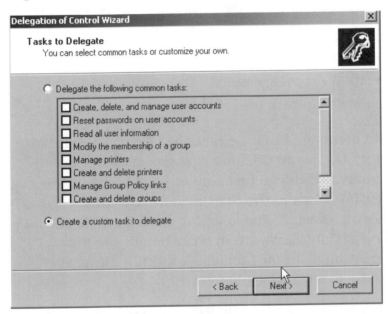

11. In the Active Directory object type window, you can select either the entire folder or a custom list of objects that are in the folder. Select Entire folder, and click Next.

12. In the Permissions box, you can select a variety of permissions (see Figure 4.11). To delegate full administrative rights, you will need to select Full Control. Then click Next.

13. The final dialog will show you a summary of the options you have selected. Click FINISH to enable delegation. If you click BACK, you can change your options. If you click CANCEL, no changes will be applied. (See Figure 4.12.)

After completing this exercise, there is a way to verify that the changes are applied. In the Active Directory Users and Computers window, select the View menu and then the Advanced Features option. You can then right-click the OU for which you delegated control, then select Properties. On the Security page, click ADVANCED.

Figure 4.11 Reset Password is an option in the Permissions box for user objects.

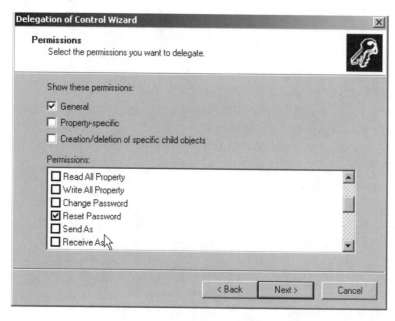

Figure 4.12 Summary dialog.

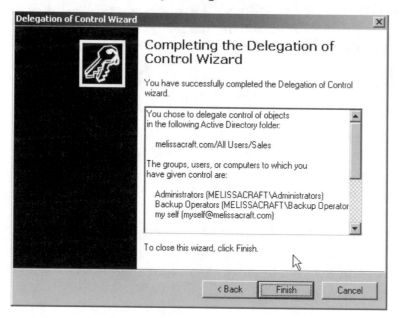

For Managers

Controlling Who Can Reset Passwords

One of the most common problems users run into is that they forget their password. Usually this happens the day after they were required to change their password. Only certain Administrators can access that type of user control in legacy environments, so this capability is typically retained by a high-level IT group. In a large organization, it can become a huge headache!

Active Directory can be an aspirin for this particular headache, if an organization has a group such as a Help Desk that is connected to the network. In this case, the Active Directory allows the delegation of only the password resetting right. The Help Desk would have no other rights to the directory and could handle the password resets immediately.

To delegate this specific right, create a group for the Help Desk. Then follow the Delegation of Control process up to the Predefined Delegations window in step 10. Here you would select the "Delegate one or more of the predefined delegations," and from the check box list, select only "Reset passwords on users accounts." It is a simple matter of finishing the wizard after that.

The Permissions tab will show you the additional permissions created for the group. If you double-click the group, you will see that it has been granted full rights to all of that OU and any OUs within it.

Another way to verify that the group has been correctly granted access is to log on as a user account that is a member of that group. Then start the Active Directory Users and Computers Wizard and try creating a new group.

There are some challenges with delegating administration. For many with experience in other directory services, the most difficult problem with delegating administration for a container is with somehow losing the delegated Administrator's password—whether the Administrator has forgotten it, or left the company, or some other mishap has occurred. For this reason, it is a good practice to always have a master administrative account that is granted access to every container, even if it is intended to be completely cut off. The account should be set aside in a secure place for disaster recovery purposes only.

Summary

Designing an Active Directory structure consists of four design objectives:

- The forest plan
- The domains and DNS strategy
- The organizational unit (OU) strategy
- The site topology

All designs should be based on the business requirements of the enterprise. When a design is based on a business requirement, it will better serve that enterprise—even though another design may be more optimal for a different company with the same size and locations but different business objectives.

Although the forest plan is a simple document detailing the number, root domain, and purpose for each forest, it is the first set of decisions that must be made toward the final Active Directory implementation. This plan must be made wisely because the forests cannot be merged, split, renamed, or otherwise redesigned after they are implemented.

The most critical decisions that will be made are those that affect the Active Directory domains and DNS strategy. DNS is compulsory for Active Directory to function. The DNS names used should be registered with InterNIC, if new ones are required for the DNS strategy. Domains are both a physical and logical structure for Active Directory. Each domain has its own DNS name. The design for the domains should be treated with as much assiduousness as the forest plan because domains have the same permanent features: They cannot be merged, split, or renamed, after they are first created.

Since an OU is a logical grouping container in the Active Directory and has no real impact on the network traffic, it can reflect the organization or another functional plan. OUs can be used for applying group policy and for delegating administration. OUs can be renamed, moved, created, and deleted at any time.

Sites are a representation of the physical network. Sites are considered to be a group of IP subnets that share fast and reliable network connections. The site should not span any slow or unreliable WAN links. Each physical campus or building can be considered a site, or when using extremely fast WAN links, a group of geographically distant but well-connected areas can become a single site.

Using OUs for delegating administration is a great tool for Administrators that prevents all the legacy Windows NT issues of creating groups of Administrators and multiple domains and trusts. An OU can be created arbitrarily, and specific rights can be assigned to a user or group for administration; this is both flexible and effective. This capability can enable an Administrator to provide password reset rights only to a group, which means that they can reset a password and not change any other information in the Active Directory. Windows 2000 Server provides a wizard to delegate control, which simplifies this activity. The Delegate Control Wizard is accessed by right-clicking an OU in the Active Directory Users and Computers MMC, then selecting Delegate Control from the popup menu.

FAQs

Q: Our group has created a forest plan that consists of three forests. We only have a single registered DNS name. We would like to use the same DNS namespace for each of the forests. Can we do this?

A: No. Each forest must have its own dedicated DNS namespaces. A namespace cannot cross forests.

Q: There are two office buildings in our organization and we have a fractional T-1 line running between them at 256 Kbps. We have a legacy Windows NT domain that covers both sites. Can we keep this same domain design?

A: Yes. The domain design is flexible enough to span WAN links, but it is preferable not to. This should not prevent an existing legacy NT domain structure from being upgraded into the Active Directory in its existing configuration. It is recommended to create two separate sites with their own DC—one site to represent each building—in the Active Directory. This will help manage the traffic crossing the WAN.

Q: Two people in our OU planning group want to recreate the org chart for the OU structure. The rest of the group wants to create a structure that reflects the administration of the network. We intend to delegate administration through the OUs. Which is the right way?

A: That depends. If the administration of the network is in a one-to-one correspondence with the org chart groups, or even if there is one administration group to several org chart groups, then the org chart method will be effective for both. If there are two groups of Administrators who are each supposed to manage a part of an org chart group, then they will end up stepping on each others toes by sharing the OU administrative rights. In this case, the OUs should reflect the administration groups, or a combination of the two.

Q: We are planning to implement three group policies separately, but want to create an OU structure that has several levels. Can we do this?

A: Yes. You can create three OUs at the top of the tree for the group policies. Then create an OU structure that makes sense below those three OUs. If you move a user, however, remember that the group policies affecting that user will change, too.

Q: Our company has eight buildings, but six of them are on a campus connected by fiber optic cabling and high-speed connections. Should we create eight sites or three?

A: In this case, you should probably create three sites. The campus really represents a single site under the definition of "collection of IP subnets that share fast and reliable links."

Chapter 5

Implementing a Domain

Solutions in this chapter:

- Installing Domains in the Active Directory
- Managing Objects in the Domains
- Installing DNS
- Integrating DNS with the Active Directory
- Managing Zones and Resource Records

Now that the domain structure design is in hand, implementation can proceed in accordance with the design strategy. This requires that the installation team has reviewed the design documents and understands them before installing the servers into the domain. Sometimes the installation team and the design team are the same set of people. Other times, they are two different sets of people with different ideas on how the domain should be structured. When design decisions are made for business-specific reasons and that is understood by all involved, the two teams can generally come to an agreement for the implementation of that design.

Introduction

Implementing a domain can be as simple as installing a single domain controller (DC). Hands-on installation usually seems a great deal easier than what the time and effort spent preparing for it would indicate. Microsoft made installation even easier for Windows 2000 than it ever was for its predecessor, Windows NT.

There are three steps for the Windows 2000 Active Directory domain installation.

1. Run the Windows 2000 Server WINNT command.
2. Configure DNS (Domain Name System) as a client or as a service on the Windows 2000 Server.
3. Run the Active Directory Installation Wizard.

The installation of a Windows 2000 Server is the simple task of running the WINNT command with the correct switches and parameters. The installation of Active Directory happens after server installation, using the Active Directory Installation Wizard. DNS is required for the Active Directory, so if it is not detected on the network at the time of the Active Directory installation, the Active Directory Installation Wizard installs the service on the Windows 2000 Server. If DNS is configured as a client, the installer must ensure that the domain's DNS name is registered in the DNS tables before installing the Active Directory domain. Dynamic updates should be turned on for the DC to register itself. If DNS is configured as a DNS server on the DC, the DNS tables must include the domain name, and dynamic updates must be turned on so that the DNS entries can be created for the Active Directory domain.

After installing a DC, the hierarchical structure within that single domain can be created, populated, and managed. This is performed by creating organizational units (OUs), creating objects within the Active Directory, and establishing a group policy system to enable role-based administration.

Installing the First Domain in Active Directory

The first DC in the Active Directory receives the honor of being the DC for the root domain of the first forest. In other words, the installation of Active Directory on the first DC is the same thing as the installation of the root domain. Performing the installation of the DC requires that you know some information about it. Table 5.1 lists the type of information needed to install the first Windows 2000 DC.

Table 5.1 Information Required for Windows 2000 Installation

Server Information	Example
Domain name	Root.com
Server DNS name	Server.root.com
Server NetBIOS name	Server
Partition and size	C: and 2 GB
Filesystem	NTFS
System directory	\WINNT
Name of license owner	M.Y. Name
Organization of license owner	My Org
Language	English
Keyboard	U.S.

Continued

Server Information	Example
License mode (per seat or per server)	Per seat
Administrator's password	Hx346xqmz3
Time zone	Arizona GMT -7

After logging on to the Windows 2000 Server for the first time, you will see a new screen as shown in Figure 5.1 This wizard has been designed to provide a single interface to assist in configuring Windows 2000 Server.

Figure 5.1 Configuring Windows 2000 Server for the first time.

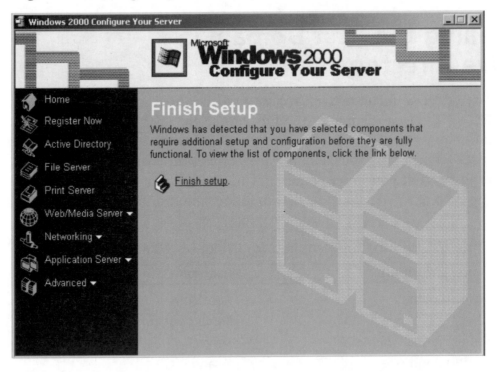

If there are further programs to install, screen also prompts you to complete the Windows 2000 Server setup. When you click FINISH SETUP, a new screen appears that displays the Add/Remove Programs utility from Control Panel shown in Figure 5.2. In fact, the original screen remains available for you to return to. As you browse through its contents, you will realize that it is simply a single compilation of all the utilities that are useful during the first installation of a new Windows 2000 Server. All of these items can be accessed through the Control Panel, the Administrative Tools, or through the command-line interface. This console utility was developed to simplify the Administrator's tasks for configuring any new Windows 2000 Server.

Figure 5.2 The Add/Remove Programs panel.

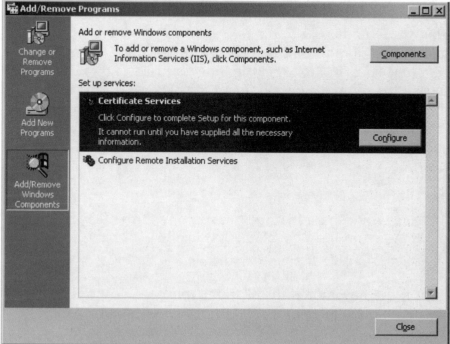

Active Directory Wizard

Windows 2000 Server installs automatically as a member server, unless an upgrade has been performed on a legacy NT primary or backup domain controller (BDC). When an upgrade is performed, the Active Directory Wizard begins automatically. The Active Directory Wizard is available from the Configure Windows 2000 Server screen under Active Directory. If the filesystem is not NTFS, it will need to be converted to NTFS before Active Directory will install. To quickly convert the filesystem, the command

For IT Professionals

Automating Installation for Windows 2000

If you have multiple servers to install that have identical hardware configuration, you can create a setup file to automate the installation of each of them. Automated installation is a function that Windows 2000 inherited from Windows NT. An automated installation will reduce the deployment time for multiple machines, but it buys little time for just a few of them because of the setup file development time involved. One benefit that is worth the extra time is that all the servers deployed with the same setup file will have the identical configuration.

In order to automate a Windows 2000 installation, you will need:

- The WINNT.EXE program
- A network share that includes a copy of the files that are on the Windows 2000 CD-ROM
- An answer file that you create

To run the automated installation, you need to boot the server to a DOS prompt and run the command winnt /u:answer.txt /s:<path to the Windows 2000 source share>

The Windows 2000 source share is the network directory that contains the installation files, including Windows 2000 files from the CD-ROM, new device drivers, and any additional files that you want to copy. The structure of the Windows 2000 source files for an Intel server would be:

\I386 Windows 2000 source directory

\i386\oem All OEM files

\i386\oem\Textmode   txtsetup.oem, scsi, and HAL files

\i386\$oem$\$$ Maps to %systemroot%

Continued

For IT Professionals

Automating Installation for Windows 2000

\i386\$oem$\$1	Maps to %systemdrive%
\i386\oem\<drivers_dir>	Plug-and-play drivers
\i386\oem\<drive letter>	Maps to a drive on the computer

You can create an answer file using the Setup Manager tool. Setup Manager will also create the network share for the Windows 2000 source files. The answer file is a plain text file that can also be created and edited in any text editor, such as Notepad.

CONVERT /FS:NTFS can be executed from the command prompt. The next time the server boots, it will convert the filesystem to NTFS.

To access the Active Directory Wizard, select Active Directory from the navigation bar in the Configure Windows 2000 screen, which will take you to the page displayed in Figure 5.3. This page will not only lead you to the Active Directory Wizard, but also offers you links to more information about DCs, domains, and forests.

The first screen of the wizard is a Welcome screen. Click NEXT to continue. The Domain Controller Type page appears asking you to select whether this will be the first DC in a new domain, or a DC in an existing domain. Since this is the first DC, select that option. After clicking NEXT, the Create Tree or Child Domain window appears, as shown in Figure 5.4. This allows you to select whether this is the first domain in a tree, or if it is a child domain. Since this is a DC for a root domain, select the "Create a new domain tree" option.

The Create or Join Forest page appears, which will allow you to create a new forest, or to place this domain tree in an existing forest. The option to select for a forest root domain is to create a new forest. The Active Directory Wizard displays its DNS component in

Figure 5.3 Active Directory screen.

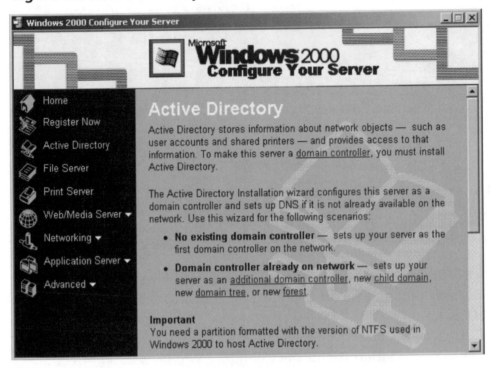

Figure 5.3 New domain tree or child domain.

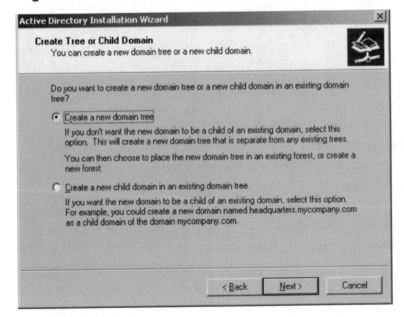

the next screen. It will detect that DNS is not running on the current computer and ask to configure the client or to install this server as a DNS server. If this server will be a DNS server, you should select the second option. If there is already a DNS server on the network, select the first option, as depicted in Figure 5.5. Regardless of which option is selected, before going further with the Active Directory Wizard, a DNS server that is locatable on the network must have the new domain's DNS name registered. That DNS server must be authoritative for the new domain as well.

Figure 5.5 Active Directory depends on DNS.

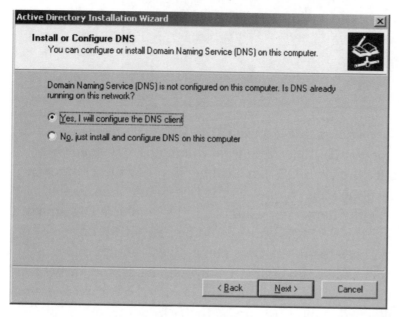

The new domain being created will need a DNS name. Unlike Windows NT, this name is not a NetBIOS name such as MYDO-MAIN, but a true DNS name such as mydomain.com. The wizard dialog that appears after prompting for the DNS configuration establishes the DNS name for the domain, as shown in Figure 5.6.

Figure 5.6 New DNS domain name.

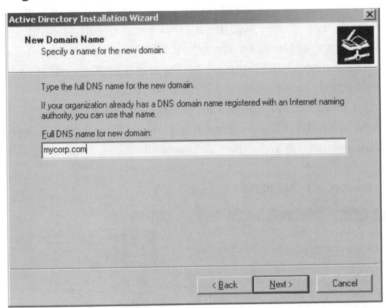

Even though the domain will have a DNS name, it will also have a NetBIOS name for compatibility with legacy domains. The following screen prompts for the NetBIOS name calling it a "downlevel name." This does not have the same format as the DNS name, nor does it have to have the same name. For example, if the domain's DNS name is mydomain.com, the NetBIOS name could be CAPNKIRK or something else totally unrelated to the DNS name. Even though this is a capability for backward compatibility, using a similar name for both the DNS and NetBIOS names will make the domain easier for users to use. For example, mydomain.com can be the DNS name, and MYDOMAIN can be the NetBIOS name. Type in the NetBIOS name and click NEXT to access the following wizard screen.

You are next prompted to select the location for the Active Directory database and logging files. Make sure that the location has enough space for growth of the directory. For optimal performance and to be able to recover the server, these two files should not be in their default locations, but on separate partitions of separate physical disks. The default locations for these files are on the system partition within the WINNT directory, as shown in Figure 5.7.

Figure 5.7 Default locations for Active Directory database and log files.

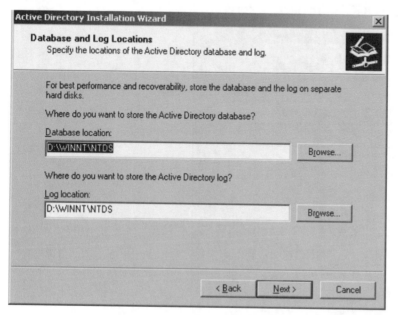

The next wizard dialog lets you select a folder for the system volume. The system volume is a folder that is replicated to every DC. SYSVOL contains the directory service information that must be replicated. Because of the replication, the SYSVOL directory must be placed on an NTFS 5.0 partition. Information that must be replicated for the Active Directory includes the files necessary to enable logon. Traditionally, this was handled by the NETLOGON share. Logon still is handled by NETLOGON, but now that NETLOGON folder is a subdirectory of SYSVOL, which means that it will be replicated with the Active Directory system information and will enable logon. The folder properties showing the NETLOGON share location are depicted in Figure 5.8. Group policy templates and information are also replicated by being placed within SYSVOL since they are required by all DCs when applying group policy. The default folder is the WINNT\SYSVOL directory. Like the database and log files, it is optimal to make sure that this folder is on a partition that will have enough space for growth, which may not be the default folder in the system partition.

Figure 5.8 NETLOGON Properties screen.

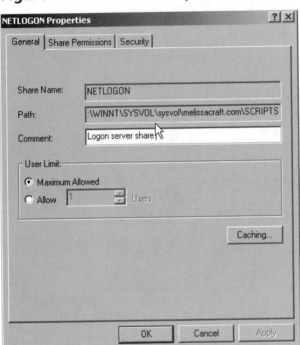

After clicking NEXT, the Active Directory Wizard will ask whether this is a mixed domain that uses Windows NT 4 RAS (Remote Access Service) servers. The issue is related to security. In order to use Windows NT 4 RAS servers, permissions must be less secure. Select the option that makes sense for your network, and click NEXT.

The following dialog will provide the Administrator password to be used when restoring the Directory Services. This is a different password than the server's local Administrator account, which means that the password can be the same or may be different. Make sure that the password is available for use in case of a disaster. Click NEXT.

For IT Professionals

Active Directory Recovery Console

Directory Service Restore mode is applicable only to Windows 2000 DCs for restoring the Active Directory service and SYSVOL directory. Restore mode is a command-line console that can be used to:

- Start or stop services
- Format a hard drive
- Copy or view files on the server's NTFS drives
- Repair the system by copying a file from a floppy or other drive
- Reconfigure a service that is preventing the system from starting

If the Recovery Console has been installed, it is available from the list of operating systems in the startup of the computer. If it has not been installed, you can run it from the Windows 2000 Setup program on the CD-ROM. This will only function if the server can boot from the CD-ROM.

To install the Recovery Console as a startup option for Windows 2000:

1. Start Windows 2000 Server and log on as Administrator.
2. Click Start | Run and type **CMD** in the box to open a command prompt.
3. Make sure that the Windows 2000 Server CD is in the drive, or that the CD's contents are available on a network share.

Continued

For IT Professionals

Active Directory Recovery Console

4. At the command prompt, change to the drive that contains the I386 directory. (If you have an Alpha server, replace I386 with ALPHA.)

5. From the I386 or ALPHA directory, type WINNT32 /CMDCONS.

6. The first dialog will allow you to bail out of the install by clicking No, or continue by clicking Yes. Click Yes to continue.

7. After files are copied, a final dialog screen appears stating that the console has been installed. Click Ok to close the screen.

8. To run the Recovery Console, restart the server and select the Recovery Console option from the list of operating systems in the Boot menu.

The wizard will display a summary page. Review this page to ensure that the options selected are the ones required for your installation. If the options are not correct, this is the last chance to click BACK to change those options. If they are correct, click NEXT, and . . . wait. The Active Directory Wizard will take a considerable amount of time to install Active Directory Services, and even longer if installing a DC that is not the first in the forest, and must replicate to an existing, populated Active Directory.

Integrating DNS into the Active Directory

Today, the only way to integrate DNS with the Active Directory is to implement the Microsoft Windows 2000 DNS service on a Windows

2000 Server. When DNS is integrated in the Active Directory, there are some immediate benefits:

- It can coexist with other DNS servers.

- It automatically supports DHCP, and no DHCP-integration testing is required.

- It will support multi-master replication of the DNS within the Active Directory.

- It will be able to scavenge stale records and keep the DNS database up to date.

If the Windows 2000 Server DNS service is implemented exclusively on the network, it will add the additional capability for using the Unicode extended character set. (Briefly, Unicode is a character set that is based on 16 bits of information. Compared to standard 7- or 8-bit ASCII or 8-bit EBCDIC, which have 128 or 256 characters, the Unicode character set can have up to 65,536 characters. This enables it to encompass most of the world's languages in one set of characters.) Additionally, the Windows 2000 Server DNS supports all the requirements for Active Directory such as Service resource records (SRV RRs) and dynamic updates.

Configuring DNS

If the server does not have DNS installed or a DNS client configured on it, it will not have Active Directory installed either, because Active Directory depends on locating a DNS server. To configure DNS before running the Active Directory Wizard:

1. Either select Start | Programs | Administrative Tools | DNS, or from the Windows 2000 Configure Your Server screen, select the Networking option in te left-hand pane and when it expands, select DNS, and finally click the Manage DNS option in the right-hand pane that appears.

2. Select the server that you will be configuring DNS on.

3. Click the Action menu.

4. Choose the Configure the Server option.

5. The Configure DNS Server Wizard appears with a Welcome screen. Click NEXT.

6. If this server will be a root server for DNS, select the first DNS server on the network as shown in Figure 5.9. If DNS is already installed and configured on the network, select the second option.

Figure 5.9 DNS Root Server.

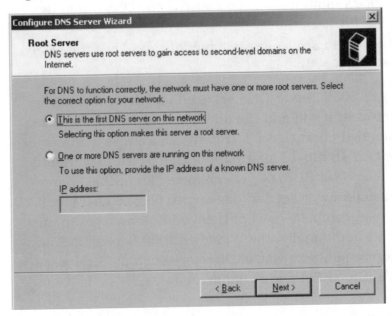

7. The Configure DNS Server Wizard will next prompt to create a Forward Lookup Zone. If Active Directory is installed, then you will be able to use the "Active Directory-integrated" option. However, if the server is a stand-alone or member server and you attempt to create a Forward Lookup Zone, you will see the Active Directory Integrated option is grayed out, as shown in Figure 5.10. Not to worry, simply select the second option to Create a Standard Primary for now, and click NEXT.

8. The Configure DNS Server Wizard will provide a Summary page. If you need to make changes, you can click BACK. If not, click FINISH to close the wizard screen.

Figure 5.10 Active Directory integration not available as a stand-alone DNS server.

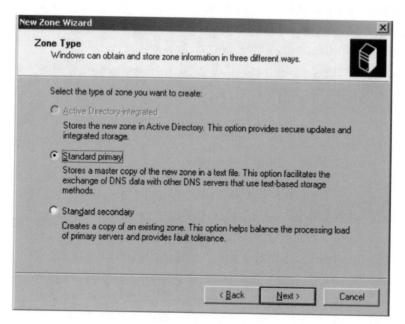

Active Directory Integrated Zones

If you install Active Directory after configuring DNS on a server, you can still create Active Directory Integrated zones. To create an Active Directory Integrated zone, do the following:

1. Enter the DNS Management Console by clicking Start | Programs | Administrative Tools | DNS, or from the Windows 2000 Configure Your Server screen, select the Networking option in the left-hand pane and when it expands, select DNS, and finally click the Manage DNS option in the right-hand pane that appears.

2. Click the plus sign (+) next to the server you are adding the zone to and expand it.

3. Select the Forward Lookup Zones folder below the server.

4. Click the Action menu, and click New Zone.

5. The New Zone Wizard will display a Welcome screen. Click NEXT.

6. The Zone Type screen will appear. Select the "Active Directory-integrated" option. (This will be grayed out if Active Directory is not installed.) Click Next.

7. Type in the name of the zone, such as myzone.com or myzone.mydomain.com. Click Next.

8. The New Zone Wizard will display a Summary page. If the summary is correct, click Finish. If not, click Back and change the options.

About Zones

The DNS namespace can be divided up into zones. Each zone stores information about a DNS domain and is the source of information for that domain. A zone can include information about subdomains, or a new zone can be created for the subdomain. When a subdomain is contained in a new zone, the parent domain's zone must still contain a few records, called name server (NS) records, to be able to delegate information to that new zone. Zones can be fault tolerant by creating secondary servers for them. Any time a zone is replicated to a secondary server, that replication is considered a zone transfer.

A forward lookup zone is the most common. This type of zone represents a query by a client based on the DNS name of another computer that is stored as an address (A) RR. The DNS server will respond to a forward lookup with an IP address.

A reverse lookup zone is used to find the DNS name of a computer with a certain IP address. It is the same as a forward lookup, but backwards. The client will submit a query with an IP address and the DNS server will respond with the hostname of that computer.

Dynamic updates function in a similar fashion to DHCP addresses. The dynamic updates self-register DNS names on a DNS server without requiring an Administrator to set the DNS name and address. This is similar to DCHP, which applies updates to the workstation without requiring an Administrator to set the IP address. In both cases, from the user's perspective, it is a transparent process. In fact, the two work quite well together. When a DNS server supports dynamic updates, clients can register and update their own A RRs with the server. With DHCP, for example, a client can receive an IP address and register it with the A RR on the DNS server. If the client does not renew the DHCP lease and is granted a new IP address the next time it accesses the network, it can update the A RR on the DNS server with its new IP address. This functionality is especially helpful for companies with active intranets published on users' computers. Until dynamic updates are enabled on the network, dynamic addressing via DHCP would make parts of the intranet difficult, if not impossible, to access and manage because the DNS servers would need to be updated each time a new address was granted to a computer. Dynamic updates must be supported by the client, as well as the server, if the client needs to register its DNS name. Legacy Windows 9x and Windows NT 4 clients do not currently support this functionality. There is a DS Client that can be installed to overcome this problem. To manage the Windows NT 4 Servers that may remain on the network, it is recommended to statically list their DNS names until they are retired, upgraded, or replaced by Windows 2000 Servers.

Windows 2000 clients will attempt to register A RRs dynamically for their IP addresses. This process can be forced by entering the command ipconfig /registerdns from the client. The DHCP service will register the IP address dynamically on the Windows 2000 client.

Scavenging is a new option within the Microsoft Windows 2000 DNS service. It enables the automatic management of RRs. What the scavenging system does is set a timestamp on all RRs. Then the DNS service attempts to refresh the record at a set interval called the "no-refresh interval." If the RR cannot be refreshed, the DNS service will wait a second period of time, called the "refresh interval," and if the record is not refreshed during that second interval, the DNS will then scavenge the record. These intervals can be set within the MS DNS Microsoft Management Console (MMC) for a server by selecting the server, clicking the Action menu, and selecting the "Set Aging/Scavenging for all zones" option. Or, a zone can have its own unique aging and scavenging properties. This is performed by selecting the zone, then clicking the Action menu, and selecting Properties. On the General tab, click AGING to see the screen similar to Figure 5.11.

Figure 5.11 Zone Aging/Scavenging Properties window.

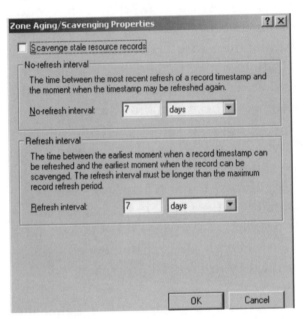

Service Resource Record Registration

SRV RRs are not created the same as a standard A RR. To create an A RR, the Administrator would simply add a new computer to the zone by right-clicking on the zone and selecting New Host. But to create an SRV RR, the Administrator must select Other New Records. This prompts a dialog box that allows the Administrator to select from a list of RR types, as shown in Figure 5.12. The Service Location record is actually an SRV RR. After selecting the Service Location option, a dialog appears for selecting the SRV RR properties.

Figure 5.12 SRV RR creation.

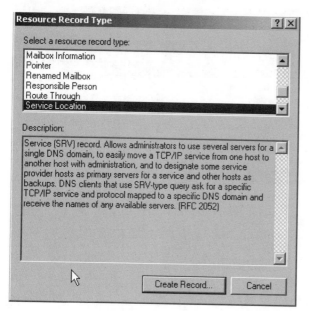

Creating Organizational Units

The hierarchy within the domain consists of nested OUs. OUs are created in the Active Directory Users and Computers MMC. Creating OUs is a privileged task, so the user who will execute this should be logged on as an Administrator, or belong to a group with explicit permissions, or have been granted explicit permissions to do so.

The following procedure is used to create OUs:

1. To invoke the Active Directory Users and Computers MMC, click Start | Programs | Administrative Tools | Active Directory Users and Computers.

2. Click the domain or OU in which you will be placing the new OU.

3. Click the Action menu.

4. Click New.

5. Select Organizational Unit, as depicted in Figure 5.13. Note that you can also right-click the parent object, select New from the popup menu and Organizational Unit from there to get the same result.

Figure 5.13 Creating a new OU.

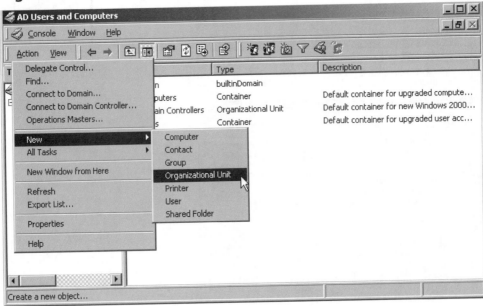

6. The New object dialog will appear. Make sure that the destination for the OU is correct by checking the "Create in:" statement at the top of the dialog. Type a name in the box for the OU, and click OK.

The OU will appear below its parent object in the left-hand pane of the window. As new OUs are created, the left-hand pane will develop a hierarchical structure as shown in Figure 5.14.

Figure 5.14 Hierarchical OUs.

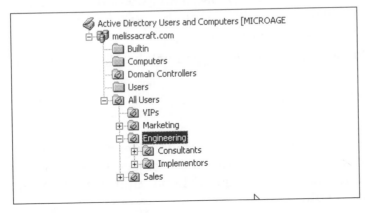

Managing Objects in Active Directory

A Network Administrator will probably spend a lot of time managing objects in the Active Directory. Each time a new person is hired, every time new Windows 2000 Professional PCs are installed, whenever someone is promoted, and whenever someone moves to a different office, a corresponding change must be made to objects in the Active Directory.

Managing User Accounts

If a person is hired at the company, the Administrator must create a user account in the Active Directory. To create a user account:

1. In the Active Directory Users and Computers console, right-click the OU, select New, and then select the User option.

2. The New Object-User dialog, as shown in Figure 5.15, will appear.

Figure 5.15 New Object-User dialog.

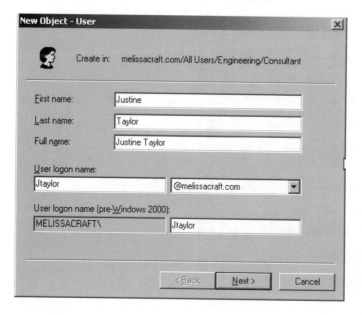

3. Complete the user's name and logon id boxes, then click NEXT.

4. Set the password, select the password options in the following dialog, and click NEXT.

5. Accept the confirmation dialog and the user account will be created and appear in the OU that was originally selected.

The New User Wizard will complete all the necessary information for the user account to be usable on the network. However, to enable the user to access resources and to store relevant information about that user, the New User Wizard is not enough. To make changes to the user's information, right-click the user account object and select Properties from the popup menu. The User Account Properties dialog is displayed as in Figure 5.16.

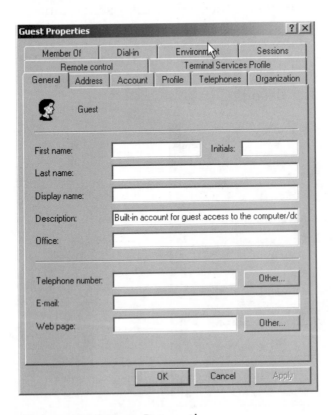

Figure 5.16 User Properties.

When a user moves to a different department, not only will user account information such as group membership need to be changed, but it is likely that the user account will need to be moved into a different OU. To move a user account from one OU to another, it is a simple matter of right-clicking the user account and selecting Move, then selecting the destination container from the resulting dialog.

Managing Groups

Creating a group in the Active Directory is the same process as creating a user or an OU. Right-click on the OU that will contain the group, click New, and then click Group. In the New Object-Group dialog box shown in Figure 5.17, type the name of the group, select the Group Scope and the Group Type. The Group Scope establishes where the group can be seen and the types of objects that can be within it. These are listed in Table 5.2. The Group Type "Security" sets whether the group can be used for the assignment of permissions to other network resources, which is why it does not cross over into another domain tree. "Distribution" is a standard group type that is used for nonsecurity-related tasks.

Table 5.2 Group Scope

Group Scope	Group Type	Where Seen	Content Objects
Domain Local	Security Distribution	Domain	Users Global groups Universal groups
Global groups	Security Distribution	Domain Tree	Users Global groups
Universal	Distribution	Forest	Users Global groups Universal groups

Figure 5.17 New Group.

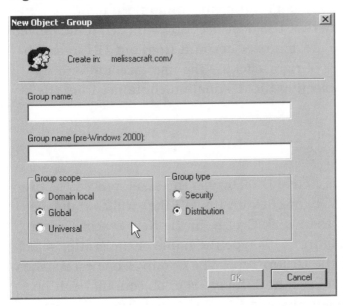

There are two ways to add users to groups. One is from the Group's Properties. The other is from the User account Properties. To add a user to a group from the Group's Properties, right-click the group and select Properties. Click the Members tab, then click ADD. Use the dialog box to find the user to add to the group, then click ADD.

To add a user to a group from the User account properties, right-click the user and select Add to Group. This can be used for multiple users at a single time.

Managing Computers

When a new computer is added to the network, it has a corresponding computer object in the Active Directory. Windows 2000 PCs are capable of adding themselves to the Active Directory domain, as long as the installer has an Administrative password. In many cases, it is preferable to not give out the Administrative name and

For IT Professionals

How Native Mode Affects Groups

While universal groups are restricted to distribution in the mixed-mode domains, they are not so restricted in a native-mode domain. Universal groups can be security principals in a native-mode domain. The reason they are restricted in mixed mode is for backward compatibility to NT 4 BDCs, since they cannot be understood as security principals in the BDC's security SAM.

Not only that, but in native mode, both a domain Local group and a Global group can be elevated to Universal group status through their properties. Once the configuration has changed, however, the group cannot be changed back—once Universal, always Universal.

Best practices for groups are to avoid using Universal groups as much as possible. The main reason for this is that Universal groups are placed into the GC along with the entire listing of their contents. This is necessary in order to publish the group to the entire forest of domains, and the GC is the only database (or index) that connects the forest's multiple domain contents.

password for this purpose, but to simply create the computer account prior to its installation. To create the computer account:

1. Right-click on the destination container, and select New.

2. Select Computer from the popup menu. The first screen that appears is shown in Figure 5.18.

3. Complete the computer name.

4. If the computer is a Windows 3.*x*, Windows 95/98, Windows NT 3.5*x*, or Windows NT 4.0 system, check the box to Allow pre-Windows 2000 computers to use this account.

5. Click NEXT.

6. The second screen allows the Administrator to mark this computer as a managed PC and to set a GUID, Globally Unique Identifier, for it. If it will be managed, complete this information. If not, do not check the box stating that this is a managed PC.

7. Click NEXT to see the summary page.

8. Click FINISH to add the computer to the network.

Figure 5.18 New Object-Computer dialog.

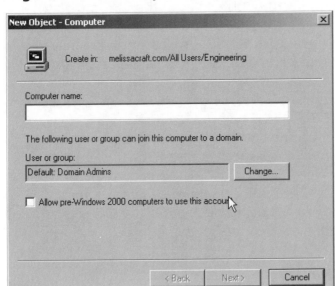

If the computer is designated as a managed PC, the Administrator can invoke the Computer Management MMC Console from the Active Directory Users and Computers console. To do this, the Administrator simply needs to right-click on the computer object and select Manage from the popup menu, as shown in Figure 5.19. This action will invoke the console shown in Figure 5.20.

Figure 5.19 Invoking computer management.

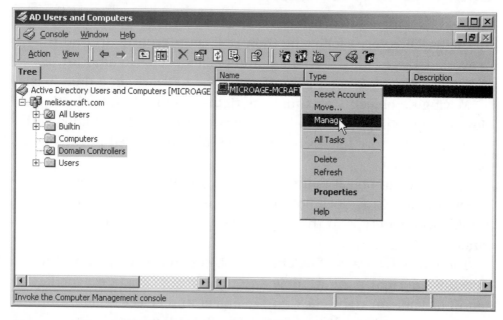

Figure 5.20 Computer Management MMC Console.

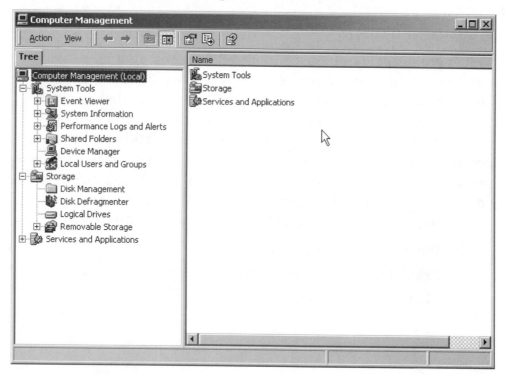

Common Object Management

With ever-changing network environments, objects will move around the Active Directory—following their real counterparts around the network. Objects wil be renamed and deleted, too. No amount of planning will prevent changes affecting the network on a daily basis.

Moving an object is as simple as right-clicking it and selecting Move from the popup menu. This will produce the Move dialog with the Active Directory hierarchy available to be navigated to the destination container.

Renaming an object is just as simple. Right-click the object and select Rename. This does not produce a dialog box, but allows the Administrator to type in the new name of the object directly into the window.

There are two ways of deleting an object. You can click on the object in the right-pane window and then press DELETE on the keyboard, or you can right-click on the object and select Delete. Both of these actions will result in a Delete Confirmation box.

Nesting Groups

Nested groups cannot be used in mixed domains; that is, those domains that include Windows NT 3.5x and Windows NT 4.0 DCs and member servers. They can only run in domains that are in native mode. A nested group is one that is a member of another group. By nesting groups, the child group automatically inherits the permissions of the parent group, plus it can have its own additional permissions. Nesting groups makes it easier to manage them, but only if they are carefully planned.

To create a nested group, start with the parent group.

1. Right-click the parent group.
2. Select Properties from the popup menu.
3. Click the Members tab.

4. Click Add and navigate the hierarchy to the child group.

5. Select the group, and click ADD. The group should appear in the Members window.

Role-Based Administration

Administrative roles are useful for enterprises that have a distributed network management structure with different levels of access required for the Administrators. For example, distributed network management is used by a business that establishes a single group to have access to full administrative rights to a domain, a second group to have the administrative rights to add, delete, and change user accounts, and a third group to reset passwords. Distributed network management is implemented in the Active Directory through created roles for Administrators, or *role-based administration.*

Microsoft Management Console

Microsoft created the Microsoft Management Console (MMC) to be a better tool with which to administer Windows 2000 Servers. It was developed to simplify administration through the use of a consistent interface. Microsoft is expected to continue the development of MMC and extend its capabilities to be usable by third-party software tools.

The interesting thing about the MMC is that it is not the management application itself. Instead, the MMC provides User Interface (UI) for the administrative application. The snap-in is the administrative tool. The snap-in will also create menu items, popup menus, and drag-and-drop actions that are specific to that administrative tool. Extensions provide even further capabilities to a snap-in. Windows 2000 Server provides a set of preconfigured MMC consoles. More are added when Windows 2000 Server additional components are installed. MMC consoles appear under the

Administrative Tools menu when you click Start | Programs | Administrative Tools.

MMC can run in two modes:

- User mode
- Author mode

User mode limits the functionality of the MMC so that its configuration cannot be saved. It also prevents the user from adding or removing snap-ins. Author mode lets the user do everything including adding and removing snap-ins, creating a new window, viewing all portions of the console tree and saving the console's configuration.

Administrative Roles

In order to economize, most large enterprises create a tiered structure for administration. A three-tiered structure might resemble Table 5.3.

Table 5.3 Tiered Support Structure

Tier Level	Support Experience	Example
First tier	Minimal	Help Desk: Reset passwords
Second tier	Mid-level	Desk-side support: Adds, deletes, changes user accounts and computer accounts, install member servers
Third tier	Highly experienced	Network Design and Engineering: Manages the site topology, hierarchical structure, and advanced troubleshooting

Obviously, an enterprise would not want their first tier to have the ability to change the way the MMC worked. It is probable that they would not want the second tier to have this ability either. Therefore, they should ensure that those administrative roles are restricted to user mode for the MMC. The way that this is done is through applying a group policy. For those organizations that wish to restrict some MMC consoles to user mode and allow others to be in author mode, it can be done. Individual snap-ins can be restricted via group policy. To learn more about applying group policy, see Chapter 9, "Group Policies and Security."

Summary

When the first domain controller (DC) is installed on a network, so also is the first domain in the first forest of the Active Directory. The DC is the source of Active Directory management. Installing a DC is a two-step process:

1. Installing Windows 2000 Server
2. Installing the Active Directory service

The process of installing Windows 2000 Server will create a member server. The Windows 2000 Server is functional as a member server with a local database of user accounts and groups that can access and use it. However, to use the Active Directory functionality, the member server must join an Active Directory domain or become a DC for an Active Directory domain.

To install the Active Directory service, the installer can invoke the Active Directory Wizard from the Configure Your Server screen that starts when the server starts. The Active Directory Wizard guides the installer through the options for installing the Active Directory. The information required for installing the Active Directory Service includes the DNS information for the computer and its domain. DNS is required by Active Directory. DCs must be configured as DNS clients, or they must provide the DNS service itself.

Configuring DNS as a service is a simple matter of starting the DNS administrative tool, selecting the local computer, and selecting Configure this server from the Action menu. If the Active Directory is not installed on the local computer, however, the DNS service cannot create Active Directory-integrated zones. If the

Windows 2000 Server is a DC, and is running the DNS service, it can create Active Directory-integrated zones and bring the following benefits to the network.

■ It can coexist with other DNS Servers.

■ It automatically supports DHCP, and no DHCP-integration testing is required.

■ It will support multi-master replication of the DNS within the Active Directory.

■ It will be able to scavenge stale records and keep the DNS database up to date.

The DNS console application is started by clicking Start | Programs | Administrative Tools | DNS. The first task is to create a DNS zone. The second task is to create the resource records (RRs) , both A, or address records, and SRV, or service location records.

The majority of the Active Directory management will occur in the Active Directory Users and Computers console. In this console, the organizational units (OUs) can be created in a hierarchical structure. New users, computers, and groups can be created within the OUs and then moved, renamed, and deleted as needed. Most actions can be executed by right-clicking the object and selecting the appropriate action item, or by manipulating the object's properties.

FAQs

Q: We have multiple DNS servers on UNIX machines in our network. We want to use the multi-master replication of Active Directory-integrated DNS. Can we keep the existing servers?

A: No. They will need to be migrated to Windows 2000 DNS. In order to have Active Directory-integrated DNS, DNS must be running on Active Directory servers. This, in turn, requires that Microsoft's Windows 2000 DNS service must be running.

Q: Our plan is to create a nested set of groups. We want to keep some Windows NT 4.0 domain controllers (DCs) for the first six months after installing the Windows 2000 Servers with Active Directory. Will we be able to use the nested groups right away?

A: No. Active Directory must be running in native mode, as opposed to mixed mode, in order for nested groups to work. That means that the Windows NT 4.0 DCs will need to be migrated before using nested groups.

Q: How do you switch a domain from mixed mode to native mode?

A: Click Start | Programs | Administrative Tools | Active Directory Domains and Trusts. Right-click on the domain and select Properties. The General tab should be the first screen shown. Click CHANGE MODE on the General tab page. Click YES to confirm. Either click APPLY or OK to change the mode. This exercise must be repeated on each DC in the Active Directory domain and is irreversible once changed.

Chapter 6

Building Trees and Forests

Solutions in this chapter:

- Understanding the Characteristics of an Active Directory Forest
- Right-Sizing the Active Directory Storage Space
- Implementing the Tree Structure
- Using Tools to Manage the Tree Structure

Installing a single domain is the first part of the Active Directory implementation. The next step is to create a forest and ensure that the namespace is installed correctly. The Domain Name System (DNS) namespace is the core of the Active Directory, and care must be taken in its implementation.

Introduction

Each time a domain controller (DC) is installed, it must be installed into a domain. If it is a new domain, it must be installed into an existing tree in an existing forest, form a new tree in an existing forest, or form a new tree in a new forest. The forest is the largest holder of the schema, configuration, and global catalog (GC). It is the ultimate division for an enterprise. Building a forest can be as simple as installing a single domain with a single DNS namespace, or it can be as complex as installing multiple domains with multiple child domains and namespaces among them.

A forest is a collection of domain trees that do not have to form a contiguous DNS namespace. For example, one tree may have the root.com namespace and another tree may have the corp.com namespace. Each tree can consist of multiple domains, but they must all share the same namespace. The domains that appear in the root.com tree may be root.com, trunk.root.com, branch.root.com, bark.root.com, and leaf.branch.root.com. This is depicted in Figure 6.1.

The forest is created with the installation of the root domain's first DC. When installing a new Windows 2000 Server to be a DC, it must be promoted to a DC after the operating system is installed. The Active Directory Wizard is the application used for promoting the server to a DC. It prompts for which forest to join the new domain to, or if this will be a new forest. The command line for the Active Directory Wizard is DCPROMO.EXE.

Figure 6.1 Active Directory forest.

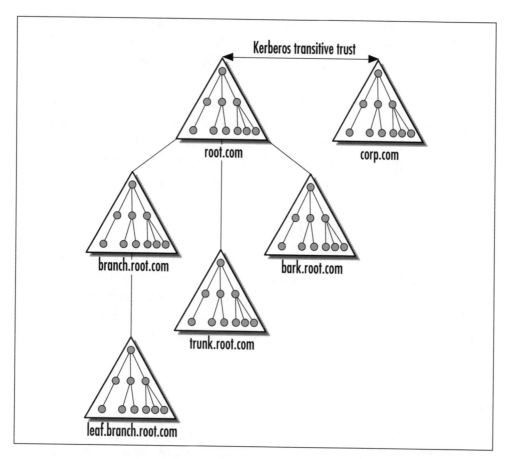

Forest Characteristics

The forest is a collection of domain trees with multiple namespaces that share a common schema, configuration, and GC. Technically, a forest can exist as a single domain with a single namespace. In essence, the Active Directory forest lets an organization use domain names that are not part of the same DNS namespace to work seamlessly together. For example, a forest could contain a domain tree with the root.com namespace and another domain tree with the tree.com namespace. There can be as many namespaces as needed in a forest.

Common Schema

Each forest shares a common schema. The schema is the list of all the object types, called *object classes*, that can exist in the Active Directory. The schema list the objects, and lists the attributes that each object class can have.

Since it is possible to add object classes or attributes to existing object classes, the schema is not necessarily going to be identical between two different forests. However, within the forest, the schema is replicated throughout the forest, and all object classes and attributes will be available at any point in the forest.

Common Configuration

The configuration for a forest is a naming context container object of which every DC in the forest contains a copy. Information that must be applied to the entire forest is stored in the configuration container object. The configuration container is used to generate the replication topology because it contains data about the underlying network infrastructure.

Global Catalog

Each forest has a single GC that contains information about each object within it. The GC is basically an index of the Active Directory database. It has a partial replica of all forest-contained objects. The GC has a larger scope than that of the domain since it will cover the entire forest. A GC server processes all UPN (User Principal Name) logons for a single forest, when the UPN suffix is different than the domain to which the computer being logged onto belongs.

Some DCs are also GC servers for the forest. The first DC installed into a forest will become the forest's first GC server. All other DCs must be specifically designated as GC servers.

When a DC processes the logon request and needs to find Universal group memberships, it queries a GC DC. If a GC server is not available when a domain controller tries its query, the logon is rejected completely to guard against security blunders. For example, if a user GARY with group membership in the Universal group, NONPAY-ROLL, that denies access to a resource share for SALARY.XLS, and the GC server cannot be contacted, GARY would potentially have access to SALARY.XLS if allowed to log on. Instead, the DC will reject GARY's logon request until a GC server can be reached.

The impact of this tactic is at the design level. The most logical place to put GC servers is one in each site. Because sites are groups of well-connected IP subnets, and because well-connected implies LAN connections, it follows that there would be fewer network fail-ures within a site than between sites that are implied to be WAN connections. If a site does span a WAN connection, even if it is a high-bandwidth link, the network designer may want to place a GC server on each side of that link.

GC DCs generate more replication traffic than regular DCs because they are replicating the GC as well as the contents of the Active Directory domain. The GC contains a read-only, partial copy of the Active Directory database for every other domain in the forest. DCs already have a read-write, complete copy of their own domain's Active Directory database.

Keep in mind the following GC rules:

- The GC includes only a single forest's set of objects for users to browse. If users need to access objects in another forest, they must know which domain in that other forest to query.

- Query traffic is generated to GC servers, when users browse the "entire network" or use search commands to find network resources.

- The settings in the schema will determine whether an attribute is available within the GC. If it is not, users will not be able to see it.

Contiguous Namespace

Domain trees are a set of domains that have a contiguous name-space. The forest can have multiple domain trees. A continuous namespace is a set of DNS names that have the same root name-space. As shown in Figure 6.2, the contiguous namespace is hierarchical. A forest can have multiple domain trees, but only contains a single root domain. The first domain installed into a forest, regardless of the number of different namespaces, will always be the root of the forest. Each domain tree will have a root DNS namespace, but that does not designate that domain as a root of the forest.

Figure 6.2 Hierarchical namespace.

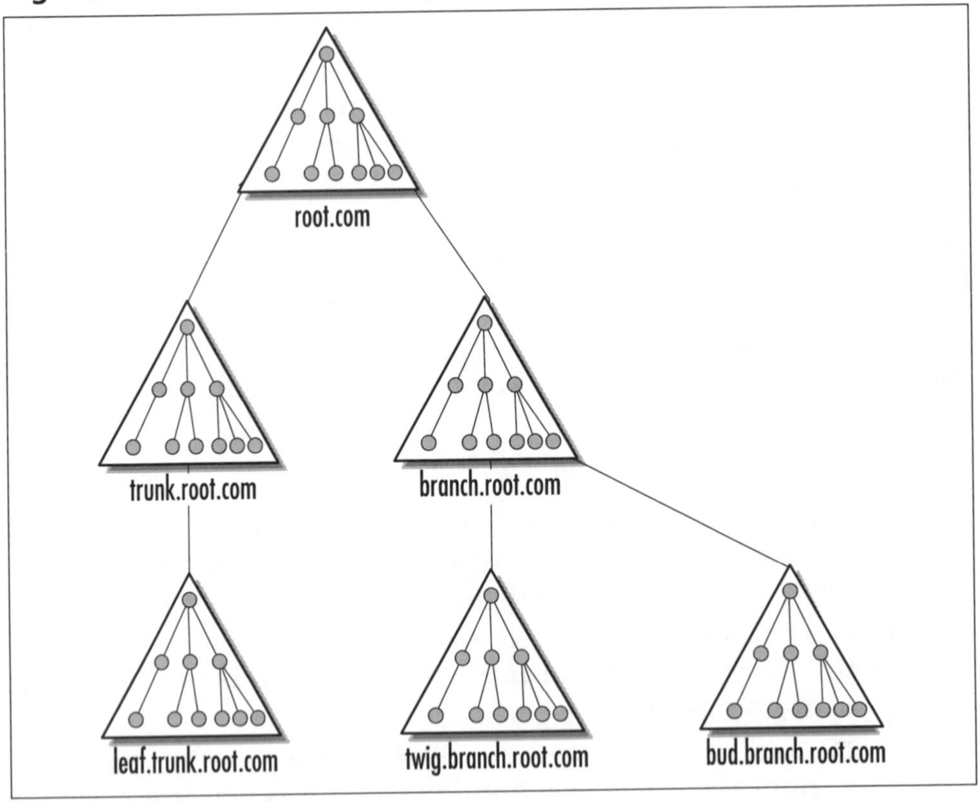

Trust Relationships

Legacy Windows NT domains enabled access to each other's users via trust relationships. These trust relationships were explicitly set between domains. Not only that, but trusts were one-way. That is, domain A trusted domain B in a single trust, but domain B did not trust domain A unless a second trust was established. Not only were trusts one way, but they were nontransitive. That is, when domain A trusted domain B, and domain B trusted domain C, then domain A did not automatically trust domain C. This system had limitations that the Active Directory fixed.

Transitive Bidirectional Trust

Active Directory trust relationships are different from the legacy NT domain trusts. First of all, within a forest, the trust relationships are created automatically. They are bidirectional and transitive. If a forest contains domain A, domain B, and domain C, then domain A trusts both domain B and domain C, and they both trust domain A and each other, as illustrated in Figure 6.3.

The Active Directory forest contains multiple domain trees that are connected via a transitive, bidirectional Kerberos trust relationship. Child domains always have Kerberos transitive trusts between themselves and their parent domain. A forest always contains entire domain trees. The domain tree cannot be split between multiple forests.

Figure 6.3 Transitive trusts in Active Directory forests.

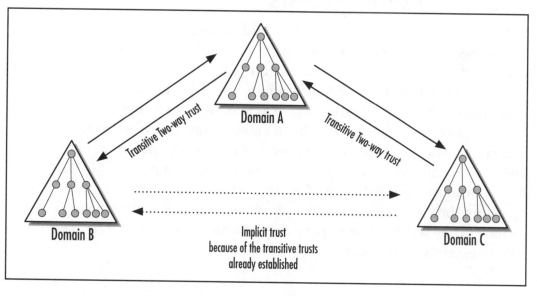

When migrating from a legacy NT domain to an Active Directory domain structure, there will be changes in the way that the domains trust each other. Before migrating NT domains to Active Directory, the Network Administrator should review the existing trust relationships and make sure to note any trust relationships that should not exist after migration. By default, domains that are migrated to the Active Directory forest will connect to each other through transitive trusts. Any domains that are not moved into the new forest will require explicit, nontransitive, trust relationships to be created between themselves and any new domains within the forest. However, any upgraded domains will retain their existing trust relationships as nontransitive, one-way trusts.

Because of the way that trust relationships work during migration, a legacy NT domain structure that uses a Master or Multi-Master domain model will require that the Master domains are migrated to Windows 2000 first. Resource domains should be migrated to Windows 2000 after all Master domains have been completely migrated. Resource domains are best migrated as child domains of already migrated Master domains.

Trusts that Cross Forests

Within a forest, there is no need for establishing trusts because of the Kerberos transitive two-way trusts. However, sometimes users in one forest need to access resources in another. Or during migration, users may need to access resources in a legacy NT domain. For example, the XYC Corporation has two forests that were created for the sole purpose of separating the global catalogs (GCs), schemas, and configurations. One forest is dedicated to a lab environment and the second forest is dedicated to the production network. When Administrators are working in the lab environment, they still need to access their corporate e-mail and manage the production forest domain. They will be able to perform their job functions if they are able to establish a domain trust relationship.

Trust Utilities

There are two tools that are useful for handling trust relationships in Windows 2000:

- NETDOM
- Active Directory Domains and Trusts Management Console

NETDOM is a command-line tool found in the Windows 2000 Resource Kit that can list existing domain trust relationships, establish new trust relationships, and manage machine accounts in a domain. Establishing a trust relationship with NETDOM can be executed with the following command:

NETDOM /DOMAIN:RESOURCE MASTER MASTERDOMAIN PASSWORD /TRUST

For IT Professionals

NETDOM

Command-line programs such as NETDOM are confusing at first because they do not usually have easily understood help options. However, these programs are a blessing when you need to automate procedures to happen after hours or without user input. If you do need to get help for NETDOM, just type **NETDOM HELP** at the command line.

There are five major commands: NETDOM BDC, NETDOM MASTER, NETDOM MEMBER, NETDOM QUERY, and NETDOM RESOURCE. Each of these commands has a group of options that affect how they work. In general, the options are:

- **/Domain:domainname**: The command is executed on the PDC or DC of the domain listed.
- **/User:domain\user**: The command uses this user account.
- **/Password:password**: The command uses this password for the user account.

Continued

For IT Professionals   NETDOM

- **/noverbose**: The command does not display much text on the screen.

The syntax of the commands is as follows:

- NETDOM [/options] BDC [\\BDC] [/Command]
- NETDOM [/options] MASTER [masterdomain] [password] [/command]
- NETDOM [/options] MEMBER [\\member] [/command]
- NETDOM [/options] RESOURCE [resourcedomain] [password] [/command]

NETDOM QUERY is unique—it has a single option, /noverbose, and all you needt o type at th ecommand prompt is **NETDOM QUERY \\computername,** where computername is the name of the DC that you want to list trust relationships for.

Notice that at the end of each of the NETDOM commands other than NETDOM QUERY ends in /command. The available commands for this are as follows:

- **/Add**: Adds a machine account.
- **/Delete**: Deletes the machine account.
- **/Query**: Finds out domain information.
- **/Fullsync**: Starts a full synchronization of the domain.
- **/Partialsync**: Starts a synchronization with the PDC.
- **/Trust**: This is only available with the NETDOM RESOURCE and NETDOM MASTER commands. This command establishes the trust relationship for the domains.
- **/joindomain**: This is only available with the NETDOM MEMBER command. It joins the member to a domain.

Continued

For IT Professionals

NETDOM

- **/joinworkgroup**: This is only available with the NET-DOM MEMBER command. It joins the member to a workgroup.

One of the ways to use the NETDOM command is when migrating servers to Windows 2000. For example, GRAY Corp. decides to restructure domains when deploying Windows 2000. Each new Active Directory domain is a new domain name deployed on new servers. The old servers in the legacy domains are to remain on the network until each legacy domain has been completely migrated to a new Active Directory domain. The Network Administrator needs to join each of 5000 Windows NT 4.0 Workstations and Windows 2000 Professional computers to the new Active Directory domains.

The Network Administrator decides to create a login script for each group of migrated clients rather than go to each desktop and run through the domain joining process, and rather than giving an Administrative password to users and walking them through the process.

The Network Administrator edits the login script in the old domain to add the line: NETDOM /Domain:newdomain /User:newdomain\admin /Password:password /Noverbose MEMBER /JOINDOMAIN

This line will join the computer that the login script is executing for to the domain named NEWDOMAIN. It will use the Admin account in the NEWDOMAIN, but will not display any text on the screen due to the /Noverbose command. Even so, using the Admin account and password in a script is not recommended because security can be breached simply by a user viewing the login script if it is in a noncompiled format.

Once the computer has joined the new domain, it will have a new login script and it will not attempt to join the domain again.

This command will establish a one-way trust in which the domain named RESOURCE trusts the domain named MASTERDO-MAIN. It can be used across forests, or between legacy NT domains and Windows 2000 domains.

The Active Directory Domains and Trusts management console is the main utility that Network Administrators will use to manage trust relationships and, oddly enough, the UPN suffix for the forest. The default UPN suffix is that of the forest's root domain's DNS name. This is where they would establish a trust between two domains in two separate forests. The steps to take in establishing the trust relationship are as follows:

1. Click Start | Programs | Administrative Tools | Active Directory Domains and Trusts. You will see the console shown in Figure 6.4.

Figure 6.4 Active Directory Domains and Trusts management console.

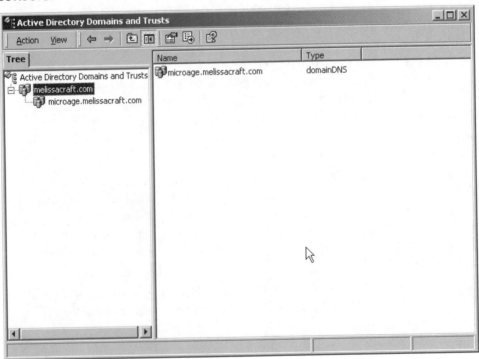

2. Right-click the domain to which a trust will be added.

3. Select the Properties option from the popup menu.

4. Click the Trusts tab. The resulting screen will resemble Figure 6.5.

Figure 6.5 Establishing trusts for domains.

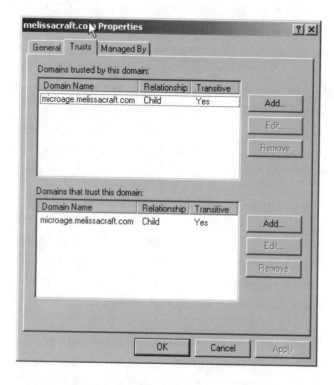

5. If the domain that you are editing is the resource domain, click ADD under "Domains trusted by this domain." If this domain will be the Master, click ADD under Domains that trust this domain.

6. Select the appropriate domain, and click OK.

7. Repeat this action on the other domain to establish the trust. Both sides of the trust must be established or the trust is invalid.

Planning a Forest Structure

There are some general design principals to keep in mind when planning forests:

- Incorporate areas in the forest plan that will enable growth of the organization.
- Design as simple a structure as possible to reduce administrative overhead.
- Understand the incremental bandwidth overhead that is incurred when implementing multiple forests.
- Keep all domains that are allowed to trust each other within a forest.
- Refer to the existing network configuration and documentation to support decisions about the forest structure.

The primary purpose of the forest plan is to determine how many forests are required for the network. Since each forest can contain multiple domains, a single forest structure is typically sufficient for any enterprise network. The situations in which multiple forests should be created are those in which there must be separate schemas or GCs, or in which there should be absolute division in administrative authority.

For example, in a corporation that implements Windows 2000 and Active Directory to support the Internet and also implements it for the internal, private enterprise network, it may be necessary to separate the private forest from the Internet forest so that the private GC is not available publicly. Another example is when a company implements a lab network in which various technical scenarios are tested before being implemented on the production network. If changes to the schema need to be tested before being deployed, they must be tested on a separate forest or else the changes will be made enterprisewide automatically through the multi-master replication of Windows 2000. The advantage to having a separate lab network is that most labs are confined to a single geographical area, and many do not share the same cabling and infrastructure that is used on a production network. When a lab is constructed this way, a separate forest for a lab will not impact traffic on the network to any great degree. A final reason that an organization may decide to have multiple forests is when there is a clear separation of administrative authority. In this case, a company may have two clearly separate business units that use completely separate administrative groups and change management methods. Although administration is best delegated through OUs or even through separate domains, it may become necessary to have separate forests for each of the administrative units.

When multiple forests do exist to separate schemas or GCs, there is an impact to administration. Either a trust relationship must exist between the forests and Administrators granted administrative authority in both forests, or separate Administrator accounts must be created for each Administrator who must manage both forests.

Administrators must also become aware of the impact they may have on the network within any particular forest. This means that they must work well with each other and make each other aware of large changes planned for the Active Directory. When there are multiple forests, they must be able to identify which forest will be changed. For instance, rapidly performing moves, adds, and changes on objects within the forest creates a large amount of replication of the GC (which contains a partial copy of every forest object) among DCs forestwide. This can cause users to not be able to log on to the network, or to be unable to access network resources. Additionally, every change to the schema, to the configuration container, and additions or removals of entire domains has a forest-wide consequence.

Multiple forests impact how users work, too. If users remain within a single forest, they can browse or query the GC to find resources. The GC makes the forest structure transparent to users. When a user must access a network resource that exists in a different forest, that resource will not be found in the GC since it is not shared. In this case, the user must know about the other domain where the resource exists. Not only that, but there must be a trust between the domain where the resource exists and the domain where the user exists. This type of a trust is an explicit, one-way, nontransitive trust. Basically, it is the same type of trust relationship that legacy Windows NT domains relied upon. Because it is a one-way trust, the direction of the trust matters. The rule of thumb is that a domain that contains a resource must trust the domain that contains the user account, as illustrated in Figure 6.6.

Figure 6.6 Multiple forests with interdomain trust relationships.

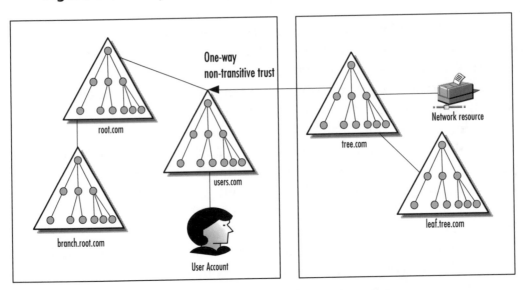

Multiple forests will affect how users log on, too. A UPN using the format user@domain.com can only be applied to a single forest. If there are multiple forests, one will use the UPN of user@domain-one.com, and the other will use the UPN of user@domain-two.com. UPNs are stored in the GC and must be unique within the enterprise network.

The Domain Tree Structure

The domain tree is a set of domains that are arranged in a hierarchical structure due to their DNS names. The forest can have multiple domain trees. Each domain in a domain tree is separate from the parent and child domains. A domain tree makes use of a single DNS namespace, enabling multiple domains to exist within it. This reduces the need for registering several DNS namespaces. For example, a company named XYZ can have seven domains in their forest, but only needs to register a single DNS namespace if all the domains are within that namespace, such as xyz.com, one.xyz.com, two.xyz.com, three.xyz.com, four.xyz.com, five.xyz.com, and six.xyz.com, as illustrated in Figure 6.7.

Figure 6.7 Wide and flat domain tree structure.

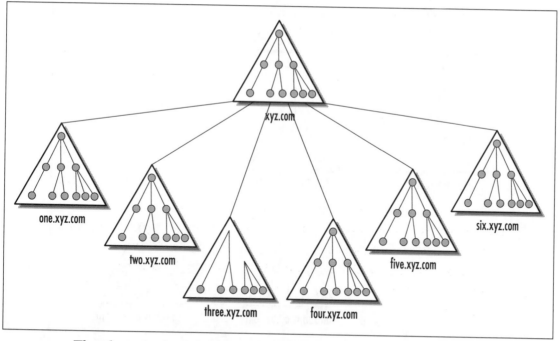

The domain tree can be wide and flat as depicted in Figure 6.7. The domain tree can also be tall, with multiple subdomains, as shown in Figure 6.8. The configuration of a domain tree is entirely up to the network designer since the Kerberos, two-way, transitive trusts essentially make a domain tree into a group of domains that completely trust each other and trust all other domains within their designated forest.

Figure 6.8 Tall domain tree structure.

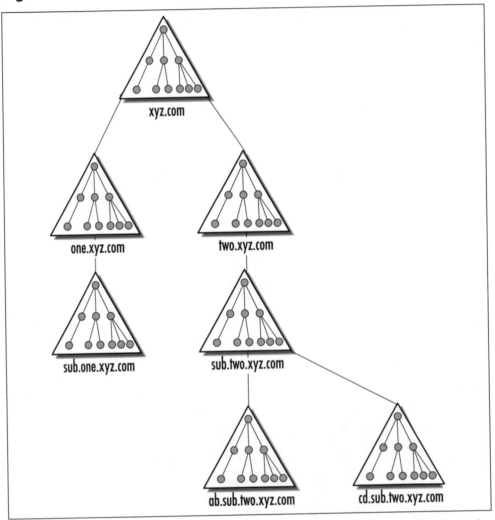

Each domain in the Active Directory forest defines a partition of the forest's database. The partition is a subset of a larger database that is distributed to multiple DCs. This method of partitioning makes the Active Directory scalable from small to extremely large enterprise networks. There is also a benefit found in having redundant replicas of the domain partitions when multiple DCs exist for each domain.

A DC can only contain a copy of the database partition for its own domain. That means that copies of different domain database partitions cannot be contained on a single Windows 2000 Server. However, the forest configuration and schema are hosted by all DCs throughout the forest.

Adding a Child Domain

Child domains are installed with the first DC of the child domain in a domain tree. When that child domain is formed, Active Directory creates a two-way transitive Kerberos trust automatically between it and the parent domain. Schema and configuration data for the forest are copied from the parent domain to the new child DC.

The relationship of a parent domain to a child domain is strictly one of the DNS subdomain name and trust relationship. For example, a parent domain in a domain tree would be PARENT.COM. The child domain would be CHILD.PARENT.COM. The trust relationship is bidirectional and transitive. An Administrator in PARENT.COM does not have administrative authority in CHILD.PARENT.COM. Instead, the Administrator in PARENT.COM must be granted administrative authority to CHILD.PARENT.COM. Likewise, group policies set in PARENT.COM are not applicable to CHILD.PARENT.COM.

Another change to the Active Directory occurs with a new child domain—a new replication topology is created. More about replication can be found in Chapter 8, "Planning and Implementing Sites."

Sizing the Active Directory Store

Each DC contains a copy of the Active Directory Store for the domain. Some of the DCs are also GC servers. They contain a copy of the GC for the entire forest. Other DCs have a copy of the forest configuration. Determining the size requirements for DCs is somewhat of an art form.

One thing to remember is that the Active Directory store does not automatically shrink in size when its objects are deleted; it typically stays the same size or grows. If space within the store is freed up, it remains available for new objects and properties to fill. Space is freed up when objects are deleted, but not immediately. Deleting an object creates a tombstone. The tombstone marks the record for deletion, but does not delete it immediately. The tombstone is replicated to the other DCs. The tombstone has a lifetime value, known as a *tombstone lifetime*, to it. When the object reaches the lifetime value, it is physically deleted from the Active Directory Store.

The ADSIEdit utility is used to view or change the tombstone lifetime value. ADSIEdit is included in the Windows 2000 Support Tools setup.exe. It is comparable to the regedit utility that has access to the Windows 2000 registry. When starting the ADSIEdit utility, it will most likely not be in the area of the registry that accesses the tombstone lifetime. In order to access the configuration container, right-click on the domain and select Settings as illustrated in Figure 6.9. Then select the Configuration container.

Figure 6.9 Accessing the Configuration container in ADSIEDIT.

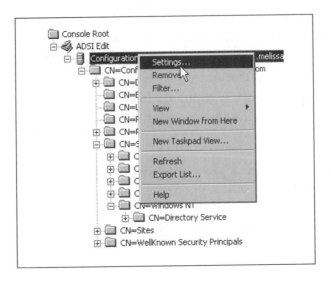

Once the Configuration container is visible in the left pane, navigate through CN=Configuration/CN=Services/CN=Windows NT/CN=Directory Service, as shown in Figure 6.10.

Figure 6.10 Navigating to the Directory Service container.

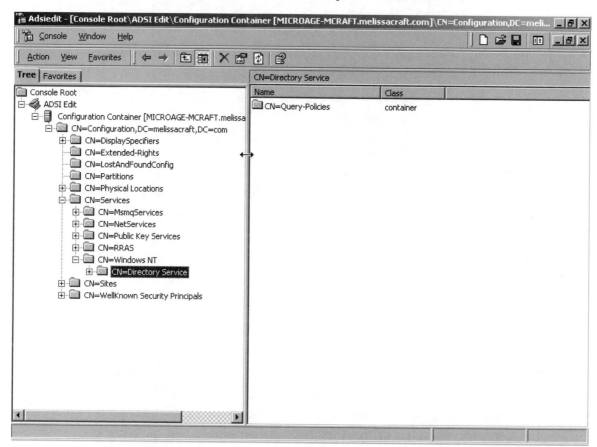

Right-click on Directory Service and select Properties from the popup menu. The Properties dialog will appear as shown in Figure 6.11. Under the "Select which properties to view" drop-down list, select tombstoneLifetime. To change the value, type in a number in the Edit Attribute box, and click SET.

Figure 6.11 Directory Service Properties and tombstoneLifetime value.

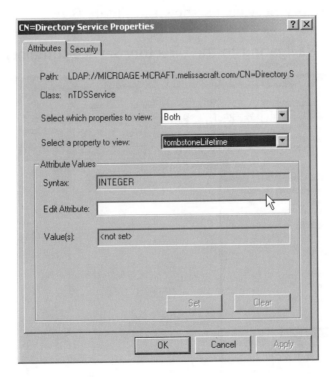

Garbage collection is the process used to free up space. It deletes expired tombstones and defragments the Active Directory database. Each DC runs garbage collection independently of the others, and the default 12-hour value can be changed in the ADSIEdit Resource Kit utility in the same place that tombstone values are changed in the Directory Service Properties dialog. To change the garbage collection period, select garbageCollPeriod from the drop-down list and place a number in the Edit Attribute box, which is shown in Figure 6.12. Garbage collection frees up space in the database, but does not reduce the size of the database.

In order to truly reduce the size of the Active Directory store, use NTDSUtil. NTDSUtil.exe is an offline defragmentation utility. After it is executed, the Active Directory database will reduce in size.

Defragmenting with NTDSUtil requires that the server be taken down from the network to run, and should be used sparingly.

Figure 6.12 Changing the garbage collection interval.

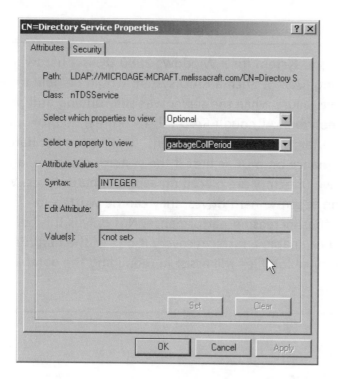

Security principals such as user objects and groups use approximately 3.5KB of space in the database. Nonsecurity principals, such as an OU object, use about 1KB of space each. When sizing the database, count the number of security principals and multiply by 3.5, count the number of nonsecurity principals, and add the two figures. Divide this sum by 1000 to receive the number of MBs. Add approximately 1000MBs for the base size of the store. Then double the final amount to account for growth. To find what is needed for the entire server hard drive, add in the amount required for Windows 2000 Server, the amount needed for applications, and additional space for growth.

If there are 100,000 security principals and 20,000 nonsecurity principals, the result will be 370,000KB, or 370MB. Added to the 1000MB, the result is 1370MB. Double this for growth and the minimum size reserved for the Active Directory store would be 2.7 GB.

NOTE

The optimal storage system for a Windows 2000 DC is a hardware-based RAID system using RAID 5. Such a RAID system would be able to recover from a hard drive failure while the server was still running and providing services to the network. Although RAID 5 is recommended for speed and redundancy, it certainly is not a requirement. If using regular hard drives, however, performance on a DC is best if the system, database, and log files for the Active Directory are placed on separate hard drives. When these files are on separate hard drives, they can be written to simultaneously, thus increasing performance. Not only is this helpful with speed, but this will enable a faster recovery if one of the hard drives happens to fail, since log files will assist in rebuilding the database to a current state.

Managing the Forest

The most obvious place to manage the forest is within the Active Directory Domains and Trusts management console, shown in Figure 6.13. This console, found in the Administrative Tools menu on a Windows 2000 DC, displays all of the domain trees in the forest and can view, change, or create any trust relationships that exist outside the forest. The forest's UPN format is also configured in this console.

There are many other utilities that can manage the forest aside from the Active Directory Domains and Trusts console. One of these utilities is MOVETREE.EXE. This utility is found in the Windows 2000 Support Tools setup.exe. It is used to move objects within one

Figure 6.13 Domains and Trusts management console.

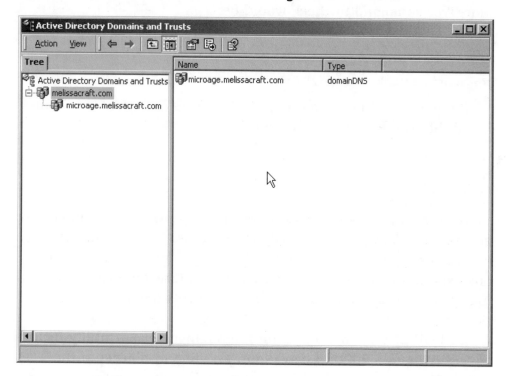

domain to another domain, as long as both domains exist in the same forest.

Objects that are domain-specific, such as domain Global groups or Local groups, cannot be moved by the MoveTree utility. If MoveTree executes a move for the OU that contains these groups, then the groups remain behind in a container called LostAndFound in the domain. Some things are not objects within the domain, but are domain-specific data that exists within the Active Directory. This includes logon scripts, policies, and profiles. These will not be moved by MoveTree either.

MoveTree is a command-line utility that can execute in batch mode. One of the switches for MoveTree is /check. This switch runs MoveTree but does not complete the move of the objects. Instead, it verifies that it will work. If MoveTree /check executes without errors, then the same command will be successful in /start mode.

For example, if moving a user from one.xyz.com to two.xyz.com, the MoveTree command to check would be:

```
Movetree /check /s server1.one.xyz.com /d server2.two.xyz.com /sdn
cn=user,cn=users,dc=one,dc=xyz,dc=com /ddn
cn=user,cn=users,dc=two,dc=xyz,dc=com
```

If the command does not report any errors, the MoveTree command that can execute the move is:

```
Movetree /start /s server1.one.xyz.com /d server2.two.xyz.com /sdn
cn=user,cn=users,dc=one,dc=xyz,dc=com /ddn
cn=user,cn=users,dc=two,dc=xyz,dc=com
```

Another utility can be used to move objects outside a domain to any domain. The Lightweight Directory Access Protocol (LDAP) is a standard supported by the Active Directory Service. LDAP is an open standard supported by many different directory services. This makes it an ideal interchange point between two different directories, or even between two different forests.

LDIFDE.EXE is an LDAP Data Interchange Format utility included with Windows 2000. It can export and import objects in the Active Directory using the LDAP protocol. The process to export objects from the current domain using LDIFDE, which can be found in the WINNT\SYSTEM32 directory, is as follows:

1. Log on to a DC in the domain from which you want to export objects, as a user with Administrative authority.

2. Open a command prompt window (Start | Run | cmd).

3. Type **ldifde—f filename.1df**, and press ENTER.

The screen should look like Figure 6.14.

The resulting file is a plain text listing of the objects in the Active Directory. It will include records that look like the following user account object:

```
dn: CN=my self,OU=Sales,OU=All Users,DC=melissacraft,DC=com

changetype: add

accountExpires: 9223372036854775807
```

Figure 6.14 LDIFDE.

```
D:\>ldifde -f c:\ldifde.ldf
Connecting to "MICROAGE-MCRAFT.melissacraft.com"
Logging in as current user using SSPI
Exporting directory to file c:\ldifde.ldf
Searching for entries...
Writing out entries.......................................................
............................................................................
136 entries exported

The command has completed successfully

D:\>_
```

badPasswordTime: 0

badPwdCount: 0

codePage: 0

cn: my self

countryCode: 0

displayName: my self

dSCorePropagationData: 19990816040611.0Z

dSCorePropagationData: 16010101000001.0Z

givenName: my

instanceType: 4

lastLogoff: 0

lastLogon: 0

logonCount: 0

```
distinguishedName: CN=my self,OU=Sales,OU=All Users,DC=melissacraft,DC=com

objectCategory: CN=Person,CN=Schema,CN=Configuration,DC=melissacraft,DC=com

objectClass: user

objectGUID:: SxvFlyYMEkmBBksImyTCqQ==

objectSid:: AQUAAAAAAUVAAAAiqcyPyPz9mP4n7R0dQQAAA==

primaryGroupID: 513

pwdLastSet: 125781260326329120

name: my self

sAMAccountName: myself

sAMAccountType: 805306368

sn: self

userAccountControl: 512

userPrincipalName: myself@melissacraft.com

uSNChanged: 2084

uSNCreated: 2077

whenChanged: 19990803035352.0Z

whenCreated: 19990803035334.0Z
```

The LDIFDE command used to import objects is:

```
Ldifde FDE command used
```

LDIFDE can be used to perform mass changes across all objects in a particular OU or across an entire domain. The LDIFDE command has extensive capabilities for managing the Active Directory.

Since LDIFDE is a command-line tool, it can be executed in batch mode. To find out what options are available, type **LDIFDE /? |more** at the command prompt.

Summary

An Active Directory forest is a collection of multiple domains using multiple DNS namespaces. Each domain within a forest shares a common configuration, schema, and global catalog (GC). The Configuration container and schema is replicated to every domain controller (DC) in the forest. The GC is a partial copy of every object in each domain that belongs to the forest.

Domain trees within a forest use a contiguous DNS namespace. A top-level domain in the domain tree would have the DNS name parent.com, and directly below it the child domain would have the DNS name child.parent.com.

Each domain within a forest is connected to others via a two-way transitive trust relationship. This results in each domain trusting every other domain within a forest.

When planning a forest, the main decision is whether or not the network will have multiple forests. Multiple forests are necessary if there is a reason to have:

- Separate schemas
- Separate configuration
- Separate GC
- Completely separated administration

There is some impact in having multiple forests on the network. Additional bandwidth is required for replication of a separate GC and Active Directory databases. Users are affected in how they work across forests. The resource domain must trust the domain that the user belongs to in order for the user to access the resource. If the resource domain is in a different forest, then the Administrator must establish that trust explicitly. Trusts between forests are one-way and nontransitive. A user must know which domain the resource belongs to and be able to query that domain directly.

Creating a domain tree in a forest is simply the process of adding new child domains using subdomains of the same DNS namespace. The tree can be wide and flat, or tall.

When a new DC is added to manage a new domain, its storage space should be adequate to support the objects that will exist in the Active Directory. Storage requirements are larger for DCs that contain a copy of the GC because they will have two databases on them.

Several utilities are used to manage the Active Directory forest.

- NETDOM is used for domain trust management.
- NTDSUtil is used to defragment the Active Directory database while the DC is offline.
- ADSIEdit provides the ability to edit specific internal parameters of the Active Directory.
- Active Directory Domains and Trusts offers a graphical view of all the domains within a forest and enables trust relationship management.
- LDIFDE is used to import and export objects from an Active Directory domain.
- ClonePrincipal is used to clone objects from a domain.
- OVETREE is used to move objects from one domain within a forest to another domain within the same forest.

FAQs

Q: I am concerned about the extra traffic that multiple forests can have on wide area network (WAN) links. However, I want to have a separate forest for my lab network, which is confined to a single room. Will creating two forests, one that is confined to that room and another that is used for production, cause significant WAN bandwidth consumption?

A: No. In the situation described, the lab forest would not span any WAN links and would have no effect on the bandwidth utilized across the WAN.

Q: I have a group of people in CORAZON.COM who must access a printer in New York that is in the CARTA.COM domain in a different forest. Which domain must trust the other in order for the users to be able to print?

A: CARTA.COM must trust CORAZON.COM. Resource domains must always trust the account domain in order for the users to access the resources.

Q: We want to move the domain Global groups from one domain to another in the same forest. What is the best utility to use, ClonePrincipal or MoveTree?

A: ClonePrincipal can clone security principals, such as users and groups, from one domain into another. MoveTree cannot move domain-specific objects such as domain Global groups.

Chapter 7

Modifying the Schema

Solutions in this chapter:

- Understanding the Schema
- Planning Changes to the Schema
- Managing Schema Extensions
- Querying the Active Directory

What is a schema? How do you modify the schema? How often should you modify the schema? Who should modify the schema? At the very least, the schema is a source of concern to Network Administrators as they contemplate their new Active Directory.

Introduction

The Active Directory is a database that uses multi-master replication. The database has a list of objects that it can contain. Whenever a new object is created, it is selected from that list. Each object has its own attributes, such as a user account First Name. This list of objects and all their possible attributes makes up the *schema*.

Active Directory is an extensible system. The originally installed list of objects can grow over time to include others. New applications can be created to take advantage of its existing schema, and they can create new objects or properties of objects to be added to the schema. Network Administrators may want to add attributes to objects to meet their own specific business requirements. Whether an application or an Administrator makes the change, this process is called *extending the schema*.

About Objects and Attributes

The schema defines classes of objects and their attributes for the Active Directory. An object class is simply the type of object, such as a user account, and all its applicable attributes, such as the user's first and last names. When the Active Directory is populated with objects, the new objects are considered *instances* of the object class.

Each object class contains both Mandatory and Optional attributes. The attributes also have a syntax, which explains what type of data can be contained in an instance of the object class. The postalCode attribute for an instance of a user object can only have a numeric value; therefore, its syntax is string(numeric).

The definitions of the Active Directory objects and attributes are contained in schema objects. A classSchema object defines an Active Directory object, and an attributeSchema object defines an attribute. When a classSchema object lists attributes under mustContain, those attributes are mandatory. Those listed under mayContain are optional. Figure 7.1 illustrates the relationship between objects and attributes.

Figure 7.1 The relationship between objects and attributes.

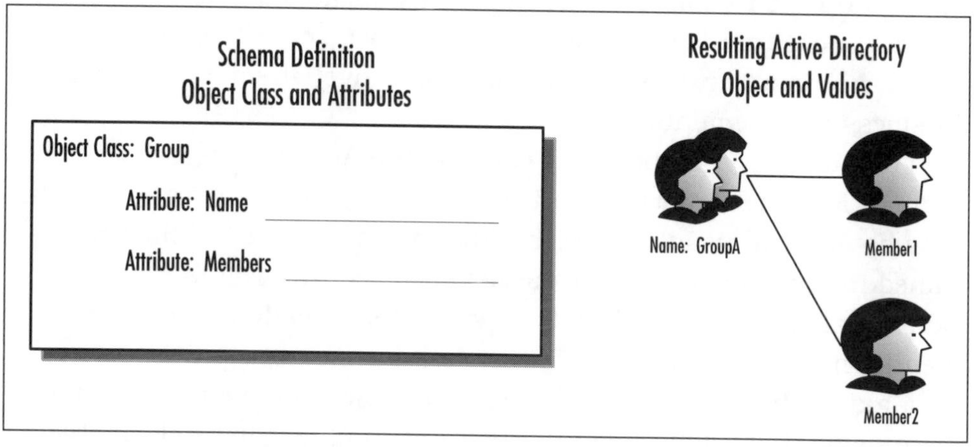

Planning Schema Modifications

Modifying the schema is not something that every user should be able to do. There are limited capabilities for removing object classes and attributes that are native to the Active Directory schema. The limits are in place to prevent disasters. What if the unthinkable happened where there were no precautions in place against schema modification, and a user removed the User object class from the schema by deactivating it? (Don't worry, the default schema cannot be deactivated because the Active Directory protects against that, but objects that you add later *can* be deactivated. Back to the hypothetical situation . . .) The network would completely shut down. No users could log on; not even the Administrator. Why? Because there would be no user objects defined anymore. What a disaster! This is merely a hypothetical situation to illustrate how important the schema objects are. This situation demonstrates the need not only to plan when to modify the schema, but also *who* should be granted this capability.

Why Modify the Schema?

Knowing that making a change to the schema could be a disaster, one might wonder why it would ever need to be modified. Microsoft created the Active Directory to be a customizable service that would provide more than simple logon and network security service. Network Administrators can modify the Active Directory to meet business requirements.

For example, a corporation can use the Active Directory for Human Resource information tracking. For some corporations this may be an ideal usage, since the identity information will be maintained in a single place with the network security rights. Additionally, the Active Directory will automatically replicate the identity information throughout the enterprise network.

Making changes to the schema can be destructive to the enterprise network if mishandled. Whenever possible, the existing objects and attributes should be used instead of creating new ones.

When to Modify the Schema

Change management procedures should always be followed when modifying the schema. Modifying the schema is a task that can interrupt how the Active Directory works, especially if there is a failure of some sort. Use the following evaluations to determine when to modify the schema:

- Review the existing schema to ensure that the attributes or objects required are not already available in the Active Directory.

- Make sure to plan the schema changes before testing and implementing them.

For IT Professionals

Think Twice Before Modifying the Schema

Modifying the schema is an advanced administrative right for a good reason. There are impacts and potential problems that can raise their ugly little heads whenever a change is made. The issues revolve around:

- This is a test
- Creating invalid objects in the Active Directory
- Replication impacts to the network

No one intends to create invalid objects. But take a user account named Joe. It has an attribute that is called Spouse that the Administrator added to the schema and then placed the value "Mary" into the Joe object instance. Later on, it is decided that the Spouse attribute is not required, so the Administrator deletes it from the schema. Joe's object is not like the rest because it has the Mary value in an attribute that does not exist. Active Directory lets Joe's object remain in the forest, but it does not clean up the invalid attribute. Instead, the Administrator must perform a query and delete that attribute manually.

Replication (discussed in Chapter 8, "Planning and Implementing Sites") is affected whenever a schema change is made. That change is replicated to every domain controller (DC) in a forest. Latency inherent in the propagation process and exacerbated by replication schedules will cause a temporary inconsistency in the schema between various DCs. Objects that are created during the inconsistency period can be replicated before the schema changes, which results in a failure. Active Directory responds to the failure by initiating a new, explicit schema replication from the DC where the schema was changed.

- Always test a schema modification on a separate forest before implementing.

- Reserve universal changes for weekend implementations. Universal changes are those that affect a majority of users in a majority of sites. Schema changes fit this definition.

- Only modify the schema when necessary, because the changes cannot be reversed.

Who Should Modify the Schema?

There is a Schema Admins global group in the Active Directory that has full control over the schema. The properties for this group in the Schema Management console are displayed in Figure 7.2.

Figure 7.2 Schema Administrators Group properties.

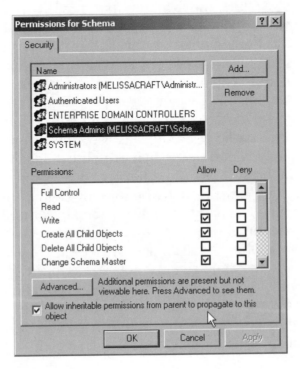

To ensure that schema changes are controlled so that unexpected changes are not propagated throughout a production network, there should be guidelines established for all members of the Schema Administrators group to follow. These guidelines include:

- The criteria for changing schema
- The criteria for being able to join the Schema Admins group
- The membership of the Schema Admins group
- How users can apply for a schema change
- The evaluation of the schema change

Finally, the Schema Admins group should consist of a small, select group of Administrators with the skills and authority to make changes to the schema.

Schema Management Console

The Schema Management console enables the Schema Administrators to access and change the schema in the Active Directory using a graphical interface. Not only does it enable the Schema Administrators to edit or create schema object classes and attributes, it also lets them select which object classes and attributes should be available in the Global Catalog (GC). This console is depicted in Figure 7.3.

In the Schema Manager, the left pane displays the scope of the schema, and the right pane displays the results. The top container, or node, in the left pane is the root node containing the forest schema, and the two below it are the class node and the attributes node, which contain schema specifiers for classes and attributes, respectively.

Flexible Single Master Operation

Make sure that the Schema Manager console specifies the Operations Master for the schema of your forest. The Operations Master for the schema is a role that is granted to a single DC for

Figure 7.3 Schema Management console.

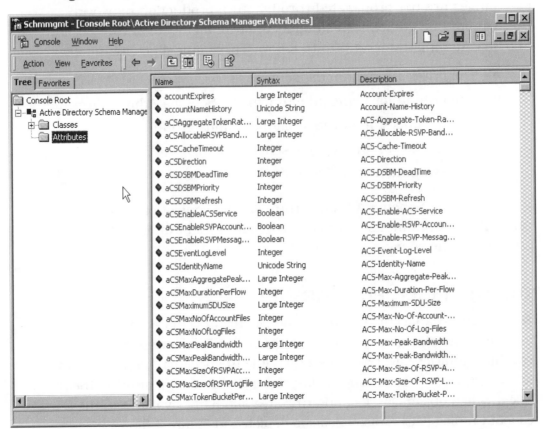

making updates to the schema. Only one DC at a time can occupy this role. After the changes are completed, they are replicated to the remaining DCs in the forest. To see the Operations Master role, open the Schema Manager console, right-click on Active Directory Schema Manager root, and select Operations Master from the popup menu. Make sure that the box for "The Schema may be modified on this server" is checked, as shown in Figure 7.4. Checking this box sets the value "Schema Update Allowed" to 1 under the registry key HKLM\System\CurrentControlSet\Services\NTDS\Parameters. This method of enabling any DC to be a single master of the schema is called the Flexible Single Master Operation model, or FSMO (pronounced FIZZ-MO, a name which, I believe, reflects the excessive consumption of Jolt Cola at Microsoft).

Figure 7.4 FSMO Schema Master.

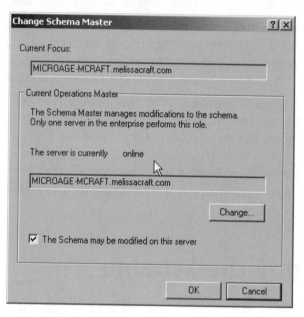

The Schema Manager is not a utility that shows up in any menu, it is installed by executing the command REGSRV32SCHMMGMT.DLL. Then, open the Schema Manager (schmmgmt.exe) and select the Console menu. Click Save As and save the file to the Documents and Settings\<your username>\Start Menu\Programs\Administrative Tools directory. You may rename the file from schmmgmt to Schema Manager at the same time.

There are five FSMO roles in Windows 2000:

- **Schema Master:** Controls schema updates.
- **Domain Naming Master:** Controls all the additions and removals of domains from the Active Directory.

- **RID Master:** Controls the allocation of Relative IDs (RIDs). Relative IDs are allocated as a sequence of numbers to each domain. The RID is concatenated with the domain's SID (Security Identifier) whenever a new object is created and then assigned to the new object as a unique object SID.

- **PDC Emulator:** In mixed mode, the primary domain controller (PDC) emulator controls backup domain controller (BDC) replication and backward compatibility. In native mode, the PDC emulator controls password updates.

- **Infrastructure Master:** Controls group-to-user references, so that updates of group memberships are propagated throughout the Active Directory

You can view various FSMO roles whenever you see the Operations Master option in an Active Directory console menu or popup menu.

How to Modify the Schema

The schema can be modified through the addition, deletion, or updates, to any objects or attributes within it. The schema is the structure of the Active Directory and manages how the content of the Active Directory is presented to users, Administrators, and applications. When changes are made to the schema, the Active Directory validates the changes to make sure that the entire Active Directory database retains integrity.

Class

It is recommended to create attributes before creating classes so that new attributes can be designated as Mandatory in the class. A new class can be created without creating any new attributes, however. Before creating a new class of object in the schema, the information listed in Table 7.1 should be determined.

Table 7.1 Object Class Information Needed for New Object

Class Object Dialog Options	LDAP Property Name	Function	Example
Common name	Cn	Name of the class of object. This name must be unique in the schema.	My Object
LDAP Display	LDAPDisplayName	This name, similar to the common name, is by programmers and is guaranteed to be unique. It has a format of being multiple words concatenated with capitals separating each	myObject
X.500 Object ID			
X.500 OID	objectIdentifier	This is a unique number where each set of numbers is separated by a period. It is guaranteed to be unique worldwide for standard object classes since it is usually issued by a standards organization, including the ISO, ITU, and ANSI. If creating a new class, the OID (Object ID) can be obtained from these standards groups. It is not recommended that you make up a number for this, since it could conflict with other classes that are added later.	1.1.111.111 111.1.1.111
Parent Class	PossSuperiors	The class from which the new class will inherit default attributes. If a new object is a subclass of Person, it will inherit all the Person attributes. Person is a subclass of top, and inherits all the top attributes.	ParentClass

Continued

Class Object Dialog Options	LDAP Property Name	Function	Example
Class Type	objectClass	The class type is an X.500 class type. There are three from the 1993 X.500 definition: **Abstract**: Template class for all three types of classes. **Auxiliary**: List of attributes that can be included in Structural and Abstract classes. **Structural**: True object class that will enable new objects to be created within Active Directory.	Abstract Auxiliary Struct- ural

There is one class type from the 1988 X.500 definition: 88. 88 does not have the same structure as the other classes, and is not available within Active Directory.

NOTE

When applying for an X.500 Object ID in the United States, you can contact ANSI (American National Standards Institute) via the Internet at www.ansi.org. ANSI will assign a subset of the X.500 OID hierarchy, which is termed an arc. This is essentially a set of numbers that can be further subdivided into subarcs, and used for multiple X.500 objects and attributes.

Follow these steps to create a new class in the Schema Manager console:

1. Right-click the Classes Node in the Schema Manager.

2. In the popup menu, click Create Class...

3. A warning will appear, as shown in Figure 7.5. Click CONTINUE to bypass it.

4. In the Create New Schema Class dialog box illustrated in Figure 7.6, complete the information that was listed in Table 7.1, and click NEXT to continue.

Figure 7.5 Class object creation warning.

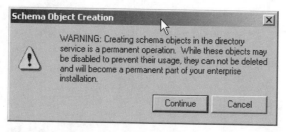

Figure 7.6 Create New Schema Class dialog.

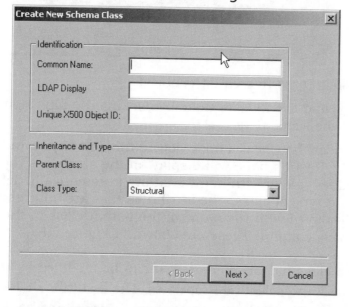

5. In the next dialog, shown in Figure 7.7, you can select the attributes that will be part of this class. For any attributes that an Administrator *must* fill out when creating one of the instances of this object, add them to the Mandatory section by clicking ADD next to the section and selecting the attributes. Add any discretionary attributes to the Optional section by clicking ADD next to the Optional section. You do not need to add any attributes, although some will be added by default.

Figure 7.7 Adding attributes to a new class.

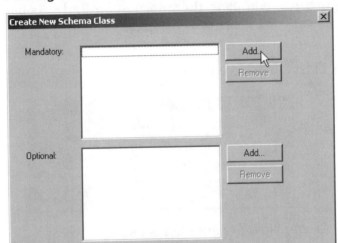

6. Click FINISH to create the object.

7. Expand the Classes node by clicking the plus sign to its left in the scope pane.

8. Under the Classes node, locate the new object and select it. The Results pane will display all the attributes that were added, along with many that are automatically defaults of that type of class. The attributes that are inherited are displayed with the name of the parent class in the Source Class column. These are shown in Figure 7.8.

Once a class has been created, it can be modified by right-clicking the class and selecting Properties. The resulting dialog allows the Administrator to change the selected attributes, the description, the possible superiors, and security. It also lets the Administrator deactivate the object or enable it to be browsed in the Active Directory by checking the boxes for these options on the General tab, which is displayed in Figure 7.9. Note that some of the properties are grayed out, and therefore cannot be changed. These include the Common Name, the X.500 Object Identifier, and the Class Type.

Figure 7.8 New class object and default attributes.

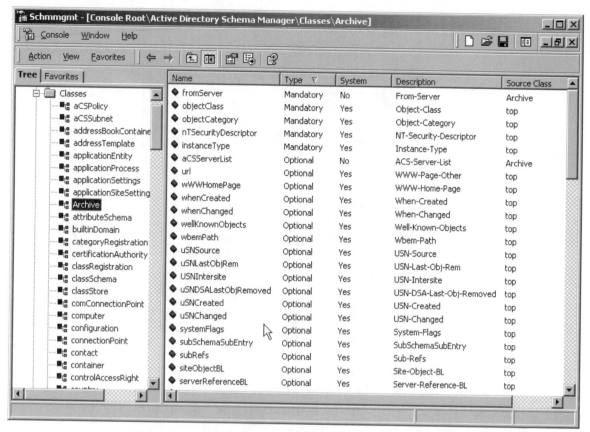

Inheritance occurs when one object class is designated as a parent to another. This designation enables the attributes of that parent class to flow down to the child class. For example, if making a new class a child of a User class, all the attributes of Users will be available as part of the new class. To change the inheritance of the object or the attributes that it uses by default, select the Relationship tab. Click ADD next to Auxiliary classes in order to select a list of attributes that should be included in this class. Then select an Auxiliary class from the list of available schema objects and click OK. The new attributes will be added to the defaults in the results pane when you are finished.

Figure 7.9 Class properties.

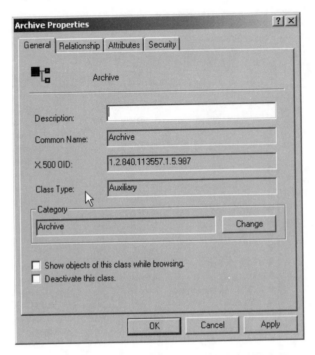

To add the inheritance from parent classes, click ADD next to the Possible Superiors box, and "Add a class" from the list that appears. After clicking OK for either of these operations, the possible superior's or auxiliary class's X.500 Object Identifier will appear in the window, as illustrated in Figure 7.10.

To select or deselect attributes for the class, click the Attributes tab, which is shown in Figure 7.11. You cannot add or remove any Mandatory attributes, but you are able to add or remove Optional attributes, even if they were added during the object's creation. The process is the same as during the creation of the class.

Figure 7.10 X.500 OID appears when adding a possible superior or auxiliary class.

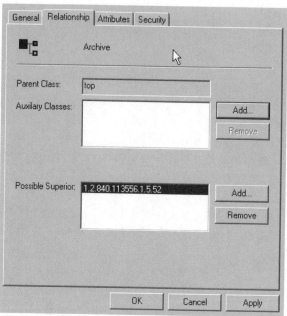

Figure 7.11 Adding attributes after class creation.

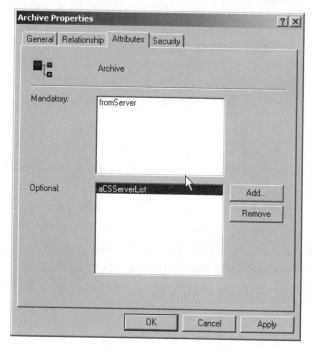

For IT Professionals

Deactivating an Object Class

The objects in the original Active Directory schema cannot be deactivated; however, those that are added later can be. Deleting a schema object is not supported by the Active Directory because of the inconsistencies that could result. Deactivation is the next best thing since the object class is unusable, but the instances of the class can still exist, just not be newly created.

The object class can be deactivated by checking the box in the Schema Manager. The object class can be reactivated by unchecking it later.

When a class is deactivated, it cannot be added as an instance afterward. Those existing instances cannot be modified. Queries made by users, or deletions of the Active Directory instances, can still occur as though nothing has happened.

After deactivation, schema updates will only modify the isDefunct attribute of the schema object. The isDefunct attribute is set to true when the object is deactivated. No other modifications will be made except for that isDefunct attribute value.

Attributes

When creating new object class that includes new attributes, it is recommended that the attributes be created first. Then, the new class can use the new attributes immediately upon creation. The attribute requires the same common name, Lightweight Directory Access Protocol (LDAP) display name, and Unique X.500 Object Identifier that is required by a new class object. Additionally, the new attribute will require the information contained in Table 7.2.

Table 7.2 Required Information for a New Attribute

Dialog Options	Purpose
Syntax	The syntax determines what type of information can be contained. This field is a drop-down list with several options, including Octet string (such as an IP address) and Boolean (true and false values).
Minimum	This is the lower limit on the syntax's value. For example, if using an Integer syntax, the default lower limit is 0, but placing 1 here will eliminate 0 from being used.
Maximum	This is the maximum limit on the syntax's value. If using a String syntax, the maximum limit would be the length of the string. Placing 50 in this field would limit a String syntax attribute to 50 characters.
Multi-Valued	When checking this box, it means that the attribute can have a one-to-many relationship with the resulting properties. For example, a multi-valued item is the Possible Superiors attribute. There can be many superior class objects. However, each Boolean attribute (true/false) can only be single-valued, since an item should not be true and false at the same time.

In order to create a new attribute, you must start with the Schema Manager.

1. Right-click on the Attributes node in the Scope panel.

2. Select New Attribute.

3. Click CONTINUE to bypass the warning. (It is identical to Figure 7.5.)

4. The Create New Attribute dialog box will appear, as illustrated in Figure 7.12. Type in the Common Name, LDAP Display, and X.500 OID, as well as the information determined for the items in Table 7.2, and click OK.

5. The object will be created and will appear in the Results window in the Attributes node.

The attribute can be modified somewhat after it is created. This is done by double-clicking the attribute in the Results pane, or right-clicking it and selecting Properties. Note that the Common

Name, X.500 OID, and Syntax are grayed out and cannot be changed. There is a statement about whether the attribute is multi-valued or single-valued, and that cannot be altered either. The remaining items can be updated.

Figure 7.12 Create New Attribute dialog.

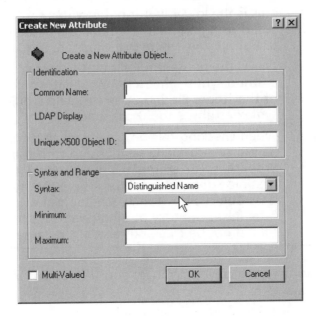

System Checks After Schema Modification

Two types of safeguards have been put in place to ensure no problems will result from schema modification:

- Safety checks
- Consistency checks

The safety check reduces the possibility of schema modifications interrupting an Active Directory application that uses the object class or attribute that has been changed. Safety checks are simply the items that cannot be modified after a class has been created, and the items that cannot be changed on default schema objects, such as adding a new Mandatory attribute on a class.

Consistency checks are the method that Active Directory undertakes to ensure that certain values must remain unique, such as the LDAP Display, Common Name, and X.500 OID. An addition of a new object will only be successful if these items and any other unique attributes are verified as unique throughout the Active Directory forest. Aside from these and other verifications, the Consistency check will ensure that:

- All attributes and classes designated during object class creation or modification already exist within the schema.
- All classes designated as Auxiliary have an Auxiliary class specification.
- The rDNAttID attribute uses the syntax for String(Unicode).
- The minimum value of an attribute is lower than the maximum value.

NOTE

The rDNAttID attribute defines the naming convention used in the Active Directory schema. Because its applicability is universal, it is critical that it is consistent.

Schema Container

The Schema container holds the entire schema, inclusive of attribute and class definitions. It must be replicated to each DC that is part of the same forest. The Schema container is located in the Configuration container, at cn=Schema, cn=Configuration, dc=mysubdomain, dc=mydomain, dc=com. The Schema Configuration container cannot be viewed with the default Windows

2000 Active Directory tools; however, it can be seen using the following utilities:

- Schema Manager
- ADSI Edit
- LDP

The first time that ADSI Edit is executed, the user must connect to a naming context. This requires right-clicking the ADSI Edit container and selecting "Connect to" from the popup menu. The ADSI Edit tool must be pointed to the schema in order to see it. This requires right-clicking the root and selecting Settings, then changing the Naming Context to Schema. The result will be the screen shown in Figure 7.13.

Figure 7.13 ADSI Edit displays the Schema container.

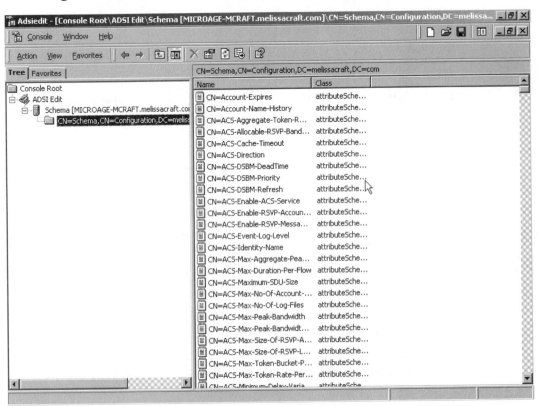

The Cache

When a DC initializes, it reads the schema from the Schema container into memory. This version of the schema sitting in RAM is called the *schema cache*. Whenever changes are made to the schema, they are validated against the schema cache rather than the schema on the hard drive to enhance performance. Whenever replication or changes are made, they are first made to the schema on the DC's hard drive and then are automatically updated in the cache five minutes after the first change was made. The file on the hard drive that initializes the schema when it is first installed is the SCHEMA.INI.file located in %systemroot%\system32. The Active Directory database is the NTDS.DIT that is located in the %systemroot%\ntds directory by default. NTDS.DIT contains the entire Active Directory, including schema and GC.

The tables in the schema cache are called ATTCACHE and CLASSCACHE, and represent each attribute and class in the schema. There are hash tables of ATTCACHE and CLASSCACHE to enable lookups in the cache. The table sizes are dynamic, based on the number of items (attributes and classes) that exist in the schema. The table sizes increase or decrease based on the schema changes made.

The schema cache is updated every five minutes. This means that changes made to the schema may not appear immediately. To update the schema cache from the hard drive without waiting for the five-minute interval to pass, in the Schema Manager, right-click the Active Directory Schema Manager root node and select Reload the Schema as illustrated in Figure 7.14.

Figure 7.14 Updating the schema cache.

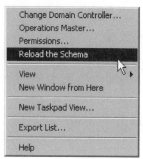

Schema Utilities

The Schema Manager is not the only utility that can update the schema, although it is probably the most user-friendly. LDIFDE and CSVDE are two command-line tools that can also update it, as well as ADSI Edit.

LDIFDE and CSVDE are two data format exchange utilities. The first, LDIFDE, uses LDAP Data Interchange Format. The second, CSVDE, uses a Comma Separated Value. Both of these utilities take files that contain data to be added or modified in (LDIFDE can modify, CSVDE can only add) the Active Directory, then import it to the Active Directory. Both of these utilities can also export directory data from the Active Directory.

It is recommended that the Schema Manager be used to update the schema. But for die-hard command-line utility users, the following is an LDIFDE file format representing an addition to the schema. Because CSVDE does not have as many features as LDIFDE, it is recommended that LDIFDE be used for the command-line format tool.

```
dn:
CN=myAttribute,CN=schema,CN=configuration,dc=microage,dc=melissacraft,dc=com

changetype: add

objectClass: attributeSchema

ldapDisplayName: myAttribute

adminDisplayName: my-attribute

adminDescription: A new schema attribute

attributeID: 1.2.840.113557.8.8.999

attributeSyntax: 2.5.5.12

omSyntax: 64
```

```
isSingleValued: TRUE

systemOnly: FALSE

searchFlags: 0

showInAdvancedViewOnly: FALSE
```

Querying the Active Directory

The schema affects end users in a fundamental way. It provides the basic layout of information about users, computers, and other Active Directory objects. This layout is copied fully within each domain and partially to the forest's GC.

First, an attribute has to be replicated to the GC. This is accomplished in the Schema Manager by double-clicking any attribute and selecting "Replicate this attribute to the Global Catalog," as shown in Figure 7.15.

Figure 7.15 Making attributes available in the GC.

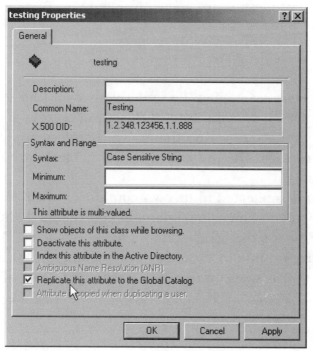

Display Specifiers

The user interface can be specified for each object within the Active Directory. The user interface information is stored in an Active Directory object called a *display specifier*. The storage of the user interface information (UI) plus the ability to secure who sees which attributes allows the Active Directory to adapt to the needs of both end users and Administrators.

For example, a Network Administrator JUNE may create a display specifier for CUBE NUMBER as an attribute for a user account that only Administrators need to see. The PAYROLL business unit may also want to add display specifiers for SALARY and VACATION HOURS, but would not want JUNE to see the values for those fields. Both JUNE and the PAYROLL unit can add the display specifiers and then apply security to them so that JUNE cannot see SALARY and VACATION HOURS, and PAYROLL cannot see CUBE NUMBER.

Display specifiers are Active Directory objects stored in cn=Display Specifiers, cn=Configuration, dc=mydomain, dc=com. They include property sheets, context menus and icons, and more. Display specifiers are available in the ADSI Edit utility. A Display-specifier object's properties are shown in Figure 7.16.

Summary

The Active Directory schema is the underlying layout for the Active Directory database. It is comprised of classes of objects and attributes. The objects that are within the Active Directory are instances of the schema classes. The properties of these objects are the schema attributes.

The schema is replicated in its own container, which is located in the Configuration container, to all domain controllers (DCs) within a forest. Each DC loads the schema into a memory cache. This cache is updated at five-minute intervals with any changes that are made to the schema that resides on the DC's hard drive. Only after the

Figure 7.16 Display-specifier object.

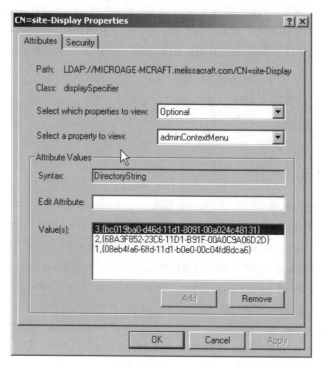

schema cache is updated will the new updates be seen in the schema.

The schema is a critical underlying support factor to the Active Directory. It controls the structure and content that users and Administrators see when browsing the Active Directory. Active Directory-aware applications and Administrators both may need to extend the schema to include more objects or attributes.

The only group that has access to the schema is the Schema Admins group. There can only be a single DC with the capability to extend the schema, since it uses the Flexible Single Master Operations (FSMO) method. FSMO lets any DC become the Operations Master for the schema, but only one DC at a time.

Planning for changes to the schema should be managed with a change management policy that establishes who has the capability to change the schema, and under what conditions. The changes are best implemented during times when the internetwork is least busy. If possible, schema changes should be tested on a separate lab forest before being placed into use on a production network.

Additions and modifications to the schema can be made in several utilities:

- Schema Manager console
- ADSI Edit
- LDIFDE
- CSVDE

It is recommended that the schema changes are made in the Schema Manager console because of its user-friendly interface. When a new class or attribute is added, it should have the complete information documented prior to its implementation, since the schema safety and consistency checks will not allow some changes to be made to the attribute or class after its creation. Classes and attributes cannot be deleted, but they can be deactivated. Classes and attributes within the default schema that Active Directory starts with cannot be deactivated.

When a new attribute is created, it must be replicated to the Global Catalog (GC) in order for users to search for objects based on that attribute. This is available as a property of the attribute. Users and Administrators can easily search for objects within the Active Directory Users and Computers console.

FAQs

Q: What is the schema?

A: The schema is the blueprint for every object and attribute in the Active Directory. It manages the values that each attribute can be found, and whether the attribute can be found in the GC.

Q: I looked for the Schema container in the Active Directory Users and Computers, the Active Directory Sites and Services, and even the Active Directory Domains and Trusts utilities. Where is it located?

A: The schema is such a critical component to the Active Directory that it is protected by not being easily accessible through standard utilities. To access the Schema, use the Resource Kit utilities for the Schema Manager or ADSI Edit.

Q: I made a change to the schema, but the change did not appear on the network right away. Why is that?

A: What you see when you look at the schema is actually the schema cache in RAM of the DC. When changes are made, they are made to the schema located on the hard drive. There is a five-minute interval for the schema cache to be updated by the changes made to the schema on the hard drive. This interval can be bypassed by manually reloading the schema from the Schema Manager console.

Q: How can I change the schema FSMO to the current DC?

A: In the Schema Manager console, right-click the root and select the Operations Master. If the current DC is not listed, click CHANGE and select the current DC. Then, return to the Operations Master dialog and select "The Schema May Be Modified on this Server."

Planning and Implementing Sites

The infrastructure system of network connections is one of the ever-changing aspects of any network. Likewise, the site topology will constantly be changing.

Introduction

Active Directory Services brings new traffic to the network in the form of:

- Query traffic
- Authentication traffic
- Replication traffic

Consider a network with multiple offices around the globe. Some offices are close to each other and have fast network links between them with T-3 lines and more than 45 Mbps of available bandwidth. Other offices are simply connected with slow network links such as ISDN 128 Kbps or Fractional T-1 lines at 256 Kbps. There is a concern about the way the added network traffic caused by Active Directory Service may affect the available bandwidth on these connections. Using sites can alleviate this concern.

Active Directory's method of managing network traffic centers around its use of sites. Sites are considered to be regions within the enterprise network that share high-bandwidth connectivity. In essence, they are an assembly of well-connected Internet Protocol (IP) subnets.

The Function of Sites in Active Directory

The main concept surrounding sites is that they should be created based on the geography of the network because they centralize the domain controllers (DCs) to which traffic should be directed. A site should be a concentration of network servers and computers in a single geographic location. For example, if a corporation had a headquarters office in Boston, Massachusetts and a satellite office in

London, England, its Network Administrator should create two separate sites: one for Boston and the other for London.

Sites can span domains. This means that several domains, or parts of domains, can exist within a single site. This occurs when a domain design separates each domain by its location. This design is illustrated in Figure 8.1. When a site spans multiple domains, there is an increase in the replication traffic within that site because two domain databases must be replicated in addition to the schema, configuration, and Global Catalog (GC) for the forest.

Figure 8.1 Sites span domains.

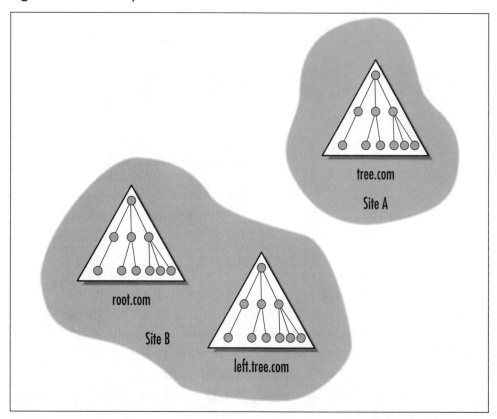

Domains can span sites, and there can be several sites within a domain. This design results from domains spanning multiple geographic locations. It is illustrated in Figure 8.2.

Figure 8.2 Domains span sites.

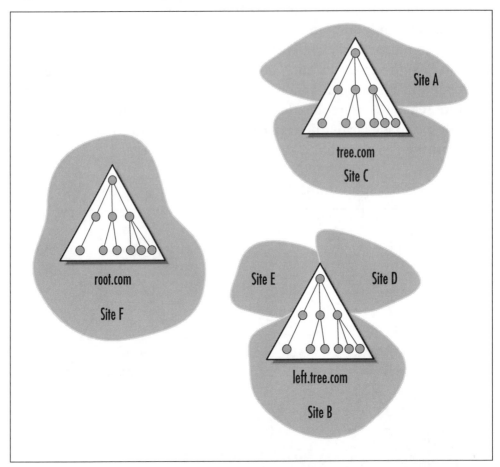

Sites are specific to a forest. If there are multiple forests in the same location, a site must be created in each forest for that location. There are few limitations on how a site or domain is designed, and sites can be created, deleted, or changed at any point in time, which may result in a rather confusing arrangement. In fact, a single forest can have sites spanning domains, and domains spanning sites, as shown in Figure 8.3.

Sites are not part of the DNS namespace; they simply set a geographic boundary for managing network traffic. Sites determine the proximity of network computers for those that are sending Active Directory-based data, such as replication, authentication, and query

Figure 8.3 Domains and sites span each other.

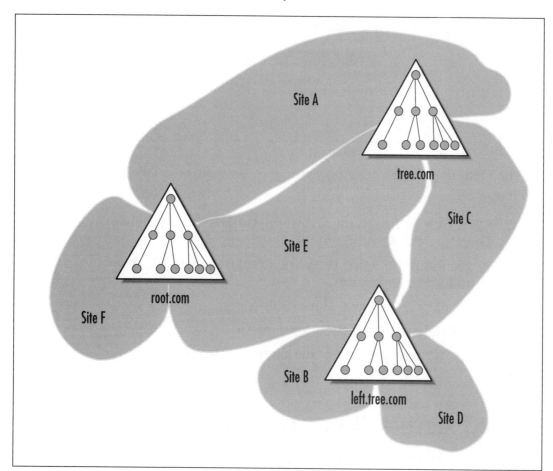

traffic. For instance, clients will be directed to DCs within their designated site when authenticating or querying.

Default-First-Site-Name

Amazingly, or maybe not so amazingly, the first DCs that are
installed within the Active Directory are automatically placed within
a site called Default-First-Site-Name, as shown in Figure 8.4. This
can be viewed in the Active Directory Sites and Services utility
found in Administrative Tools.

Figure 8.4 Default-First-Site-Name.

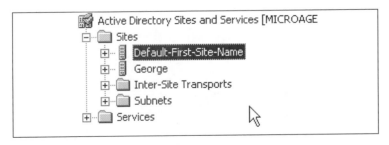

The Default-First-Site-Name name can be changed. To change the name:

1. Click Start | Programs | Administrative Tools | Active Directory Sites and Services.

2. In the left pane, click the plus sign (+) next to the Sites container to expand it.

3. Right-click the Default-First-Site-Name.

4. Select Rename from the popup menu.

5. You can then type the name directly into the pane.

Replicated Active Directory Components

Several components within the Active Directory must be replicated. Some of these are replicated solely within a domain, whereas others are replicated to all parts of a forest.

Domain Partitions

The Active Directory database is partitioned for each domain. The DCs maintain a replica of the partition for their own domain and no other. This replica is identical to all other domain replicas until an Administrator makes a change to the domain. At that point, the change is replicated to all other domain replicas. The domain partitioning enhances performance for the database, since smaller database parts enable faster response to queries and more efficient processing.

Figure 8.5 Domain partitions.

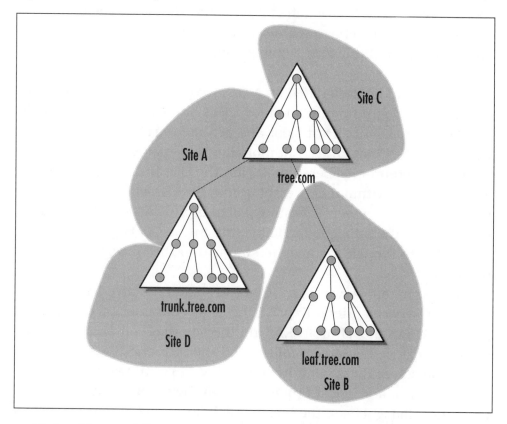

Using Figure 8.5 as an example, if a change is made to a user account in tree.com, the replication is only affected in tree.com. Neither leaf.tree.com nor trunk.tree.com are impacted. The sites that are affected with the update replication are site A and site C. Sites B and D are not affected because they do not contain any DCs for tree.com.

Global Catalog

When there is a single domain within the Active Directory, there is no real need for a GC server since all users have the same context (and User Principle Names (UPNs) are not required), and Universal groups are mostly useful in distributing objects between domains (and so would not be required). The entire Active Directory forest is represented by the GC, which is a database that contains a partial replica of every object in each Active Directory domain within a single forest. The GC provides a single database to search for users or resources.

Any DC can be designated as a GC server. Because the GC server provides logon authentication for UPNs and the source data for queries, there should be at least one per site to retain query traffic within the site boundaries. Additionally, Universal groups publish their entire group memberships within the GC. If there are thousands of users within a Universal group, the GC will increase tremendously. However, if nesting global groups within Universal groups, then the published membership in the GC is greatly reduced even though the membership within the Universal group is the same.

To designate a server as a GC server, use the Active Directory Sites and Services utility. Expand the Sites container by clicking the plus (+) sign to the left of it. Expand the site that contains the server, then expand the Servers folder, and then expand the server itself. Below the server there is an item called NTDS Settings. Right-click NTDS Settings and select Properties from the popup menu. In the Properties dialog, check the box for Global Catalog server, as shown in Figure 8.6.

Schema and Configuration Containers

All DCs in an Active Directory hold a copy of the schema and the configuration for their designated forest. Both the Schema and Configuration containers must be replicated to ensure consistency throughout the entire forest.

Site Replication Components

Several components must be configured within an Active Directory forest in order to enable replication:

- Site objects
- Connection objects
- Site links
- Site link bridges
- NTDS Settings

Figure 8.6 NTDS Settings for a GC server.

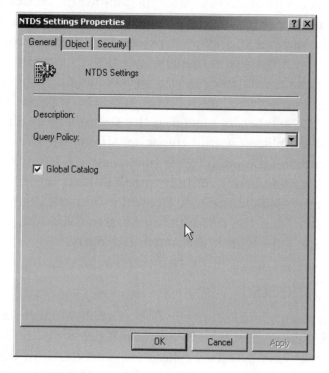

Site Objects

A site object represents an Active Directory site. A site is a set of well-connected IP subnets. Furthermore, well-connected means that the subnets are linked together and have substantial bandwidth available to those links.

There are no hard-and-fast rules regarding which links are considered well-connected and which are not, so designating an IP subnet to a particular site can be somewhat of a confusing decision. The characteristics of sites can help make this decision. Microsoft designed sites to reduce bandwidth consumption between sites, yet still enhance performance of the replication topology.

Workstations attempt to contact DCs within their own site for logon. The Knowledge Consistency Checker (KCC) will designate more replication connections between DCs within a site than with DCs in other sites. When replication occurs between different sites, the replication traffic is compressed to reduce the bandwidth consumption. Where replication occurs within a site, the replication traffic is not compressed to increase the speed of processing the replication. Finally, the replication within a site is triggered whenever a priority change is made to the domain database, as well as on a default five-minute interval, and replication between sites occurs based on a preset schedule.

The first DC installed is placed in the Default-First-Site-Name. All other DCs are placed within the same site as the first DC, or into a site designated as the default site for the Active Directory forest. If another site is created that contains an IP subnet to which a new DC's IP address belongs, the new DC will automatically join the other site rather than the default site. After installation, new DCs can join various sites within the Active Directory.

Connection Objects

A connection object represents the flow of replication between DCs within a site. Connection objects are found below the replication target DC, and they point to the replication source DC. In this way, the connection object flows in a single direction. The only way to have replication occur in both directions is to create two connection objects, one for each target DC.

An Administrator can create a connection object, or it can be created by the KCC on the destination DC. The KCC connection objects are created automatically and are sufficient for replication. The only time that an Administrator needs to create connection objects manually is to reduce latency between sites. The KCC will not delete any manually created connection objects, nor will it create a duplicate connection object where a manually created one exists.

Site Links

Without site link objects, DCs in different sites would not be able to communicate. Site link objects guide traffic between sites using a protocol, such as IP or Simple Mail Transfer Protocol (SMTP). Each site link object represents a link of a particular type and all the attached sites to that link, and should have an equal cost. For example, a frame relay network may have several sites attached to it, and that frame relay network would be represented by a single site link object.

The site link object contains information such as availability for replication, cost of using the link. and how often replication can occur for the link, as shown in Figure 8.7. The site link object offers a way for the Active Directory to understand how to use the connection. Site link objects are used to connect DCs from different sites together.

The properties that influence how a site link object is used are:

- Cost
- Replication frequency
- Schedule of availability

Cost is the logical expense of using a site link object. When a cost number is high, then the logical expense of the messages is high, and that cost of messages is directly translatable into the amount of bandwidth that is available for them. Microsoft designed replication to select a link more frequently for low-cost messages and less frequently for high-cost messages.

In routing scenarios, cost is traditionally established in inverse proportion to frequency or priority of a link's usage. Since the site link object represents an actual network connection, replication frequency should be increased as the cost decreases in any particular object. When this value is configured, provide a value for the number of minutes, between 15 and 10,080 minutes. When there are redundant site links representing redundant network connections, the Active Directory will select only the site link with the lowest cost.

Less bandwidth = higher cost = less frequent replication

The schedule can intervene in an automatic replication system by simply setting up whether the link can be accessed. The schedule enables the link for certain blocks of time, then disables it during the remaining hours.

Figure 8.7 Site Link Object properties.

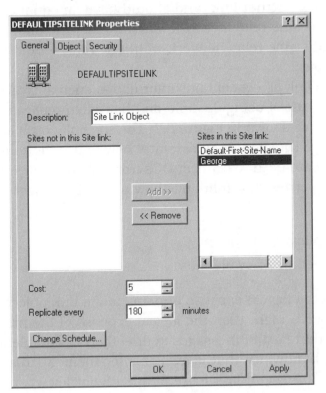

Site Link Bridges

A site link bridge object creates a forwarding system, which models multiple segment routing, between site link objects that have sites and protocols in common. A site link bridge cannot exist between site links that have no mutual sites. When a site link bridge is created, the cost of the site links is additive.

For example, Joe's Parts, Inc., shown in Figure 8.8, has three sites: one in London, one in Sydney, and the third in Tokyo. Joe's Parts' Administrator creates a site link between London and Sydney called LONSYD, and another site link between Sydney and Tokyo called SYDTOK, because those site links represent the WAN links on the network. To ensure that replication will flow through from London to Tokyo, the Administrator must create a site link bridge between LONSYD and SYDTOK. If LONSYD has a cost of 2 and SYDTOK has a cost of 3, then the site link bridge has a cost of 2+3=5.

Figure 8.8 Joe's Parts, Inc. site link bridge.

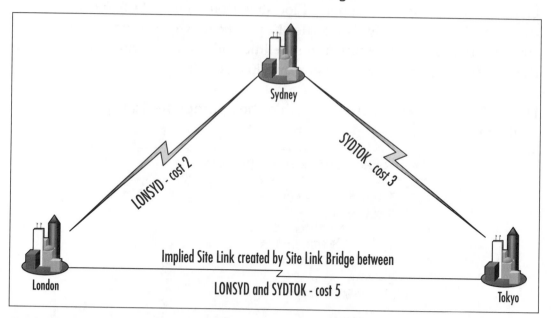

Replication Protocols

Two protocols are used for replication traffic:

- Remote Procedure Calls (RPCs) over IP
- SMTP

RPCs over IP are used for traffic within a site between DCs over connection objects, and for replication traffic between sites across site links. RPCs are a Session-layer API that executes applications on remote computers but appears to be executing them locally. RPCs can be executed over other protocol stacks, such as Vines and IPX. However, in the Active Directory, RPCs are only supported when executed over IP. In order to execute an RPC, the underlying network protocols must be in complete working order. If a DC's network interface card (NIC) or DNS configuration is not working correctly, an RPC error may be the result.

IP seems an obvious choice for a replication traffic protocol, but SMTP is not. SMTP was selected as the protocol to use solely for intersite (between sites) replication. SMTP, in this case, is asynchronous and appropriate for slow or low-bandwidth WAN links. SMTP-based replication is not supported for sites that contain DCs from the same domain; it only can be used to replicate GC, schema, and configuration data. Site links and site link bridges are created below the transports they utilize, as shown in Figure 8.9.

Figure 8.9 Site links are created within the appropriate Transport container.

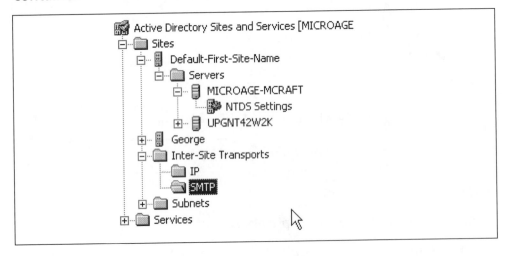

Replication in Active Directory

The function over which sites have the most control is replication. Replication is an essential component to a distributed database system, which the Active Directory is. When copies of the database exist in multiple locations, and a change is made in one copy, the other copies must be synchronized with that update. The synchronization of updates is accomplished through replication. The result is that users are able to access the Active Directory at any time, in any site or domain within the forest. Replication in the Active Directory will:

- Select efficient connections and site links
- Use multiple routes through the internetwork to provide fault tolerance
- Minimize the cost of replication by updating only the changed information
- Provide a method of conflict resolution

Replication will occur between any two DCs with the minimum of the Schema and Configuration containers being replicated. Replication between any two GC servers includes the schema, configuration, and GC. Replication between two DCs within the same site consists of the schema, configuration, and domain database. If those two DCs are also GC servers, then the replication traffic will have schema, configuration, domain database, and GC.

Replication traffic will treat bridgehead servers with preference. A bridgehead server in a site will receive all updates from within the site and exchange those updates with other sites via site links and site link bridges. The bridgehead server will receive replication traffic from other sites and then replicate that to DCs in its own site. To establish a server as a bridgehead server, in the Active Directory Sites and Services management console, right-click the server and select Properties from the popup menu. Click on a transport (either IP or SMTP), and then click ADD to make this server a bridgehead server for the selected transport, as shown in Figure 8.10.

Figure 8.10 Setting up a bridgehead server.

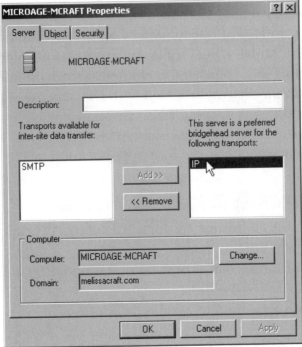

Replication Topology

The replication topology is the configuration of connections within a site, and the site links between sites. The intrasite (connections inside a site) configuration is automatically generated by the KCC. The KCC is a service that operates on each DC. It creates the connection objects between DCs that are located within the same site and executes every 15 minutes to reconfigure the replication topology.

The KCC ensures that replication occurs by reviewing the replication topology and creating additional connection objects to provide redundancy or to overcome a failure in the replication. To do this, the KCC attempts to establish a replication topology that includes a minimum of two connection objects to each DC and no more than 3 hops in a replication circle. Although the KCC automatically generates a replication topology, it can be overwritten by an

Administrator creating new connection objects. The replication topology manages how DCs communicate with each other.

The replication topology between sites must be manually created by an Administrator. The use of bridgehead servers and site link bridges can enable an efficient design. Scheduling the intersite replication can further make the replication topology effective.

Each naming context has its own replication topology. This is mainly due to the fact that each context has a separate place to be replicated to.

- The schema and the configuration's naming context applies forestwide, so they share a single replication topology across all sites and domains.

- Each domain has a separate naming context, and its replication topology applies across all DCs within it, and any sites to which they may belong.

The replication topology is built on top of the sites in a single forest. There is no replication between forests. Within each naming context, a bidirectional ring is created and the spanning tree algorithm is used to prevent routing loops of replication traffic when redundant links exist.

The optimum site topology is one in which domains and sites are in a one-to-one correspondence. For example, if domain A is completely within site A, and domain B is completely within site B, the intersite traffic only consists of GC, schema, and configuration information, and the intrasite traffic is limited to a local domain plus the GC, schema, and configuration traffic.

If a site consists of four DCs that are within the same domain, the replication topology resembles Figure 8.11. Note that in these diagrams, wherever one or more double arrows exist between DCs, two connection objects must exist, one in each direction.

The replication ring for a single site with two domains in it is more complex. This replication topology demonstrates the incremental bandwidth overhead of sites that span multiple domains. The replication topology is depicted in Figure 8.12.

Figure 8.11 Replication topology in same site for same domain.

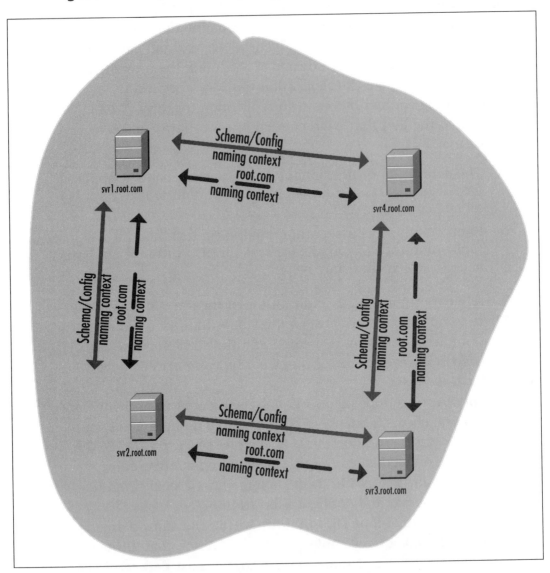

The replication topology becomes more intricate as multiple sites are added. As you have seen in each of the previous figures as well as the following, there is no stated path for the GC namespace. GC replication is somewhat counterintuitive, since the data for the GC will simply follow the same path that the domain namespace follows.

Figure 8.13 illustrates a replication topology for two sites that each contain DCs from two separate domains. Note that in Figure 8.13, two DCs in each site have been designated as bridgehead servers.

Figure 8.12 Replication topology in single site for two domains.

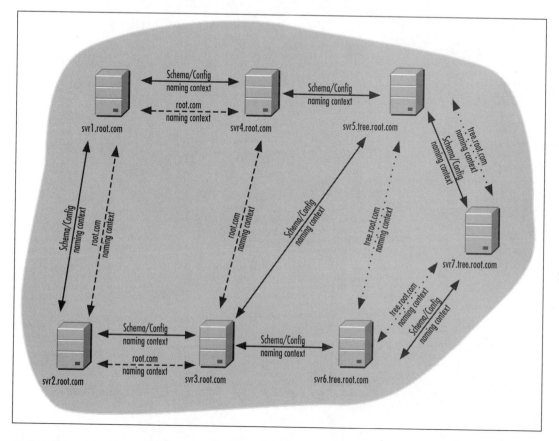

Planning a Site Structure

One of the first planning decisions is whether to establish multiple sites, and if so, how many. Separating the network into sites gains the following:

- Traffic from workstations and servers is localized.
- Replication traffic is optimized between DCs.

Figure 8.13 Replication topology for two sites with two domains.

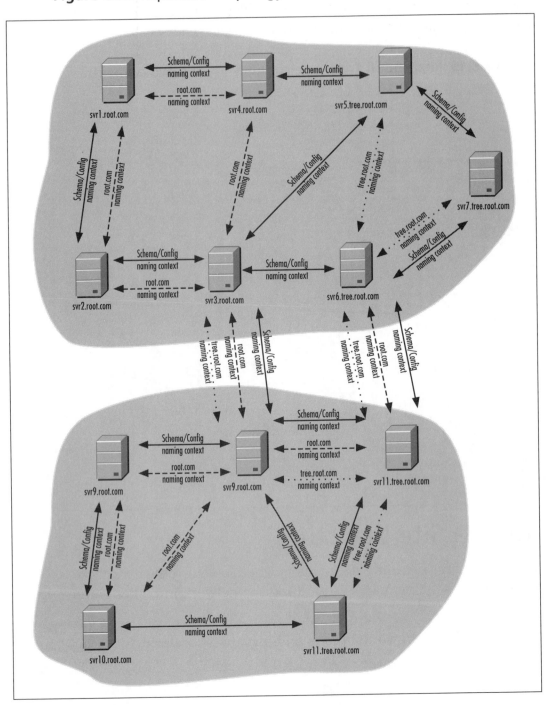

- Response performance from DCs is increased, typically resulting in reduced response time.

- Overhead traffic is reduced over WAN links.

All of these items translate into enhanced performance from the perspective of the end user. The reasons to create a new site would be to gain performance and reduce overhead on the network. A site should only be created separately from the default site if it has a DC dedicated to it, since otherwise it would not be involved in the replication topology. A separate site should be created for any office that has enough users to rate a dedicated DC. A site that has more than 30 users probably would benefit from having a DC. A site with less than five users would probably not. These are only suggested guidelines. The actual decision to place a DC and create a new site is one built of business requirements, usage, and performance requirements.

Site links should be created to provide reliability and fault tolerance to the intersite replication topology. A single site link is sufficient to send data between two separate sites. However, multiple redundant site links can make the topology fault tolerant.

When planning the site structure, the main organizing factor is the physical network infrastructure. The infrastructure is typically built to mirror the geography of the organization's places of operation. For example, Grape Drapes has its headquarters in Paris a manufacturing plant in Florence, and sales offices in New York and London as depicted in Figure 8.14. The infrastructure would most likely have a hub and spoke configuration, with links between Paris and all other locations. A single domain could encompass the entire corporation, and separate sites dedicated to each location would be most effective to centralize traffic. Since the KCC automatically generates each site's internal replication topology, the only thing that must be planned are the site links, site link bridges, and bridgehead servers between the sites.

Figure 8.14 Grape Drapes' network infrastructure.

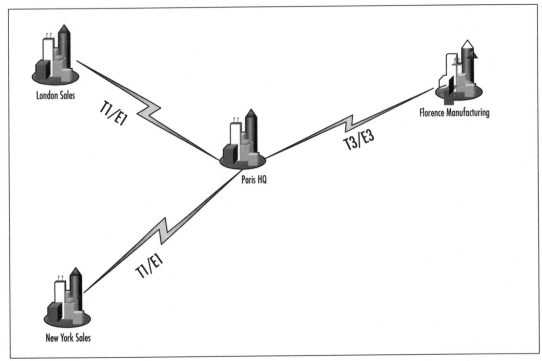

In the Grape Drapes scenario, there are three WAN links, for which three site links should be created. Remember, a site link represents a network connection and the sites involved in that connection. Each link will require cost and frequency of replication. Florence has the fastest link to Paris with the T3/E3 link, whereas the other two links have much less bandwidth in T1/E1 links; therefore, the Florence cost should be lower and the frequency should be higher. The New York sales office is not available for replication during 10 A.M. to 2 P.M. in order to reduce the cost of the overseas link. The three site links can be created as shown in Table 8.1.

Table 8.1 Site Links for Grape Drapes

Site Links	Cost	Frequency of Replication	Schedule
London–Paris	5	45 minutes	Available all hours
NY–Paris	5	45 minutes	Available 12:00 A.M. to 10:00 A.M., and 2 P.M. to 11:59 P.M.
Florence–Paris	1	20 minutes	Available all hours

This will enable replication to occur between any site and Paris, but does not enable replication traffic to occur between New York and Florence, New York and London, or London and Florence. To enable this type of connection, site link bridges must be created. The site link bridge should use Paris as the site in common. The site link bridges in Table 8.2 would be created for Grape Drapes will include all the sites links shown in Table 8.1 and have a total cost of 11.

WARNING

SMTP is asynchronous, and will normally ignore the schedule set on the site link properties. The only time that the SMTP site link schedule should be set is when the underlying network link itself is only live during certain time periods.

Placing Domain Controllers

There should be at least one DC in each site for each domain that exists in that site. This will provide an efficient localization of traffic for queries and authentication. Every site must have at least one site link associated with it.

Each site has to be associated with a subnet in order to be functional. Since a site is defined as a collection of well-connected subnets, each subnet associated with the site will automatically place a client workstation, server, or DC that is on that subnet into the site. It is recommended that the sites and their subnets are designed and implemented prior to installing any machines; except, of course, for the first DC in that forest.

When using a firewall, or when a site is connected to other sites only through a low-bandwidth network connection, a bridgehead server should be designated for intersite replication traffic. If using any SMTP-based site links, then a Certificate Authority (CA) service must be installed in the forest. The CA signs the SMTP packets, which enables their acceptance by the receiving DC.

Where to Place Global Catalog Servers

There should be at least one GC server on a DC in each site. The main issue with the GC is how large the forest is. The larger the forest, the larger the GC, and the greater the replication traffic. This replication traffic is simply between GC servers.

When there are fewer GC servers, there is less replication traffic, but there is more traffic for queries and authentication from workstations. When there are more GC servers, there is more traffic for replication, but less for queries and authentication from workstations. Replication traffic can be controlled between sites via the frequency and scheduled availability for the site link, so the most effective placement of GC servers is to ensure at least one server in each site.

Another issue to consider when placing GC servers is that there will need to be an Infrastructure Flexible Single Master Operations (FSMO) server for the forest. This Infrastructure FSMO cannot be run on the same DC as the GC. Since the Infrastructure FSMO is "flexible" and can be moved from DC to DC as needed, each site that may possibly host the Infrastructure FSMO must also have a separate DC for the GC.

The GC cannot be run on the same DC as the Infrastructure FSMO because the FSMO is responsible for cleaning up stale references from objects in its domain to objects in other domains of the forest. The stale references are those objects that have been moved or renamed. This means that the local data is out of sync with the GC. The only way that the two can synchronize is by the FSMO server verifying the objects' validity against the GC. If the Infrastructure FSMO and GC are housed on the same server, it will never recognize any references as stale, and cleanup will not occur.

Implementing a Site Structure in Active Directory

Implementing sites is accomplished through the Active Directory Sites and Services management console found in Administrative Tools. Since the first DC in the forest automatically created the Default-First-Site-Name site, then the console will display this site.

After that first DC is installed, the entire site structure can be created before installing any other domains and DCs.

The following examples use Bland Blinds as an example organization with the network infrastructure and designed site structure shown in Figure 8.15.

The first item is to rename the Default-First-Site-Name. Since the first DC installed is la1.blandblinds.com, then the site name should change to LA. In the Active Directory Sites and Services console, right-click Default-First-Site-Name and select Rename from the popup menu. Then change the name to LA.

The next thing we can do is create the PHX and LON sites. In the Active Directory Sites and Services console, right-click the Sites container and select New Site. Type in the name for PHX, and select a site link—DEFAULTIPSITELINK is fine for now, we will edit the site links later. Then click OK. You should see a dialog similar to the one shown in Figure 8.16. Click OK to bypass it. Repeat this procedure for the LON site.

The next step is to add the correct IP subnets to the site. Even though the Default-First-Site-Name was used as the LA site, it will

Figure 8.15 Bland Blinds' network infrastructure.

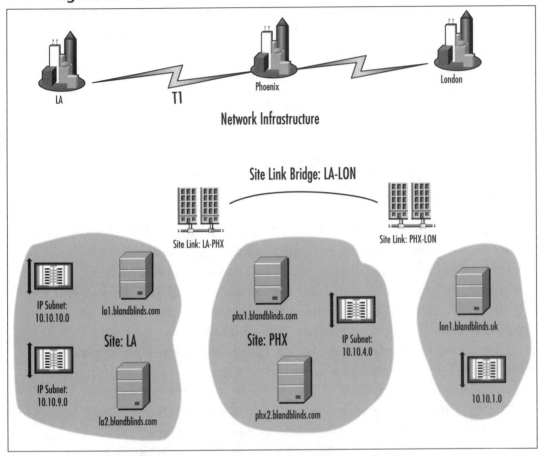

Figure 8.16 Create an Active Directory site.

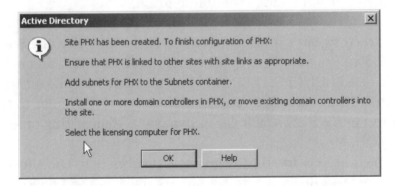

not have any IP subnets assigned to it. Right-click the Subnets container and select New Subnet. In the LA site, one of the subnets is 10.10.10.0. Although it is not listed here, the subnet mask is 255.255.255.0. In the New Object-Subnet dialog shown in Figure 8.17, type in the address and subnet mask, click on LA in the Site Name box, and click OK.

Figure 8.17 Create an IP subnet object.

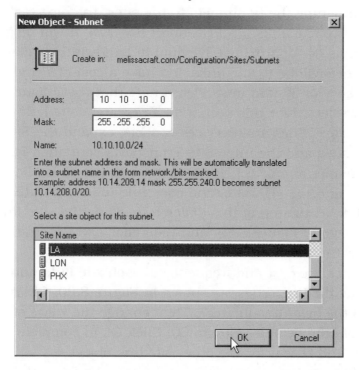

The name will build as you type in the subnet mask; it is merely a different notation for subnetting that is commonly used for Variable Length Subnet Masking (VLSM). The /24 represents the number of bits assigned to the subnet mask. To generate the remaining IP subnet objects, repeat this process and assign the subnets to the appropriate sites. The final IP subnet set for Bland Blinds should resemble those shown in Figure 8.18.

Figure 8.18 Resulting IP subnets for Bland Blinds.

Name	Site	Type	Description
10.10.10.0/24	LA	Subnet	
10.10.9.0/24	LA	Subnet	
10.10.4.0/24	PHX	Subnet	
10.10.1.0/24	LON	Subnet	

After assigning the IP subnets to the sites, the next task is to create the two site links: LA-PHX and PHX-LON. It will be assumed that the links are approximately equal in bandwidth availability, and that they will be IP site links and have a cost of 7 and a replication frequency of 60 minutes. (Please note that these figures were arbitrarily selected for this scenario.) To create a site link, in the Active Directory Sites and Services console, expand the Sites container, then expand the Inter-Site Transports container. Right-click the IP container and select New Site Link. In the dialog box, select the LA site and the PHX site, and click ADD to incorporate them into the site link. At the top of this dialog box, name the site link LA-PHX as shown in Figure 8.19. and then click OK. Repeat this process for the second link.

To change the cost and frequency of each site link, double-click it to display the Properties, as shown in Figure 8.20. Change the Cost from the default value to 7. Then change the value of the frequency from the default value to 60. Click OK to complete the configuration, and repeat for the other site link object.

Now that site link objects are configured, the site link bridge from LA to London can be created. This is a nearly identical process to creating a site link. In the same IP container below the Inter-Site Transports container, right-click the IP container and select New Site Link Bridge. In the resulting dialog, similar to that shown in Figure 8.21, select each of the new site link objects in the left-hand pane and click ADD to move them to the right pane. Give the site link bridge a name, and click OK.

Figure 8.19 Site link creation.

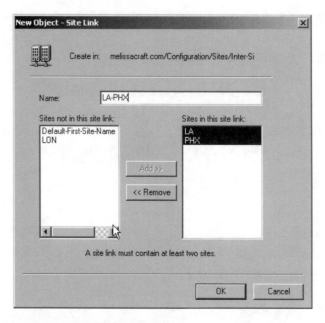

Figure 8.20 Site link configuration.

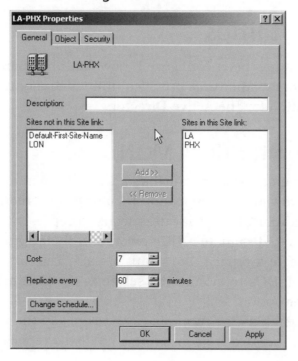

Figure 8.21 Site link bridge creation.

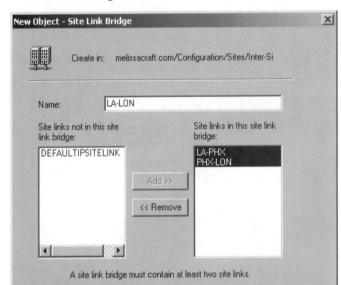

Replication Utilities

Once replication has been configured, how can an Administrator verify that it works? Microsoft provides utilities to monitor and manage the replication for the Active Directory.

Replication Monitor (REPLMON)

The replication monitor is installed as part of the Windows 2000 Support Tools to view the replication topologies and monitor the traffic. It is a graphical tool that uses icons to represent server roles, such as a globe to designate a GC server, and their status, such as a red X to indicate a replica that is out of date. The Administrator can select which DCs to monitor by selecting the Edit menu and the Add Site/Server option.

This utility enables the Administrator to specify the naming contexts and sites, then track each naming context's replication traffic for each DC by creating log files. Statistics are placed in the log files for each replication partner and each replication topology (e.g., naming context level).

Administrators should use the replication monitor after establishing the site structure to verify that it is working. If testing various site structures, which is entirely possible given the fact that sites are easily moved, changed, or deleted, Administrators can use this tool to validate the best replication topology set for their environment.

Replication monitor also serves as a troubleshooting tool. If there are persistent errors with replication, or if there are bandwidth utilization concerns, the replication monitor can provide the statistics. The replication monitor can be used to recalculate the replication topology by triggering the KCC. Additionally, if a naming context appears to be out of sync on separate DCs, the replication monitor can be used to force a synchronization.

Replication Administrator (REPADMIN)

REPADMIN is installed as part of the Windows 2000 Support Tools. This tool can provide the same functions as replication monitor; as a command-line tool it is less intuitive, although it can produce some very precise results.

DSASTAT

Although not specifically geared toward replication or sites, the DSASTAT command-line tool can help diagnose problems with naming contexts. This tool would be used if there were no obvious source of problems from the replication monitor log files.

DSASTAT compares naming contexts on different DCs. Additional statistics regarding the Active Directory store capacity, at a granular level, can further detect divergence of replicas.

Understanding Time Synchronization in Active Directory

Time synchronization is an important subject in distributed databases. One reason is that most distributed databases use a "last write" date and timestamp to determine which change should be considered final when there are conflicts.

If, for example, a change is made on a replica in New York at 3:08 P.M., and another change is made on a replica in Los Angeles at 12:09 P.M. (which would be exactly one minute after the New York change given the time zones), the change that would "win" during replication would be the change made in Los Angeles. However, if the DC's time clock had drifted to 12:07 P.M., the New York change would win. A change to a user object that was made in error at one site and then corrected on the other site could be the difference between that user being able to log on the next day or not. This is not the best situation, especially if that user happens to be a vice president of a corporation, which that user always seems to be when these types of glitches occur.

So how does time synchronization work with the Active Directory? The goal of time synchronization is to eliminate the consequence of drifting computer clocks and enable a common time for all participants on the internetwork. Common time does not necessarily refer to correct time, such as the atomic clock can provide. Rather, a common time is simply the same designated date and time that all computers agree upon. Keep in mind the following factors that are looked at by Active Directory when evaluating a conflict in replicated data:

1. The version number of an attribute has changed. If a user's password is changed in two locations (once by the user, once by the Admin), the attribute's version number is incremented by 1 on that DC. The change with the highest version number wins during a conflict. If the version numbers are equal such as when the changes are made within two different sites, then...

2. The change timestamp is evaluated. If the timestamps are equal, then...

3. The Globally Unique IDs (GUIDs) of the originating write Directory Service Agents (DSAs) are evaluated.

Active Directory reaches this goal through the W32TIME service running on Windows 2000 Servers. A simple command, NET START W32TIME, will start the service, which is implemented as SNTP (which is described in RFC 1769 and is available on each Windows 2000 Server or Professional machine). The service designates two types of machines:

- Time servers
- Time clients

The first installed DC acts as a primary SNTP server. Other DCs are also time servers for all time clients. Time servers implement synchronization between sites when Active Directory replication initiates a connection between DCs. If the time server is pointing to another Active Directory-based time server, the time source can be validated, but this cannot happen if pointing to a standard SNTP time server.

Time clients contact the time servers at logon. There is a five-minute difference in time allowed by Kerberos. Time is checked in eight-hour intervals after logon to verify time compliance. If the time client's clock is off, it will adjust its clock to match the time server's clock, log the change into its event log, and cut the interval check to every four hours.

The legacy NET TIME command is still available, but is not the same as the SNTP-compliant W32TIME service. However, NET TIME can use NTP services.

Summary

A site is defined as a set of IP subnets that have a high amount of bandwidth available between them. The purpose of a site is to localize traffic from queries, authentication, and replication. Replication is the process of synchronizing all the copies, or replicas, of the distributed Active Directory database. Queries and authentication traffic is generated at the will of clients. Replication traffic occurs actively and frequently within a site, but can be managed through intervals and scheduled availability between sites. Because of the nature of replication traffic, sites typically define a single geographic location.

When planning a site structure, make sure to place at least one domain controller (DC) and at least one Global Catalog (GC) server (they can be the same server) in each site. The configuration that will have the least amount of traffic between sites is that where sites and domains are in a one-to-one correspondence. This ensures a minimum of intersite and intrasite traffic, making this an optimum topology.

The replication topology is the configuration of the physical flow of information between DCs. Each naming context (schema, configuration, and domain) has a separate replication topology. Replication traffic increases when sites span two or more domains. The Knowledge Consistency Checker (KCC) generates the replication topology within a site by creating a bidirectional ring for each naming context. Each direction in the ring is represented by a one-way connection object that can be found below each DC.

The replication topology between sites can be manually created by an Administrator. The Active Directory Sites and Services console is used to create the replication topology. Within it:

- Sites are created and assigned to a transport type, currently IP or SMTP.

- IP subnets are created and assigned to sites.

- Site links are created to connect those sites that have actual network connections between them.

- Site link bridges are created to connect sites by hopping over sites in common when two sites do not have network connections between them.

- Servers can be moved into sites, or if installed after the site has been assigned IP subnets, they will install into the site that contains their IP subnet.

Three utilities can assist in managing replication traffic:

- Replication Monitor—REPLMON
- Replication Administator—REPADMIN
- DSASTAT

These tools are capable of monitoring traffic on selected DCs, as well as forcing a replication synchronization and other troubleshooting options.

Time synchronization has an impact on replication in that if all Active Directory DCs do not agree on a common time, then updates may be applied out of order, resulting in possible logon failures and other access problems. Time synchronization is handled through the W32Time service, which is an SNTP-compliant time service. There are both time servers and time clients in this service. Time servers synchronize on a common time setting. Time clients check with time servers at logon to validate their time. If a time client is not synchronized, it will update its clock and log the event.

FAQs

Q: I would like to test three different site topologies on a production network. Can I do this, or must I select one and stay with it?

A: Sites are easily created and changed as needed. They were developed that way to incorporate growth and change within an organization. Therefore, any number of site topologies can be tested before selecting the optimal version. This, however, does not apply to a domain structure, since domains cannot be merged, split, or easily deleted.

Q: We have three sites, site A is in Phoenix, site B is in Mexico City, and site C is in Vancouver. Both Mexico City and Vancouver have WAN links to Phoenix. Since there is no network connection between Mexico City and Vancouver, how do we enable replication between those two sites?

A: This can be enabled by a site link bridge. A site link bridge is generated by connecting at least two site links that have at least one site in common. It duplicates a multihop routing system for the replication traffic.

Q: We want to limit the number of servers that can send replication traffic between two sites. Can we?

A: Yes. Designate each of the servers that is allowed to transmit replication traffic as a bridgehead server.

Q: We do not want to use the automatically generated intrasite replication topology. Can we delete and create some different connection objects without the KCC reconfiguring them later?

A: Yes. The KCC will not change or delete any connection objects that were manually created by an Administrator. In order to reduce the cost of administration for replication, use the KCC-generated site topology. Whenever a manually generated connection object is created, an Administrator would be required to analyze each change to the site's configuration (such as a new DC) and make appropriate changes to the connection objects.

Q: We would like to use a third-party time service that is SNTP compliant. Is this possible?

A: Yes, an SNTP-compliant time source can be used as the primary time server with the W32Time service.

Q: How can you filter group policy for a group of users that exists in an organizational unit (OU) with other users so only the first group receives the group policy and the rest do not?

A: When you want to apply a group policy object to a group of users that exists within an OU and it is not feasible to move that group into its own OU, you can rely on applying rights to filter the group policy. To filter a group policy for a select group, edit the properties of the group policy object. Click the Security tab, then remove the Authenticated Users group from the ACL. Add the selected group and make sure to grant the Read and Apply Group Policy rights. This will provide an effective filter.

Q: Where are my group policy objects? They don't appear as objects within their applied containers?

A: Group policy objects are stored in two places: in the GPT folder below SYSVOL on each replicated DC's hard drive, and within the System\Policies container in the Active Directory. The System container is not available by default in the Active Directory Users and Computers console. To view the System container and the Policies subcontainer, you can select Advanced Features from the View menu of the Active Directory Users and Computers console.

Chapter 9

Intellimirror

Solutions in this chapter:

- Understanding Group Policies
- Designing Group Policy Strategy
- Implementing the Group Policy
- Deploying Applications with Group Policies
- Understanding ACLs and SIDs

Intellimirror is a Windows 2000 feature that is enabled by the Active Directory through the use of group policies. When Intellimirror is implemented, a user's environment, even his personal documents, can intelligently follow him around the network.

If there is no other reason to implement Active Directory Services, then do it for the group policies. This is one of the most functional components of the Active Directory for Administrators—making user and computer settings easier to manage.

Introduction

When Microsoft released Windows 95 in August, 1995, a new feature called system policies was a slick way to manage Windows 95 computers and their users across a network. This functionality was included in Windows NT 4.0 when it was released later. Now, for Windows 2000, system policies have grown up to become *group policies* in the Active Directory. System policies may still exist on a Windows 2000 system, but since they have been displaced by group policies, it is not recommended that they be used.

Group policies are a constantly evolving administrative system. They can be used for managing computers and the end-users' environments. They can even be a method of deploying software to client workstations and as a configuration management tool. If an organization intends to use group policies in this manner, it is recommended that the Windows 2000 domain controllers (DCs) are established before creating the group policies and installing or upgrading client workstations. In order to use the group policies attached to organizational units (OUs), domains, or sites, the Active Directory must be functional. Otherwise, only Local group policies can be used.

What Are Group Policies?

Group policies are rules that the Network Administrator sets for users and computers on the network. Rather than a single flat file located in a file-based directory, group policies take advantage of the Active Directory distributed database. The result is a managed user environment and desktop configuration.

Group policies are stored in group policy objects. The group policy objects are associated with Active Directory containers. The settings in a group policy object are inherited by child containers. For example, a user will receive the group policy settings in all the policies leading from their current OU up to the top-level group policy, as shown in Figure 9.1. Multiple group policy objects can be associated with the same container, too. The depth of a user's location in the OU hierarchy does not affect the length of time it takes to log on. Instead, it is the number of group policy objects that must be read and applied. If there is a single group policy for each OU, and a user is located five OUs deep, it will take the same amount of time for the user to log on if the user is in a top-level container that has five group policy objects associated with it.

The group policy itself is contained within a group policy object in the Active Directory. The object is created in the Group Policy Editor, which can be launched in three different ways:

- From the Active Directory Users and Computers console, from the Group Policy tab on container objects
- From the Active Directory Sites and Services console, from the Group Policy tab on container objects
- As a separate management console using MMC and opening gpedit.msc

The Group Policy Editor is shown in Figure 9.2.

Figure 9.1 Group policy objects are inherited.

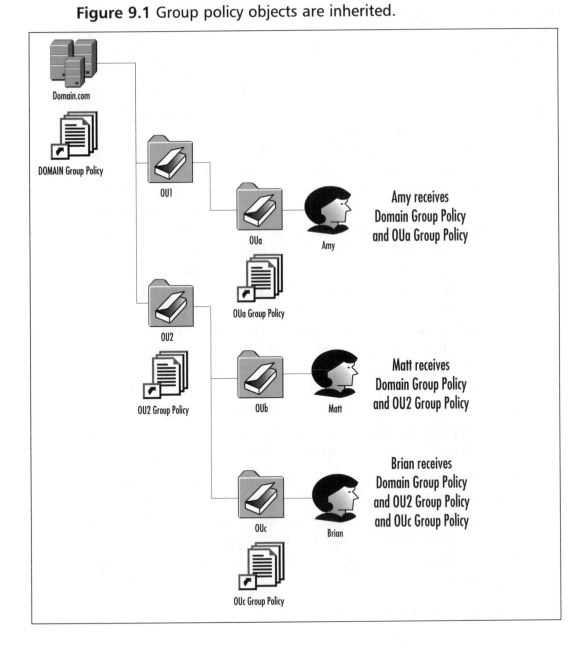

Figure 9.2 Group Policy Editor.

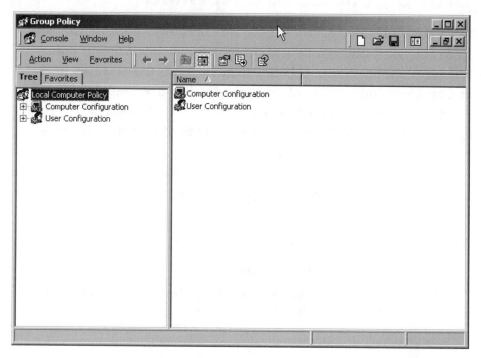

There are four containers to which group policies may be applied:

- **Local group policy:** The Local group policy object exists on each Windows 2000 computer. It contains, by default, only policies regarding security. The policy is located in the %systemroot%\system32\GroupPolicy directory.

- **Site group policy:** Site group policy objects are linked to site objects and can affect any object across the entire forest, since sites can span domains. Although linked to a site, a site group policy physically exists on a domain controller within a single domain.

- **Domain group policy:** Domain group policy objects are linked to a single domain and affect all user and computer objects within the domain.

- **Organizational Unit (OU) group policy:** OU group policy objects are linked to a specific OU. The OU group policy will affect all objects within the OU and within any OUs nested below it in the hierarchy.

How Group Policies Are Applied

When a computer boots into the Active Directory, it grabs the settings in the computer configuration of its associated group policy objects and applies them. When a user logs on, the settings in the User Configuration portion of the group policy are applied to the user's environment. No other Active Directory objects receive group policies. Computer configuration and user configuration are discussed in further detail later in this chapter.

The order of policy application will begin with legacy NT4 system policies, if they exist. If they do not, the order is as follows:

- Local group policy object
- Site group policy object
- Domain group policy objects
- OU group policy objects from the parent OUs down to the user's or computer's OU location

Refresh Interval

Both the user and computer configuration settings include options for refreshing group policies. The interval can be set for 0 to 45 days. Zero essentially establishes a constant dialog from the client computer to a DC every seven seconds to determine whether updates to group policies have been made. The default setting for the refresh intervals is every 90 minutes. To change the refresh intervals for the computer, within the Group Policy Editor, expand the Computer Configuration container, then the Administrative Templates, then System, and finally click Group Policy in the left-hand pane. In the right-hand pane, double-click on the Global Policy Refresh Interval and establish the interval. The navigation is essentially the same for the User Refresh Interval, except that the first container to expand is User

Configuration, and the item to double-click is the Global Policy
Refresh Interval for Users.

TIP

One of the ways that software developers can integrate applications into
the Active Directory is to take advantage of group policy features.
Application programming interfaces (APIs) have been created to enable an
application to lock sections of the registry in order to apply changes and
ensure that group policies do not interrupt the process. A RefreshPolicy
API enables the application to request a Group Policy Refresh. When an
application integrates group policies, it may require notification that the
group policies have been applied. Group policies create a message and log
an event when they are applied, so an application can read the event to
be assured that the policy was applied.

Blocking and Enforcing

A group policy that can be inherited from a higher level can be blocked
so that it does not pass further down the hierarchy. To block a policy:

1. Right-click the site, the domain, or the OU, and select
   Properties.
2. Click the Group Policy tab.
3. Check the box at the bottom of the dialog that states "Block
   Inheritance" as illustrated in Figure 9.3.

If there are conflicts between a policy setting in two different
group policy objects, the last group policy object will override the
setting applied previously. An Administrator can stop a policy from
being blocked or overridden. To enforce a policy:

1. Right-click the site, the domain, or the OU, and select
   Properties.
2. Click the Group Policy tab.

Figure 9.3 Blocking inheritance.

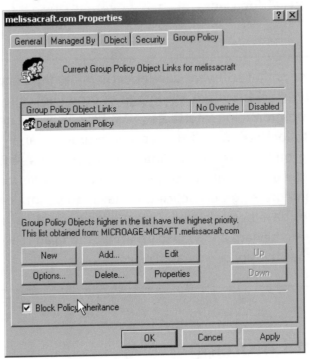

3. Click Options.

4. Check the box for No Override, as depicted in Figure 9.4.

Figure 9.4 Enforcing a policy.

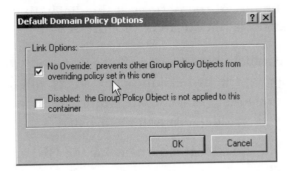

As shown in Figure 9.4, a group policy can also be disabled. An Administrator should exercise this option when retiring a group policy. By disabling the policy, the Administrator can reenable it later, should the need arise.

Group Policy Information Storage

Group policy objects store information into the Active Directory and into a Group Policy Template. The Active Directory storage is a Group Policy container that further contains subcontainers for user and computer information.

The Group Policy Template is actually an entire folder structure stored in the SYSVOL of the Active Directory DCs. The Group Policy Template top-level folder is \Policies. Below that, each group policy object is granted its own subfolder using its GUID (Globally Unique Identifier—a long, indecipherable string of numbers and characters) as the folder name. Below that there is a GPT.INI file and further folders that are created whenever changes are made to the following:

- **Adm:** Additions of Administrative Templates files (.adm files).
- **Apps:** Application deployment files for Windows Installer advertisements (.aas files), appears as a subfolder of both User and Machine.
- **Files:** Contains files to be deployed to the client, appears as a subfolder of both User and Machine.
- **Machine:** Contains the registry.pol file for the computer configuration changes.
- **Scripts:** Contains all scripts for the entire group policy.
- **User:** Contains the registry.pol file for the user configuration changes.

Both the Active Directory and the SYSVOL directory structure participate in multi-master replication. This ensures that the group policies are available anywhere within a global enterprise.

Administrative Templates

The source settings for group policies can originate from an MMC extension, or, as is more commonly used, an Administrative Template. Administrative Templates consist of ASCII text files with the extension .adm. The files include the registry settings in a format of categories with subcategories. These appear to the user in a Group Policy Editor interface as a hierarchy of settings, some with default settings already selected. Windows 2000 Group Policy can use the .adm files described in Table 9.1, as well as others. It is not recommended that the legacy system policy .adm files are loaded because they can result in persistent registry settings. Once an .adm file is loaded, it can be found in the SYSVOL directory, ensuring that it will participate in multi-master replication as well as netlogon.

Table 9.1 Administrative Templates

Template	Policy Editor	Installed by Default	Function
System.adm	Group Policy	Default	This is the default Administrative Template and is used for Windows 2000 client workstations.
Inetres.adm	Group Policy	Default	This is an Administrative Template installed by default and is used to set Internet Explorer policies for Windows 2000 client workstations.
Winnt.adm	System Policy	Not default	This is a legacy system policy Administrative Template for Windows NT 4.0 clients.

Continued

Template	Policy Editor	Installed by Default	Function
Windows.adm	System Policy	Not default	This is a legacy system policy Administrative Template for Windows 95 and Windows 98 clients.
Common.adm	System Policy	Not default	This is a legacy system policy Administrative Template for the common interface items of Windows NT4, Windows 98, and Windows 95.
Wmp.adm	Group Policy	Not default	This is a template for Windows Media Player.
Conf.adm	Group Policy	Not default	This is a template for NetMeeting.
Shell.adm	Group Policy	Not default	This is a template for additional interface options under the User Configuration options.

An Administrator can create Administrative Templates to include registry settings that are not default selections. Software developers may include .ADM files for their Windows 2000 applications. If a .adm file is included, an Administrator can take advantage of the template and establish settings for the users, and perhaps even deploy the software.

To open a .adm file, start in the Group Policy Editor. Expand the Computer Configuration or User Configuration container and right-click the Administrative Templates container. Select Add/Remove templates from the popup menu, as shown in Figure 9.5. Click ADD, then select the .adm file that you wish to add from the dialog. If you click REMOVE, you can remove an .adm template. Finally, click CLOSE. New options will appear immediately in the Group Policy Editor.

Figure 9.5 Adding an Administrative Template.

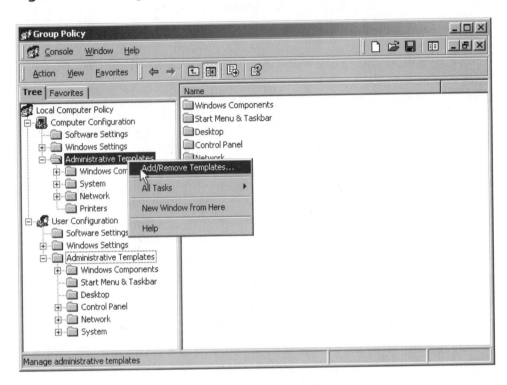

Registry.pol

While the Administrative Template files are the source for group policy settings, the actual resultant information is saved as registry.pol files. The User settings are saved in the Policies\<Group Policy GUID>\User\Registry.pol file, and the Computer settings are saved in the Policies\<Group Policy guid>\Machine\registry.pol file.

Group Policy Settings

There are two settings containers in group policies:

- Computer Configuration
- User Configuration

The Computer Configuration policies can change registry settings within HKEY_LOCAL_MACHINE. The settings in the Computer Configuration policies are applied to a computer no matter who logs on to it. User Configuration policies can change registry settings within HKEY_CURRENT_USER. The User Configuration policies are applied to any computer that a user logs on to. Aside from assigning interface preferences, group policies can apply logon, logoff, startup and shutdown scripts, distribute software, change security settings, and redirect system folder locations such as My Documents.

Since the System.adm and Inetres.adm files are default templates, the following Computer and User Configuration sections will discuss their default settings.

Computer Configuration

The Computer Configuration settings stipulate operating system behavior. All options for the desktop, security settings, and even startup and shutdown scripts can be found in this area. Since the Computer Configuration settings are applied to a computer, regardless of who logs on to it, this policy is best applied to computers that require being locked down to protect local data or applications from being misused.

The Computer Configuration portion of group policies includes a profusion of security settings, as shown in Figure 9.6. This is by design, since these policies are applied to individual computers. An example of a computer that can benefit from computer security policies would be a kiosk computer that is placed out for public use. The kiosk needs to be secured regardless of the user logged on, since anyone can log on.

User Configuration

The User Configuration settings are similar to the Computer Configuration settings. These are user-specific settings that follow a user around a network wherever that user may log on. Many of these settings are similar in content to the Computer Configuration

Figure 9.6 Computer Configuration and its security settings

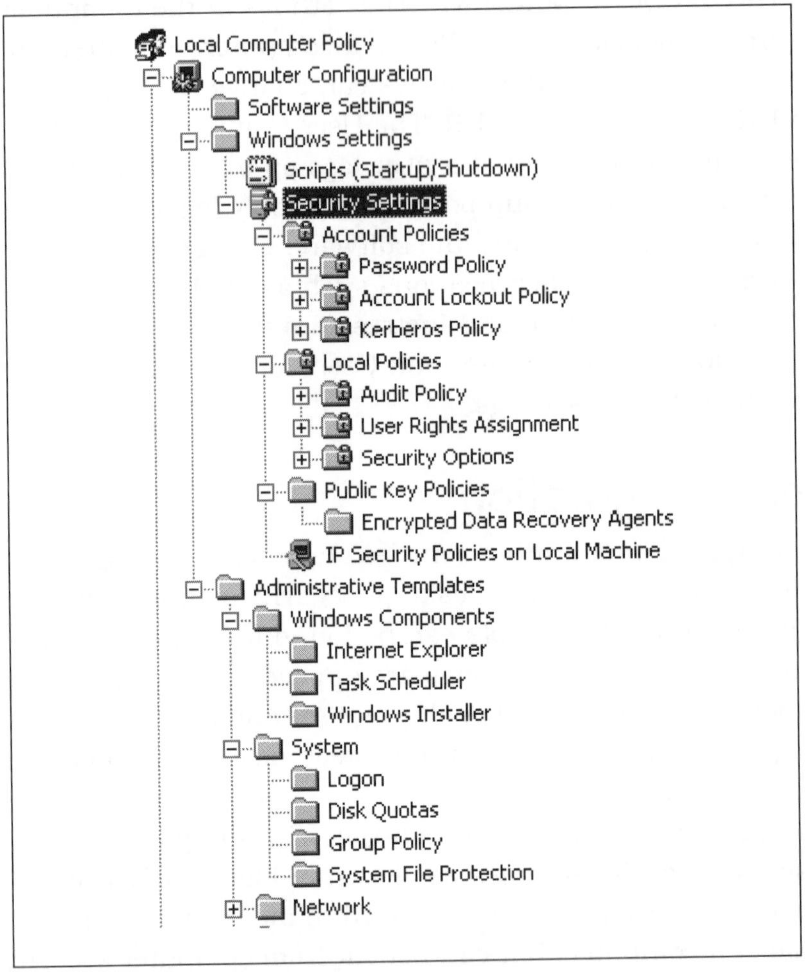

```
Local Computer Policy
  Computer Configuration
      Software Settings
      Windows Settings
          Scripts (Startup/Shutdown)
          Security Settings
              Account Policies
                  Password Policy
                  Account Lockout Policy
                  Kerberos Policy
              Local Policies
                  Audit Policy
                  User Rights Assignment
                  Security Options
              Public Key Policies
                  Encrypted Data Recovery Agents
              IP Security Policies on Local Machine
      Administrative Templates
          Windows Components
              Internet Explorer
              Task Scheduler
              Windows Installer
          System
              Logon
              Disk Quotas
              Group Policy
              System File Protection
          Network
```

set, but there are many more settings for the interface in the User Configuration set, as shown in Figure 9.7. This enables the same interface to appear wherever a user may choose to log on, which is desirable especially for roving users.

Scripts exhibit the reasons behind the selection of a setting to be placed under the computer configuration as opposed to the user configuration. Script settings for users are different from those for computers. Whereas computer settings include startup and shutdown scripts, which run automatically for a computer regardless of whether anyone has logged on, the user settings include logon and logoff scripts. Logon and logoff scripts occur only when a user accesses the network.

Figure 9.7 User Configuration and its interface settings.

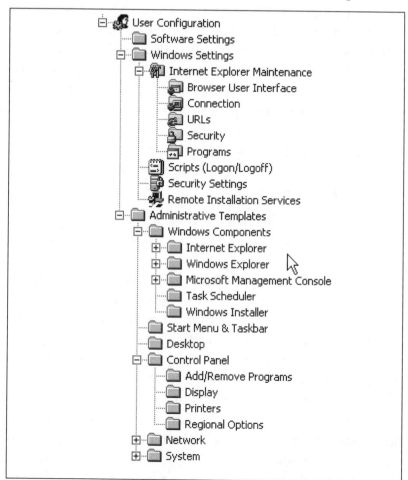

Designing a Group Policy Strategy

Group policies should be taken into consideration when designing an OU structure. The number of group policies affect the user's experience for logging in, and the placement of machines and users in the OU structure will determine how many group policies are required.

For example, FrigidMidgets is a small-sized refrigerator rental service that is located in seven cities with large universities across the United States. There is a sales group, a service group, and a collections group in the FrigidMidgets company. All of sales must have identically configured computer and security settings. If the Network Administrator designs an OU structure that places seven cities at the top, with three nested OUs for Sales, Service, and Collections in *each* of those seven top-layer OUs, then there will be seven identical group policies in each of the Sales containers, along with all the additional traffic to replicate those policies. However, if the Network Administrator designs three top-layer OUs for Sales, Service, and Collections, there will only be one group policy for the Sales OU and a considerably more efficient system.

This example demonstrates the primary rules for designing OUs with group policies in mind:

- Group similarly configured computers in the same OU.
- Group users with similar requirements in the same OU.

Additionally, the fewer settings that a group policy contains, the less time it will take to download and apply that group policy to a computer. Therefore, an Administrator should take care to only establish a group policy setting that is absolutely required. The sequence of events from the time a computer is booted to the time that the final user interface is applied is illustrated in Figure 9.8.

Multi-master replication pledges that information will be synchronized across the entire forest of DCs. However, in any multi-master replication system there exists the potential for conflicting group policy settings where one setting overrides another. This typically occurs when two different Administrators make contradictory modifications to the same group policy or make a change to a lower-level group policy setting that overrides a parent group policy setting. To reduce the risk of this happening, organizations should only empower a small number of Administrators to manage group policies.

Figure 9.8 Sequence of startup events for group policies.

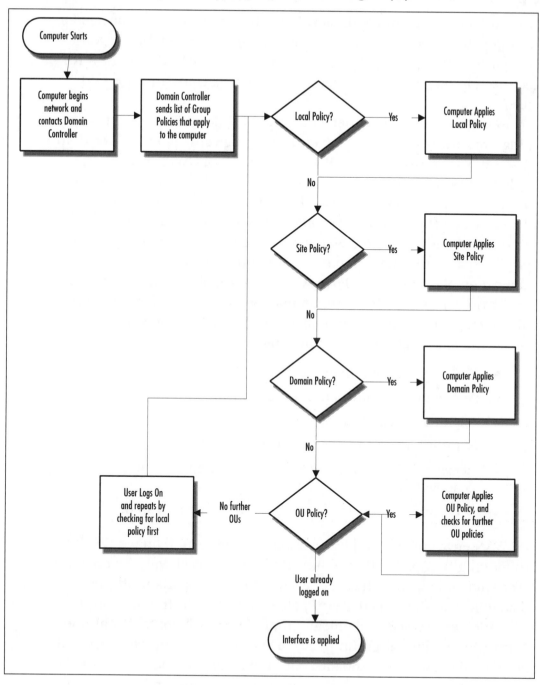

Group Policy in WAN Environments

Network environments with slow WAN links present other issues for group policy. Because of the excess time that it takes for a logon to complete when group policies are present, a slow WAN link or a RAS connection may result in exceptionally poor performance for end users.

Netlogon is capable of detecting a slow link by sending a test ping from the client to the server. If the ping returns in greater than 2 seconds, netlogon sets a GPO_INFO_FLAG_SLOWLINK value to indicate that the connection is a slow link. A slow link is considered to be 500 Kbps or less. A Network Administrator can change this default value through the *Computer Configuration\Administrative Templates\System\Logon\Slow network connection timeout for user profiles* policy and the *Computer Configuration\Administrative Templates\System\Group Policy\Group Policy slow link detection* policy. Various group policy settings may be deactivated for that particular client, but not all group policy settings. When the slow link flag is set, the following are default actions:

- Software policy remains active and cannot be deactivated.

- Application deployments are deactivated.

- File deployments are deactivated.

- Scripts remain active but can be deactivated.

- Registry-based policies remain active and cannot be deactivated.

- Security settings are active but can be deactivated.

WAN environments typically implement sites to manage WAN traffic. A group policy that is linked to a site object will be applied to every machine within that site, even if that site spans multiple domains. The site-linked group policy stays within the domain in which it was created. This means that clients will contact that one domain to apply that group policy. This can cause unnecessary traffic if the domain spans the site. Site-linked group policies should be applied sparingly, and with the traffic implications understood, so that only domains that are held entirely within a site are used as the creators of that site's site-linked group policy.

Implementing Group Policy Strategies

The Network Administrator creates the group policies using a utility called the Group Policy Editor, which is a management console that can be launched separately, or from the Active Directory Users and Computers.

For IT Professionals

Using Group Policy to Secure the Management Console

The Active Directory and its schema are dangerous things to enable people to access and use if those users have the ability to make changes to them. Accessing the Active Directory, the schema, and many other system functions in Windows 2000 is executed through a common interface: The Microsoft Management Console (MMC).

Group policy contains a section for securing the MMC. This section of the group policy, which is located in the User Configuration\Administrative Templates\Windows Components\ Microsoft Management Console, allows the Administrator to effectively stop any user from using specific console applications.

Sometimes, however, it is necessary to enable the viewing of a console, but the Administrator may not want the user to *change* anything. In this case, the Administrator will want to turn off the Author mode for that user in the group policy. This particular group policy setting is entitled: Restrict the user from entering Author mode. When this policy is enabled, the user can browse any console that the Administrator has left enabled, but is unable to make any changes within it, thus adding another layer of security to the network.

Configuring Group Policy Objects

To create a group policy object linked to a site, domain, or OU, in the Active Directory Sites and Services utility, right-click the site container to which you are linking a group policy and select Properties, as illustrated in Figure 9.9. (Use the Active Directory Users and Computers to access the properties for domains and OUs.) Click the Group Policy tab. Click New and type in a name for the new group policy object. This is illustrated in Figure 9.10. If you don't want to make any changes to the object, you can simply click Close.

Figure 9.9 Properties of a site.

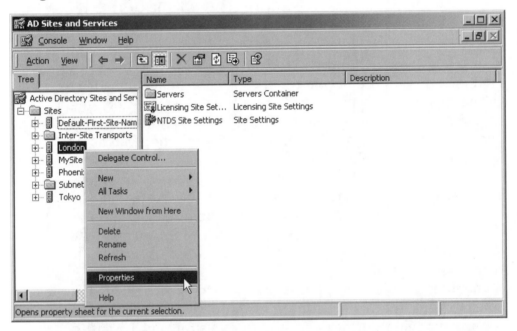

To edit the group policy object, in the Group Policy tab of the Site, Domain, or OU Properties dialog, double-click the group policy object. The Group Policy Editor will open, ready to edit that particular group policy object. The Group Policy Editor has two panes. The

Figure 9.10 New group policy object.

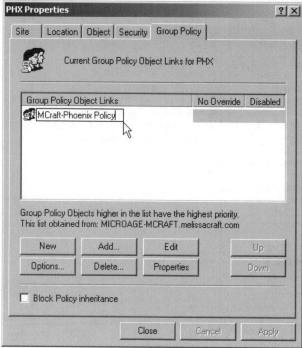

left pane is used to navigate the hierarchy of policy containers. The right pane is used to display the contents of whichever container is selected in the left pane. Figure 9.11 displays the policies available for Users regarding group policy behavior.

To edit a particular policy, double-click the policy in the right-hand, contents pane. It will display the individual policy's properties, such as Figure 9.11.

Figure 9.11 is also an example of group policy usage. The Wire Place Company installed a kiosk system in order for prospective clients to review their wire products. The kiosks use group policies to deploy applications, and to secure the kiosks themselves. Each kiosk automatically logs on to the system using a standard logon account in the KIOSK OU. Most of the kiosks use slow links, at about 56 Kbps. The Wire Place Administrator wants to ensure that all accounts within the KIOSK OU will apply the group policies

Figure 9.11 Group Policy Editor contents pane.

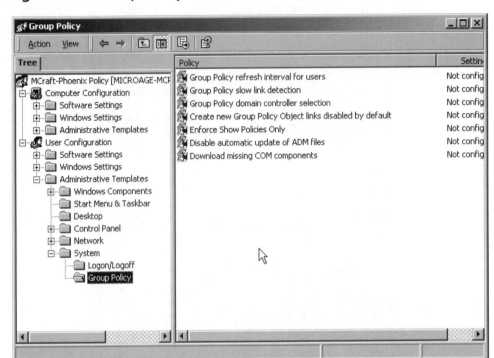

regardless of the network link speed. To do this, the Administrator disables the slow link detection by applying the group policy shown in Figure 9.12.

Sometimes a group policy object is no longer needed. Either its contents are combined with that of another group policy object, or its functions are no longer used. Many organizations undergo constant change and need to remove defunct group policy objects. To delete a group policy object, right-click it and select Delete from the popup menu displayed in Figure 9.13. Or click it and then click DELETE.

Link a Group Policy Object to a Container

An Administrator may create a group policy object in an OU, domain, or site and then wish to deploy the identical group policy

Figure 9.12 Disabling slow link detection.

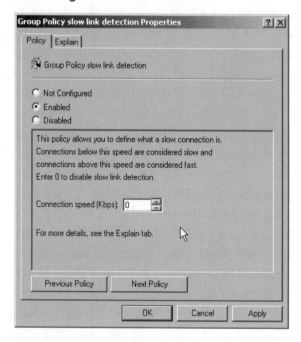

Figure 9.13 Delete a group policy object.

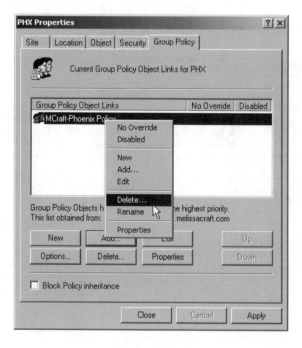

object elsewhere. Recreating the group policy object may take a tremendous amount of time if it is a complex set of policies. The optimum solution would be to link the existing group policy object to the other container, which is possible within the Active Directory. To do this, right-click the site, domain, or OU and select Properties. Click the Group Policy tab. Click ADD. In the resulting dialog box, click the All tab. All of the group policy objects for the entire domain will appear, as shown in Figure 9.14. Select the group policy object that you want to use, and click OK. The linked group policy will be added to the bottom of the list of group policies for that container. If you want the group policy to be processed prior to the others, select the group policy and then click UP. Group policy objects cannot be moved outside of the domain in which they were created; they can only be linked. This will force the users in a linked domain to contact a DC in a different domain to access the group policy, which in turn may cause undesirable network conditions. If not carefully managed, linked group policy objects can cause significant network traffic.

Figure 9.14 All group policies for a domain.

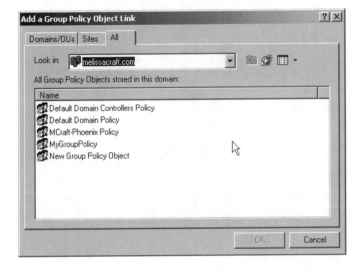

Administrators may need to find out which containers a group policy is linked to when they need to troubleshoot the group policy, or when they intend to delete the group policy. The way to go about this is to open the group policy object in the Group Policy Editor and right-click the root container of the group policy. Then select Properties from the popup menu, as depicted in Figure 9.15.

Figure 9.15 Group Policy root container properties.

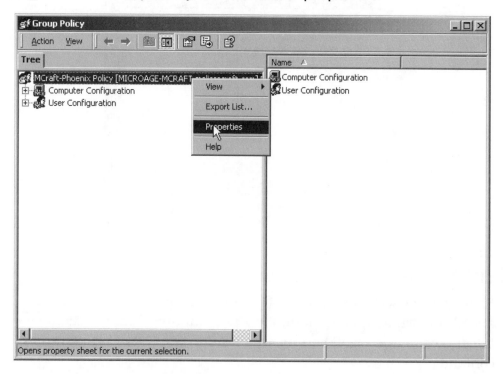

The Properties dialog for the group policy object will appear. Click the Links tab for the dialog, then click FIND NOW. All of the containers that the group policy is linked to will appear in the dialog, as shown in Figure 9.16.

Figure 9.16 Linked containers for a group policy object.

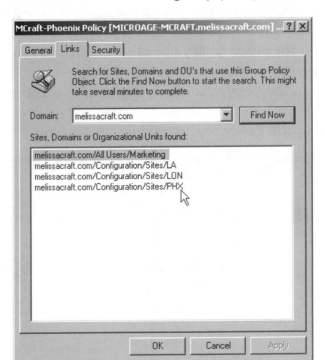

Adding Scripts

Four types of scripts can be configured in the group policy. Startup and shutdown scripts are found in the Computer Configuration container. Logon and logoff scripts are found in the User Configuration container.

Logon scripts are the most commonly used scripts. They organize a user's environment once that user has logged on to the network. A logon script, however, is somewhat user-specific. If a computer required a certain setting, regardless of which user logged on, then every logon script had to identify that computer and add that setting just in case a user of that logon script happened to log on to that particular computer. To better manage this requirement, computer startup scripts are provided. Both logoff and shutdown scripts are methods of cleaning up an environment. Additionally, other information can be captured.

For instance, Testme.com is an international testing facility. They execute timed tests via computer terminals at testing centers, and practice tests over the Internet. Testme.com delivers its practice tests through a Terminal Server window, and then provides results via Web pages. When the student logs off the Terminal Server window, Testme.com must capture the final results of the test, reset the application, and capture the time that the student was logged on. Testme.com can use a logoff script to manage this effort.

NOTE

All scripts can use any of the Windows Scripting Host (WSH) scripting tools, including batch files, VBScript, and JScript. To find out more about WSH, see Microsoft's Web site.

To establish scripts under a group policy object, they must first be copied into the Netlogon share of an Active Directory DC along with any dependent files. After the scripts are copied, edit the group policy object in the Group Policy Editor. For startup or shutdown scripts, navigate down the left pane from Computer Configuration\Windows Settings\Scripts(Startup/Shutdown) and double-click either the Startup or the Shutdown script in the right-hand contents pane. For logon or logoff scripts, navigate down the left pane from User Configuration\Windows Settings\ Scripts (Logon/Logoff) and double-click either the Logon or the Logoff script in the right-hand contents pane.

The script's properties page will appear, as shown in Figure 9.17. Click ADD. A small dialog box will appear to prompt for the script's name and any parameters required by it. After completing this dialog, click OK to save the script into the group policy.

Figure 9.17 Script properties.

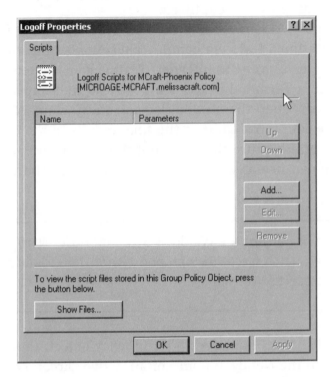

Deploying Applications

Deploying applications with group policies requires that the software uses the Windows Installer packages. Many applications include a Windows Installer package. If the application does not have one, it will need to be produced. After this is completed, a software distribution point containing the package and all required files must be established along with the rights that each user must have to be able to access and install the software.

Once the network has been prepared, the application can be deployed to end users. There are two basic options for software deployment:

- Assign the application
- Publish the application

The difference between assigning and publishing is that an Assigned application appears as an advertised application on desktops or start menus and appears to the user as able to be used, even if it has not been installed yet. If the user selects the application icon, or double clicks the document associated with the application, it will install itself the first time. The Assigned application cannot be deleted. By contrast, publishing an application enables the user to use Add/Remove Programs and see that application in the list of available programs. The user can remove the Published application at any time.

WARNING

Windows 2000 Group Policy makes it easy to deploy software. However, sometimes there are errors that can cause significant damage, usually in the form of downtime for end users, if software is not tested before being deployed to a production network. Always use a lab and test each software application on the same type of hardware that the application will be deployed to. Also make sure to apply Assigned applications only to the group policy for Computer Configuration Software Installation, so that roving users do not accidentally install software on others' workstations.

To define software installation for a user, open the Group Policy Administrator and navigate under User Configuration to Software Settings, then to Software Installation. Right-click Software Installation and select Properties from the popup menu. Select the General tab, if it is not already selected. This screen will let you establish standard settings for all future settings.

To create an individual package, you should right-click the Software Installation object and select New | Package. If you set the Default Package Location in the Software Installation properties, then you will be automatically taken to a software distribution point. If not, then you must browse to a software distribution point and select a Windows Installer Package, which has a file extension of .msi.

After selecting the package, you will be shown the dialog depicted in Figure 9.18. The dialog allows you to select whether to publish, assign, or configure advanced published or assigned features. Publishing an application means that it is available for installation via the Add/Remove Programs icon in Control Panel or by opening a file that has an extension that is associated with that particular application. Assigning an application means that the application automatically appears on the user's system and is not optional. If you want to explore the assignment or publishing options, select the Advanced option, which will lead to the Properties of the new package.

Figure 9.18 Publish or Assign dialog.

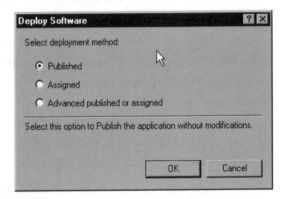

The following dialog allows you to select the details regarding the software installation. There are multiple tabs to the dialog, which are described in Table 9.2.

Table 9.2 Software Installation Options

Dialog Tab	Option	Function
General	Name	The name that the user will see when given this software option.
General	Product information	Software information taken from the package file.
General	Support information	Support information taken from the package file.

Continued

Dialog Tab	Option	Function
Deployment	Deployment type	Published (install optional) or Assigned (install not optional).
Deployment	Deployment options	Auto-Installation when the application's associated file extension is activated.
		Uninstallation of the application after the management scope expires.
		Whether to display this application in the Control Panel Add/Remove Programs.
Deployment	Installation user interface options	**Basic**: Provides a minimum display of the installation progress.
		Maximum: Provides display of all installation dialogs and screens.
Deployment	ADVANCED button	Whether to install the application if its language is different from that of the target workstation.
		Whether to install an X86 application on Alpha workstations.
		Whether to enforce removal of other installations of the same product if the Group Policy did not install it.
		Diagnostics for the deployment of the app, including product code, script location, and number of times it has been deployed.
Upgrades	Packages that this package will upgrade	Upgrades applications selected from previously installed group policy object software installations.
Upgrades	Packages in current GPO that will upgrade this package	Any applications that will upgrade this application.
Categories	Selected categories	A listing of the available categories that this package will appear under in the Add/Remove Programs.

Continued

Dialog Tab	Option	Function
Modifications	Modifications	A list of the transforms files that script the installer package to work in a specific manner. Typically these files have a .mst extension.
Security	Permissions box	Description of the default object permissions for this group policy.

All of these options can be changed after a software installation package has been added by double-clicking the package or by right-clicking it and selecting Properties. This dialog is shown in Figure 9.19.

Figure 9.19 Software package options.

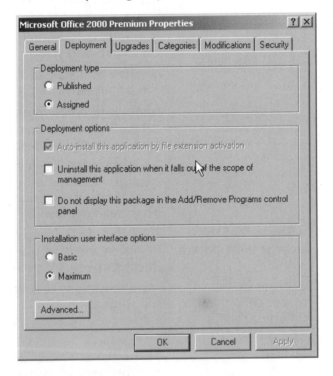

To remove a software package, right-click the package and select All Tasks | Remove. The Remove Software dialog shown in Figure 9.20 will appear. You have the option of uninstalling the software from all users' desktops, or simply preventing future installations. Regardless of which option you select, the package will be removed from the contents of the Software Installation node.

Figure 9.20 Removing a software package.

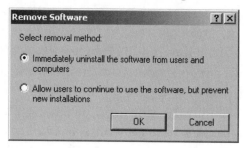

Folder Redirection

Folder redirection is the transparent relocation of a user's special folders from a Windows 2000 machine to a network server. For example, the Start menu and My Documents folders can be relocated onto a server for a user who roams from one PC to another on the network. When the user moves from PC to PC, the Start menu is always the same and the My Documents folder always contains that particular user's files. If roaming user profiles are enabled for that user, only the network path to My Documents is required to be part of the profile, rather than the folder itself. This significantly reduces the amount of data that crosses the wire when a user roams. Storage of data on servers will allow it to be backed up when the server is backed up, whereas such data is not normally backed up when it resides on a local hard drive. If you implement a disk quota in addition to redirecting these folders, then you can place limits on the amount of data a user stores in them. The following folders can be relocated:

- Application data
- Desktop
- My Documents
- My Documents/My Pictures
- Start menu

Offline folders are available to users even when the users are not connected to the network. This is useful when redirecting folders to a network share, and enabling a local copy for the user if the user travels with a laptop computer. Offline folders are local synchronized copies of files and folders that exist on the network. Using offline folders enables users to work even when they are not connected to the network, and ensures that the files are always the latest versions. When a user has made changes to an offline file, the user synchronizes after reconnecting to the network. If there are conflicts to the data, the user is given the choice of selecting his own file, the current file on the network, or saving both versions. A user must select the folders that he wants to use as Offline Folders. This is done through My Computer or My Network Places. The user can click on the selected folder and then select Make Available Offline from the File menu.

To redirect a folder, in the Group Policy Editor, navigate to User Configuration \ Windows Settings \ Folder Redirection. Select one of the folders to redirect; for example, My Documents. Right-click the folder and select Properties from the popup menu. There are three options for redirecting a folder:

- No administrative policy specified (default): Folders are not redirected.
- Basic: Redirecting every user to the same network location.
- Advanced: Each group's folders are redirected to various locations, which can be the same or different.

Obviously, using either the basic or advanced option does not give the granular control that is generally desired for files in the My Documents folder. To gain a granular control, you can incorporate the parameter %USERNAME% in the UNC name for the folder location. For example, if you wanted to place the My Documents folder into the \\myserver\myshare\myfolder location with a different subdirectory for each user, then you would use \\myserver\myshare\myfolder\%username%\My Documents.

The Settings tab for folder properties allows further configuration, as illustrated in Figure 9.21. There is an option to grant the user exclusive rights to the folder. (You would only want to select this option if you individualize the folder location.) You can select an automatic migration of the contents of the local My Documents folder to the network location. You can also specify how to handle the data in the folder when the policy is finally removed.

Figure 9.21 Folder redirection properties.

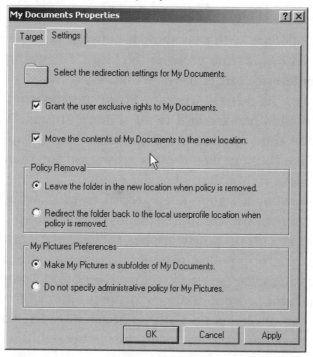

Disk quotas can be enabled for computers. When using a disk quota in addition to redirecting folders, you will want to apply the disk quota to the server that holds the special folders. Disk quotas are dependent upon using NT File System (NTFS) on the computer. To set a disk quota, navigate to Computer Configuration\Administrative Templates\System\Disk Quotas. You will want to enable the following policies to establish a disk quota:

- **Enable disk quotas:** This will allow a disk quota to be set even if a previously applied group policy denies it.

- **Enforce disk quota limit:** When this is not enabled, the user is warned about the limit; when enabled, the user is stopped from adding files.

- **Default quota limit and warning level:** This policy lets you set the disk quota limit and a warning level.

Keeping Groups from Growing Over Time

One of the challenges with managing a network is to be able to keep administrative groups from growing too large. For example, Joe may leave for a conference out of town. While Joe is away, he may have Susan take over his duties. To grant Susan access, the Administrator adds her account to all of Joe's groups. When Joe returns, no one thinks to remove Susan from the groups. Multiple occurrences like these makes groups grow, and too many people end up with more rights than actually needed.

Group policy has a way to keep groups from growing overlarge. By adding groups to the computer configuration group policy, any computer that the group policy applies to will reset permissions according to the group policy, even if changes have been made to that group through the Active Directory Users and Computers console. This does not prevent changes to the groups while the computer is up. Instead, it cleans up those changes after the computer reboots. The next time that the computer is booted, it will apply the group policy and remove any extra entries.

To use restricted groups, open a group policy object and navigate to Computer Configuration\Windows Settings\Security Settings \Restricted Groups. Add groups to the Restricted Groups node by right-clicking the Restricted Groups node and selecting New Group. After adding the groups, configure their appropriate user list.

After applying the group policy to a set of computers, only changing the group policy will change the list of users in those groups. It is recommended to use this only with sensitive groups to keep them from growing over time.

Group policy objects are not the only features in Windows 2000 that can create restricted groups. The Domain Security Policy console can also establish restricted groups to be applied domainwide (see Figure 9.22).

Figure 9.22 Domain Security Policy.

Troubleshooting Group Policies

There are three issues with group policies that need troubleshooting:

- The policy does not execute.
- The policy does not execute the way that was expected.
- Logging on takes a really long time.

Policy Does Not Execute

When the policy does not execute, it is usually a problem with the Access Control Entry (ACE) or multiple group policies that conflict with each other, or that part of the policy has been disabled. When the user does not have an ACE directing a group policy object to be applied, then the group policy is skipped completely. To check on the ACEs for a group policy object:

1. Right-click the OU or DC in Active Directory Users and Computers (or right-click the selected Site in the Active Directory Sites and Services console).

2. Select Properties from the popup menu.

3. Click the Group Policy tab.

4. Click once on the policy that is not executing to select it.

5. Click PROPERTIES.

6. Click the Security tab.

7. Select the group or the user account from the list in the upper box and review the rights assigned in the lower box.

8. To see a more detailed view, click ADVANCED.

9. Make sure that the user or a group to which the user belongs has the Read right and Apply Group policy right. Also make sure that no group to which the user belongs has been denied rights to either of these rights.

If the user has multiple group policies applied, some may conflict with others, and the result is that the last one that applies usually overrides all previously applied policies. A group policy does not override previously applied group policies if the No Override feature has been checked on one of the upper-level group policies. Upper level can be one of the policies in the list applied to that container, or a group policy that has been applied to a parent container. The best method is to start with the group policy that did not execute correctly, and ensure that it is configured correctly. Then work backwards to the top of the tree until all the policies have been reviewed. This would be in the order of OU, parent OUs, domain, site, and then the Local group policy. To check them, click on the group policy, then click OPTIONS and make sure that the No Override check box is clear.

Finally, if a policy has been disabled, it will not execute. To see if a group policy has been disabled, select it and then click OPTIONS. Make sure that the Disabled check box is clear. To see if part of the policy has been disabled, select the group policy and then click PROPERTIES. On the General tab, make sure that the check boxes for disabling either the User or the Computer portion of the policy have not been disabled.

Policy Executes in the Wrong Way

A policy may execute in an unexpected manner for a couple of reasons. It could be a legacy NT 4 system policy that was applied accidentally. A good practice to follow is to not use any legacy system policies.

If a group policy is created to install software, and the installation does not occur correctly, it could be that the software transform file is not correct. Transform files are those that custom configure Windows Installer packages. If the transform file is not added to the Modifications tab, the plain vanilla installation of the software will proceed. If the wrong transform file is added to the Modifications tab, then errors may occur or the wrong configuration of software will be a result.

It is possible that the same software application is applied to the same group policy software installation. If so, then the application may install in the wrong way. Make sure that an application only appears once within any group policy object, or within a string of nested group policy objects.

If you receive a "Failed to open the Group Policy object" error, then you will need to recheck the network connection and DNS configuration. This error indicates that the policy was not located.

Logging On Takes a Long Time

The primary thing to do when there is an extended logon period is to reduce the number of group policy objects that are applied to a user. This can be done by removing group policies, combining multiple group policies into a single group policy, or by removing the "Apply Group Policy" right from the user's Access Control Entries (ACEs).

The next thing that can be done is to disable parts of group policy objects. This is done through the Properties dialog box for the group policy. It will avoid processing the settings, even for unconfigured policies.

There may be a group policy object that is applied to a site, where the group policy object belongs to one domain and the user belongs to another. When this happens, the user must be authenticated back to the DC that "owns" that particular group policy. This excess processing causes a slower logon. Where possible, remove site-linked group policies and apply them to containers instead.

If none of these tactics work, you may need to look at the site topology and whether there are enough DCs available to service logon requests from users.

Security

Rights can only be assigned to security principals. Security principals consist of user accounts and security groups. Security groups are either Domain Local groups or Global groups. (Universal groups exist only as distribution groups in mixed mode, but can be made into Security groups in native mode.)

Unlike Novell's directory service (NDS), OUs are not security principals. You cannot assign rights to an OU and expect that those rights will be inherited by the users and groups within them. If you are an NDS Administrator and would like this same functionality, you can muddle through with strategic placement and organization of Global groups. The system is to create a Global group within each OU, and name it accordingly. Then include all the users and groups within that OU as members of the Global group. Plus, add the Global groups of the next level down OUs. This nesting system will permit rights to flow down through the tree. Assign rights to these OU Global groups as though assigning them to the OU itself. The only thing that is not achieved with this system is the ability to block inheritance. An example of this system is shown in Figure 9.23.

Groups

Three types of groups are available for the Active Directory: Domain Local, Global, and Universal. Of these types, there are several default

Figure 9.23 Nesting Global groups to flow rights down the Active Directory hierarchy.

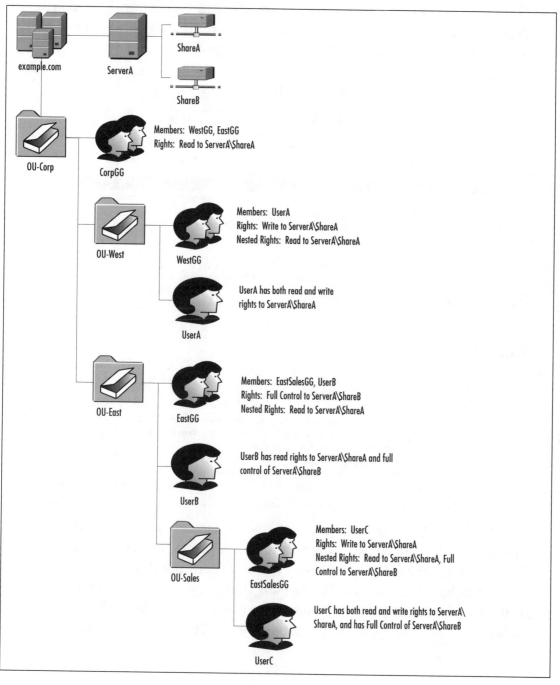

groups that are provided automatically within the Users container in each domain. These are shown in Figure 9.24 along with their descriptions. Another set of groups are placed in the Builtin container in each domain. Builtin groups are provided for local group usage and backward compatibility, and are illustrated in Figure 9.25.

Figure 9.24 Default groups within the Users container.

DHCP Administrators	Security Group - Domain Local	Members who have administrative access to DHCP service
DHCP Users	Security Group - Domain Local	Members who have view-only access to the DHCP service
DnsAdmins	Security Group - Domain Local	DNS Administrators Group
RAS and IAS Servers	Security Group - Domain Local	Servers in this group can access remote access properties of users
WINS Users	Security Group - Domain Local	Members who have view-only access to the WINS Server
Cert Publishers	Security Group - Global	Enterprise certification and renewal agents
DnsUpdateProxy	Security Group - Global	DNS clients who are permitted to perform dynamic updates on behalf of some other ...
Domain Admins	Security Group - Global	Designated administrators of the domain
Domain Computers	Security Group - Global	All workstations and servers joined to the domain
Domain Controllers	Security Group - Global	All domain controllers in the domain
Domain Guests	Security Group - Global	All domain guests
Domain Users	Security Group - Global	All domain users
Enterprise Admins	Security Group - Global	Designated administrators of the enterprise
Group Policy Creator Owners	Security Group - Global	Members in this group can modify group policy for the domain
Schema Admins	Security Group - Global	Designated administrators of the schema

Figure 9.25 Builtin groups.

Account Operators	Security Group - Builtin Local	Members can administer domain user and group accounts
Administrators	Security Group - Builtin Local	Administrators have full access to the computer/domain
Backup Operators	Security Group - Builtin Local	Backup Operators can only use a backup program to backup files and folders on to t...
Guests	Security Group - Builtin Local	Guests can operate the computer and save documents, but cannot install programs ...
Pre-Windows 2000 Compa...	Security Group - Builtin Local	A backward compatibility group which allows read access on all users and groups in t...
Print Operators	Security Group - Builtin Local	Members can administer domain printers
Replicator	Security Group - Builtin Local	Supports file replication in a domain
Server Operators	Security Group - Builtin Local	Members can administer domain servers
Users	Security Group - Builtin Local	Users can operate the computer and save documents, but cannot install programs or...

There are yet other groups available for security reasons that are not provided as an Active Directory security principal that you can add or remove users from. These are special groups that define default behavior for users. The reason that they are provided as special groups is so that the Network Administrator can define that default behavior in ACEs for various objects. The special groups are:

Anonymous Logon: This group handles anonymous logons, and is used for Microsoft Message Queuing (MSMQ). When MSMQ clients use RPCs to reach an MSMQ server, the call is considered an anonymous logon.

Authenticated Users: This represents any user who can log on to a machine or to the Active Directory. This group is automatically made a member of the Power Users Local group, so that all users are "Power Users" on Windows 2000 PCs. To reduce those users' rights to be equivalent to standard users' rights, you will need to remove the membership for Power Users and leave the membership to the Users Local group. All Authenticated Users are given the Read and Apply group policy rights to each group policy, so this will need to be removed from a group policy if the Administrator wants to filter the group policy and apply it to only certain security groups. Of course, the Administrator will need to apply explicit rights for those security groups in order for the group policy to become effective.

Everyone: This group includes all current network users, including guests and users from other Active Directory domains.

Interactive: This group includes any user who is currently logged on to a specific computer locally and given access to its resources. There can be multiple user accounts in this group when the DC is providing terminal services.

Network: This group is the antithesis of the Interactive group. It includes all users who have been authenticated and granted access to a specific computer's resources over the network.

There are other special groups that are installed with certain services. For example, a Dialup group is created for remote access services, and a Proxy group is created for Internet Information Services. Your Windows 2000 system may have additional special groups depending upon which services have been installed. The service's documentation should explain the purpose of those groups and what security may be required to manage them.

Group Strategy

The group strategy in legacy Windows NT was summarized by the acronym AGLP. This stood for **A**ccounts added to **G**lobal groups that are placed in **L**ocal groups, which are assigned **P**ermissions. The strategy for Windows 2000 is nearly identical. In this strategy, user accounts should be placed within Global groups. Here we depart from the former standard with options—the Global groups can be placed within other Global groups or within Universal groups in whatever nesting strategy is established. Then we pick up with the recommended strategy again, place the Global groups within Domain Local groups, which are assigned Permissions. The resulting acronyms? AGDLP is standard, AGUGDLP is nested.

Seeing Security Features in Active Directory Users and Computers

When viewing the Active Directory Users and Computers console, it is sometimes necessary to view who has rights to individual objects. To see the permissions for each object, click the View menu and select Advanced Features. You will see an additional two folders: Lost and Found, and System. Lost and Found holds orphaned objects. System holds other Active Directory objects such as group policy objects in its Policies subcontainer.

Not only will you be able to see the additional features, but you will have a Security tab added to the properties of Active Directory objects. The Security tab will lead to the discretionary access control list for the object. Any users or groups who have rights will be listed. You can add, remove. or edit properties for the object. Note that whenever you add a right, you add it explicitly for that object. If you want to add a right that is propagated to other objects within a container, you must select the Advanced tab and drop down the box that states "This object only" to change it to "This object and child objects."

Domain Security Console

Security for the Active Directory is configured in many places, but domainwide policies are configured in the Domain Security console shown in Figure 9.26. The Domain Security Policy is located in the Administrative Tools menu.

Figure 9.26 The Domain Security console.

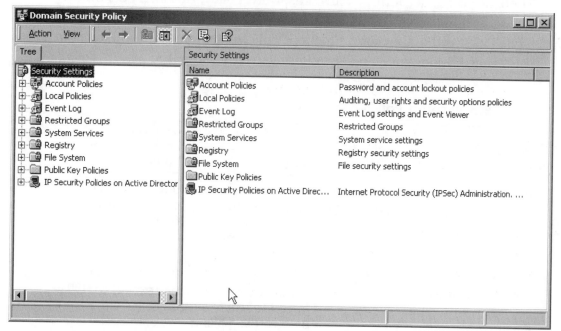

There are several containers for security policy in the Domain Security console:

- Account policies
- Local policies
- Event Log
- Restricted Groups
- System Services
- Registry

- Filesystem
- Public Key policies
- IP Security policies on Active Directory

Account Policies

There are three account policies: Password Policy, Account Lockout Policy, and Kerberos Policy. Kerberos Policy is new to Windows 2000, while Password and Account Lockout policies are similar to the ones in the legacy Windows NT Server. All are listed in Table 9.3.

Table 9.3 Account Policies

Policy Type	Policy	Default Setting	Security Feature	Minimum and Maximum Values
Password Policy	Enforce password history.	1 password remembered	Users are prevented from reusing the same password over and over.	0 (do not keep password history) to 24 passwords
Password Policy	Maximum password age.	42 days	When set to a low number, users are forced to use fresh passwords, making the system more secure.	0 (passwords do not expire) to 999 days.
Password Policy	Minimum password age.	0 days	When set to any number other than 0, users are forced to retain a password for a duration of time, preventing immediate changes.	0 (password can be changed immediately) to 998 days.

Continued

Policy Type	Policy	Default Setting	Security Feature	Minimum and Maximum Values
Password Policy	Minimum password length.	0 characters	When set to a longer number, users cannot use easy-to-guess passwords.	0 (no password required) to 14 characters
Password Policy	Passwords must meet complexity require-ments.	Disabled	When enabled, the password is required to have a combination of other characters, numbers, and upper and lower case.	Enabled or Disabled
Password Policy	Store password using reversible encryption for all users in the domain.	Disabled	When enabled, passwords are encrypted.	Enabled or Disabled
Password Policy	User must log on to change the password.	Disabled	When enabled, a user must first present existing credentials to the domain by logging on before changing the password. This presents problems for remote users.	Enabled or Disabled
Account Lockout Policy	Account lockout duration.	Not defined	When defined, the Administrator sets the number of minutes that an account is locked out after the set of invalid logon attempts.	0 (account is locked out until Administrator unlocks it) to 99,999 minutes

Continued

Policy Type	Policy	Default Setting	Security Feature	Minimum and Maximum Values
Account Lockout Policy	Account lockout threshold.	0 invalid logon attempts	The user must fail at logging on for the number of attempts specified, and then will be locked out of the system.	0 (account will not lockout) to 999 logon attempts
Account Lockout Policy	Reset account lockout counter after...	Not defined	The greater the number of minutes specified here, the more likely a user may have an account locked out. This is the duration of time during which the system counts invalid logon attempts before resetting to 0. Each successful logon resets this counter to 0.	1 to 99,999 minutes
Kerberos Policy	Enforce user logon restrictions.	Enabled	This enables Kerberos to use the logon restrictions.	Enabled or Disabled
Kerberos Policy	Maximum lifetime for service ticket.	600 minutes	The duration that a Kerberos security ticket remains valid.	0 (ticket does not expire) to 99,999 minutes
Kerberos Policy	Maximum lifetime for user ticket.	10 hours	The duration that a user's logon remains valid without contacting a Kerberos host.	0 (ticket does not expire) to 99,999 hours
Kerberos Policy	Maximum lifetime for user ticket renewal.	In order to renew a ticket, the user must contact a KDC in this timeframe.	Kerberos 0 (ticket renewal previously used	Maximum 7 days does not expire) to 99,999 days

Continued

Policy Type	Policy	Default Setting	Security Feature	Minimum and Maximum Values
Kerberos Policy	Maximum tolerance for computer clock synchronization.	5 minutes	Kerberos authentication is stamped with a start and expiration time (default of 10 hours). If the time of the KDC and the client are not synchronized, the Kerberos ticket could prematurely expire or never expire. This sets the allowable time variance.	0 to 99,999 minutes

Administrators have tough decisions in front of them when they set up the Account policies. They must decide where to trade off ease of use for security. For example, users who are forced to change passwords every day will be more likely to forget passwords and will overwhelm the help desk. However, users who are never forced to change passwords, probably won't; in which case, the network is left nearly unsecured.

When deciding on the policies for your organization, you should take into account the desired level of security and likelihood of security breaches in each area. For example, if your organization is a school with one domain for teachers and another domain for students, then it would be preferred to keep high security on the teacher's domain by enforcing monthly password changes and long, encrypted passwords.

Local Policies

Three types of policies affect the local DC:

- Audit Policy
- User Rights Assignment
- Security options

Audit policy enables the Administrator to audit the domain's activity with security events. Audited items include (but are not limited to) events such as logons, access to objects, access to system events, and policy changes. The audit can reveal whether such security events were successful or unsuccessful. An Administrator would generally prefer to know when an event has been unsuccessful since that will provide the Administrator with the knowledge of who has tried to access something denied to him or her. Administrators may also wish to know whenever a policy change attempt has been made, whether successful or unsuccessful, since that is indicative of the use of a highly secured right.

The User Rights Assignment container provides a single place to add general rights to the local DC for users or security groups. These rights control who can shut down the server, who can change system time, who can add computers to the domain, and so forth.

Security options provides a local security system that can further lock down the DC. These security options include whether to disable using CTRL-ALT-DEL for logging on to the server, whether to automatically log off any users after a logon time expires, establishing a message text for users at the time of logon, whether to shut down the server if no more security events can be logged, and more. Although many of these items are new, others were available as registry edits in the legacy Windows NT server.

Event Log

The event log settings manage the system, application, and security logs. These settings can establish the maximum size, access to the logs, and retention of the logs.

Restricted Groups

This is the same group restriction that can be set in a group policy. The setting here for restricted groups is far more secure, since a DC must be rebooted before it accesses and uses a new group policy. When restricted groups are used in the Domain Security Policy console, the DC establishes the new security settings for groups right away.

System Services

There is an associated policy for each of the default services that runs. The policy is, by default, not defined. When defined, however, the Administrator is faced with the dialog shown in Figure 9.27 where the service startup mode must be selected and the Administrator can further edit who has access to change the service. By default, the group Everyone is first offered full control of services when a policy is activated. If using Terminal Server, this should be changed to Administrators.

Figure 9.27 Editing a service policy.

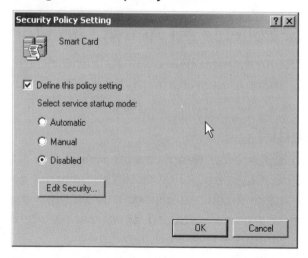

Registry

The registry policy settings can secure individual registry keys from being edited by a user. Like services, by default, the Everyone group is initially offered full control of the registry keys, which means they can change them any way they please. You can add registry keys into this policy and then secure those keys from being changed, or viewed, by changing the groups and users who are granted access to those keys.

Filesystem

The filesystem policies can configure security for files and folders. This is a more granular control over files and folders than share-level security. It offers a single point of security administration for the local DC.

Public Key Policies

Public key policies let you add automatic certificate requests and manage the certificate authority behavior. You should make sure to have your Certificate Authority server(s) installed before attempting to establish these policies.

IP Security Policies on Active Directory

If you have IP Security established on the network, these policies will manage it. There are several ways that a DC can handle IP Sec.

Security Templates

Windows 2000 has several templates for security settings that you can apply to either a group policy or to the Security console. If there are changes made to a computer's security settings and the template is the organization's standard, then reapplying the template can return the computer to a working state.

To import a policy into a group policy, open the policy in the Group Policy Editor. Then, navigate to the Computer Configuration\Windows Settings\Security Settings. Right-click Security Settings and select Import Policy from the popup menu. The security templates will appear in the window.

To import a policy into the Domain Security console, right-click the root container called Security Settings. Select Import Policy from the popup menu and select the desired security template.

Object Protection

With Active Directory, establishing permissions is more than just granting a user access to a file or a printer. It also involves permitting and denying access to objects for users and security groups.

Access Control Lists (ACLs)

Permissions in Windows 2000 are stored in an ACL. The ACL is accessible through the Security tab on various objects, such as the Properties of a group policy as shown in Figure 9.28.

Figure 9.28 ACL.

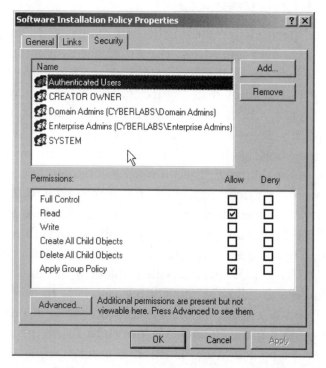

The Security dialog screen lets an Administrator specify the groups or users that have access to the group policy. The default permission for any user to a group policy is to Read and Apply Group Policy, except for Domain Admins, Enterprise Admins, and the SYSTEM groups who are not granted the Apply Group Policy right to prevent themselves from being restricted by the policy. The Administrative groups are also granted rights that enable them to edit the policy as well. The default rights set for groups is more than the minimum required, since Read access is not needed to use the group policy. It may mean a better secured environment to remove the Read right for Authenticated users from the ACL.

You can move any object from one OU to another within the same domain by right-clicking it and selecting Move from the popup menu. When you move an object from one container to another, only explicitly assigned permissions will follow the object to the new container; inherited permissions do not follow the object.

Access Control Entries (ACEs)

Each individual permission within the ACL is an ACE. To gain comprehensive control over the ACEs, the Administrator should click ADVANCED at the bottom of the Security dialog. This leads to the Access Control Editor shown in Figure 9.29.

When adding an ACE, there are several rights that can be granted or denied. Explicitly denying a right will take precedence over allowing the right. If a user belongs to two different groups and one allows a right while the other denies it, then the user is denied access.

Note that many of these rights are not applicable to the group policy object being edited. Instead, there is a check box at the bottom of the ACE editor that lets you establish these rights for the user or group. These rights are then granted to any objects within the container to which the group policy object belongs.

A good practice to follow when adding rights is to add them for groups only. Even if a single user is going to require a particular right, if you create a group and grant the right to the group, then other users can be added later, or the first user completely replaced. This facilitates administration is beneficial in the long run, even though it can be a little extra work upfront.

Figure 9.29 Access Control Entries.

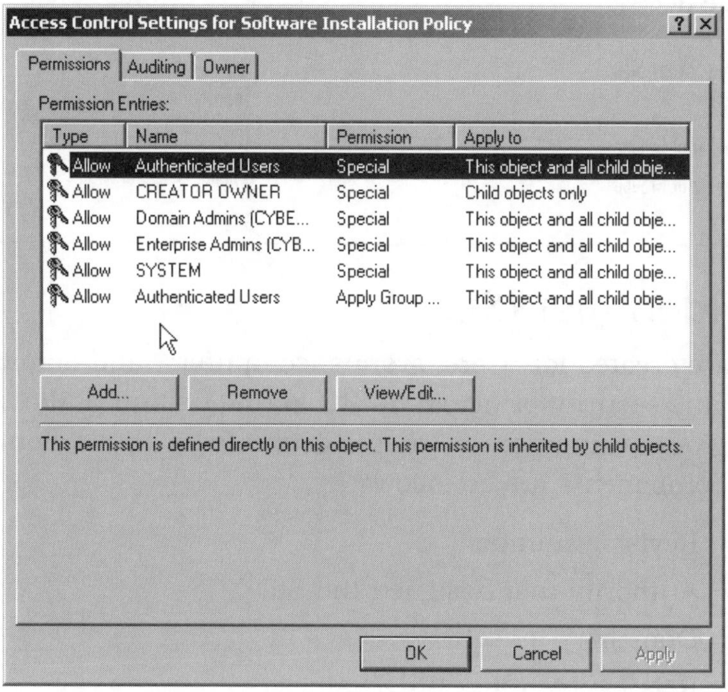
Access Control Settings for Software Installation Policy
Permissions
Auditing
Owner
Permission Entries:
Type
Name
Permission
Apply to
Allow Authenticated Users Special This object and all child obje...
Allow CREATOR OWNER Special Child objects only
Allow Domain Admins (CYBE... Special This object and all child obje...
Allow Enterprise Admins (CYB... Special This object and all child obje...
Allow SYSTEM Special This object and all child obje...
Allow Authenticated Users Apply Group ... This object and all child obje...
Add...
Remove
View/Edit...
This permission is defined directly on this object. This permission is inherited by child objects.
OK
Cancel
Apply

Security Descriptor

When a user authenticates to the Active Directory, the account is identified with its username and password. With a successful authentication, the system creates an access token including the Security Identifier (SID) (explained in the next section) and the SIDs of all the groups of which the user is a member. When the user generates a process after that, the access token is attached to the process.

The security descriptor is attached to network resources, rather than to users. It is the reverse of the access token in that it is the holder of the resource's ACL, which is compared to the user's access token when the user attempts to authenticate to a resource, as illustrated in Figure 9.30. The ACL contains the SIDs of each security principal that has been granted or explicitly denied access. It is the SID that maps the access token to the security descriptor.

Figure 9.30 Access tokens and security descriptors are used to provide access.

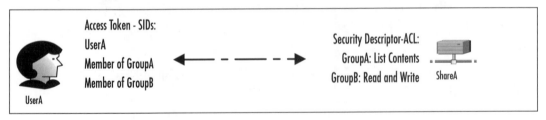

Security Identifier (SID)

SIDs are created for users, groups, computers, and domains; essentially, any security principal. A SID is unique and built when the user, group, computer, or trust is generated within a domain. A SID's components are as follows:

- Revision number
- Authority that assigned the SID
- Domain
- Relative Identifier (RID) values

SIDs are a legacy Windows NT concept. When a user is moved from a legacy domain to an Active Directory domain, it must be issued a new SID. Because the SID is the mapping mechanism between the access token of the user and the security descriptor of the resource, it has significant implications when a SID is changed. In fact, membership would need to be reestablished for each user account. When groups are moved, new rights would need to be granted to reestablish the ACLs.

There is a new attribute of security principals in the Active Directory called SIDHistory. SIDHistory retains a copy of a moved object's old SID. For example, a user that was upgraded from legacy NT to Windows 2000 would be able to access the same resources as before the move. Behind the scenes, the user would either authenticate as its NT4/SID or as its Windows 2000/SID—whichever has more rights. SIDHistory also works when moving a user from a domain in one forest to a domain in another forest. However, there are also implications when the SIDHistory is retained. If a user has been moved more than one time from an NT upgrade to Windows 2000, and from forest to forest, then there will be multiple copies of the SIDHistory in the access token and it becomes overlarge. Furthermore, troubleshooting permitted access for a security principal with multiple SIDHistories is difficult.

Security Model

Active Directory includes an inherent security model using OUs to organize the namespace into subsets. Objects are contained within separate OUs within a domain. Each object can be granted or denied access to other objects in the Active Directory. Access is so granular that it is applicable to each property of an individual object. Technologies involved in the security of Windows 2000 include Kerberos, PKI, and IPSec. Directory services are used as a repository for digital certificates, both to store and to manage them. For more information, see *Configuring Windows 2000 Server Security*, ISBN: 1-928944-01-6.

Kerberos

The Kerberos protocol is automatically installed when the Active Directory is installed on a Windows 2000 DC. Kerberos is not only the provider of transitive, two-way trusts, but it is used for logon authentication in the Active Directory. When logging on to the Active Directory, a user is issued a Ticket Granting Ticket (TGT) by the Key Distribution Center (KDC) on a Windows 2000 DC.

The TGT holds the authentication information about the user. It is encrypted with the domain master key. Whenever the user requests access to other network resources, the TGT is checked for permissions rather than executing a full authentication sequence. There is also an interdomain key shared by the domains that is used for authentication to use resources in other domains. This is a part of the Kerberos transitive, two-way trust relationship.

Public Key Infrastructure (PKI)

PKI is a security system that uses certificates as its basis. A certificate is a digital voucher containing the name of the account and a public key. The certificate can contain multiple names for the account, including the Active Directory ID, the UPN (where different), the e-mail account, and DNS names. A certification authority (CA) signs a digital certificate to attest that the account's private key is possessed by the account and is associated with the public key.

The CA issues the certificate that includes the public and private encryption keys. This system is based on standard public key encryption whereby either key can be used to encrypt, and the other key can be used to decrypt any message that the first key encrypted. Public keys are called such because they are available to the public to use when encrypting messages to be sent to the account (usually a user, but sometimes an application). The account can use the private key to decrypt the message. A second use for this system is to verifiably ensure to the public that a message sent is from the named account. This is called a digital signature. It is sent using the private key from the account, and the public, using the public key, can ensure that the message came from the named account.

Windows 2000 Certificate Services is an optional component. It works with the Active Directory by storing certificates in the directory database. When installing a CA server, remember that you will not be able to rename the server or move it outside the domain it was in after installation.

Smart Cards

Smart cards depend upon PKI to function. If you implement smart cards, you will require a Windows 2000 enterprise CA to be installed. A smart card looks like a plastic credit card and contains the private key for an account. When implementing smart cards on a network, each workstation requires a smart card reader and at least one enrollment station. Note that Windows 2000 only supports PC/SC-compliant, plug-and-play smart card readers.

For Managers

Secondary Logons

Run As is a secondary logon feature for Windows 2000. Using this feature enables an Administrator to execute administrative functions without logging on to a machine as the Administrator account. This adds a level of security because a PC could not be left running with an Administrator's credentials. Not only can a user walk up to that machine and execute functions with Administrative access, but a Trojan Horse attack that uses the credentials that currently exist on the PC to execute damaging functions would not have access to the credentials that enable those functions if using a standard user account rather than an Administrator's account.

Secondary logon exists as the Run As Service and can be managed on each Windows 2000 computer via the Computer Management console, or from the Component Services icon in Control Panel. To use the tool, you must be logged on as a user without rights to some application. Then, right-click the application while holding SHIFT down on the keyboard. Then select Run As from the popup menu, as shown in Figure 9.31.

IP Security

IP Security (IPSec) is a method of enabling Network-layer encryption and authentication to ensure private communications over any IP network, including the Internet. Since IPSec is based on open standards, it can be used to communicate with other IP networks.

Summary

Group policy is an Active Directory-integrated feature used to govern the user interface and computer settings. It is a newer version

Figure 9.31 Using the secondary logon feature.

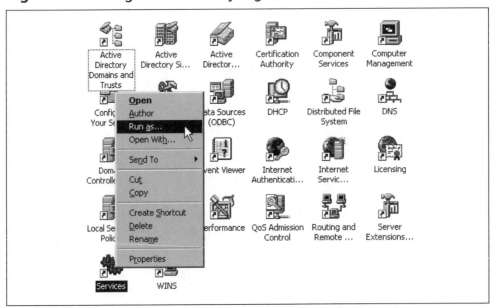

of the System Policies that originally were introduced with Windows 95, and used in Windows 98 and Windows NT 4. Group policies allow an Administrator to control how a workstation is used. Instead of being a file-based policy (like System Policies where machines must contact a server holding a particular system policy file before the policy is applied), group policy is applied to containers within the Active Directory and applied during the computer authentication to the network and user logon to the Active Directory.

Group policies are applied in a specific order:

1. Local group policy object

2. Site group policy object

3. Domain group policy objects

4. Organizational Unit (OU) group policy objects from the parent OUs down to the user's or computer's OU location

Although there is a single Local group policy, there can be multiple policies associated with a site, domain or OU. These policies can be changed in order to execute as the Administrator would require.

The last policy to execute will override all previous policies for the same item unless a policy has been designated as "No Override." The more group policies that must be applied, the longer a user's logon sequence will take. This does not pertain to the depth of the OUs, because six policies applied to a single OU will take as long to execute a logon as six OUs deep each with a single policy. Site policies will require contact with the domain controller (DC) that manages a particular group policy, and may further increase logon time. When designing group policies, do not use site-associated policies if possible, and use as few group policies as possible. To implement a group policy, start in the Active Directory Users and Computers console. From there, right-click the container to which the group policy will be applied, and select Properties. Click the Group Policy tab, and then add, remove, and edit group policies as needed.

One of the features of group policy is the capability of deploying applications to either a set of designated computers or a set of designated users. The Software Installation container can be used to add Windows Installer packages and transforms to custom script a software deployment. There are two options for software installation:

- Publish
- Assign

Publishing an application enables it to be available for users to install, even within the Add/Remove Programs icon in Control Panel. Assigning an application does not give any options for the installation of the software; instead, it is a required installation.

Security within the Windows 2000 Active Directory involves the use of Access Control Lists (ACLs) and Security Identifiers (SIDs). ACLs are lists of the groups and users who have rights to the resource, plus which rights they have been granted. SIDs are unique IDs applied to the security principal. SIDs for a user and any of the groups to which the user belongs are listed within a user's access token at the time of logon. The ACL uses SIDs to identify the users and groups. The process is simply a comparison of a user's access token to a resource's ACL. The SID is used as the mapping mechanism between the two in order to determine which rights are applicable to the user.

FAQs

Q: I want to deny a user access to a resource, but the user needs to belong to a group that is given full control of the same resource. Do I need to create a special group for this user?

A: That depends on how you want to manage this in the future. You do not have to create a special group with all the explicit rights for that user, and the user can remain in the group that is given full control of the resource. You can simply deny access to the resource to that user explicitly. The deny right will override all other rights to the resource. However, if you have this situation occur once, you may encounter it twice; in which case, it is recommended that you leave the user in the group with full control of the resource, then create a second group that is denied access to that resource. Adding the user to that second group will accomplish the same thing as denying access explicitly. If eventually you encounter another user who has the same requirements, you can simply add that user to the second group.

Q: Why do group policies contain many of the same features as the Domain Security Policy console?

A: Mainly because a group policy can be used to apply the same registry settings as the Domain Security Policy console and is flexible enough to apply those registry settings to computers domainwide, or to a subset of computers within a specific OU.

Q: How can I look at the ACE for an OU?

A: The ACEs are available from the Group Policy tab. By looking at the Properties of the group policy and selecting Security, the ACL is shown. From there, click ADVANCED. At that point, you can click ADD or REMOVE to add or remove ACEs, or View/Edit to change an ACE.

Chapter 10

Publishing

Solutions in this chapter:

- Understanding Published Resources
- Planning the Published Resources
- Publishing Printers
- Publishing Folders
- Understanding RPC, DCOM, and Windows Sockets

The term *published resource* brings to mind the rustle of newspapers and the feel of their rough-cut edges. But in the Active Directory, newspapers they are not. Instead, in the Active Directory, a published resource is some printer or network share or other network resource that has been made available to the public at large.

Introduction

Availability is not a problem until a network resource becomes unavailable. Then . . . well, it usually is a problem. Finding available network resources becomes more difficult when users are not familiar with the office they are in. This is happening more often as more enterprises support the remote office-worker paradigm. These folks may wander into an office to meet with their coworkers, but when they hook up to the network, they may find that they are unable to work because they cannot print to the printer around the corner or access the local file server.

Publishing resources within the Active Directory enables each server, whether a domain controller (DC) or not, to make its files and printers available on the network through the Active Directory in a user-friendly manner. Windows 2000 Servers can share files and printers, normally, but users must know the server and share names to locate them. The fact that the Active Directory uses the Domain Name System (DNS) as its namespace provider and locator mechanism further enables that resource to become available globally via the Internet as long as the Internet users have a compatible client software, appropriate access, *and* the network is connected to the Internet in such a way as to not prevent access.

Deciding What to Publish

Although a group policy can publish an application to a desktop, it does not publish the application into the Active Directory in the same way as other resources can be. The following items can be published within the Active Directory:

- Shared folders
- Printers

When publishing a resource, the resource is more than just an object within the Active Directory; it is also a searchable entity. That is, users can execute queries to find published resources, or they can browse around to look for them.

Not only should you determine what is going to be published, but also where in the directory should it be published. If a SalesReports user is in an OU for Sales, then publishing the SalesReports share in the Services OU would not be as helpful as publishing it in the Sales OU. Select meaningful placement of resources, and pay attention to the location from which users may be suddenly browsing. If publishing a file from New York in a container that only holds Florida users, there may be more traffic on the WAN than desired. In these cases, another option is to use File Replication Services (FRS), which is a fault-tolerant form of sharing files automatically configured for each DC through the SYSVOL share.

Sharing Folders

The first step toward making a folder available in the Active Directory is to make it available within the domain as a standard shared folder. Two utilities are commonly used both in Windows 2000 and in legacy Windows NT 4.0 to share folders:

- Windows Explorer
- Computer Management (the Windows 2000 version of NT's Server Manager)

Although this is elementary, the steps to sharing a folder in Explorer are to right-click the folder that will be the root of the information shared. Then select Sharing from the popup menu. Configure the share any way you desire.

Best practices are not to share the root of a partition (e.g., C:\) since that share will have all the information ever placed on that partition within it. Problems particularly exist when sharing the system partition, because system files may be deleted or damaged.

Computer Management is found in the Administrative Tools menu. In the Computer Management console shown in Figure 10.1, navigate to System Tools and then to Shared Folders. Click Shares within the Shared Folders. Right-click in the contents pane and select New File Share. The Create Shared Folder wizard will begin. You can walk through the steps to configure a share.

Figure 10.1 The Computer Management console.

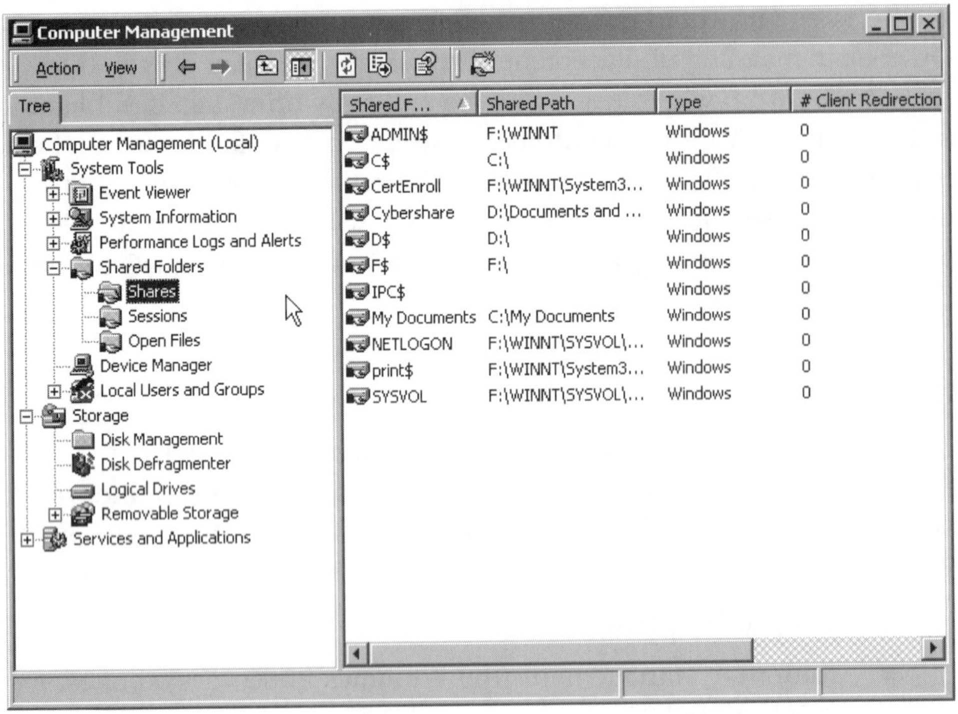

Publishing a Folder in the Active Directory

Sharing a folder is only the first step toward publishing it in the Active Directory. The next portion of the process follows in another console, the Active Directory Users and Computers. In this console, navigate to the organizational unit (OU) in which you will be storing the published resource. Right-click the OU and select New, then Shared Folder from the popup menu, as illustrated in Figure 10.2.

Figure 10.2 Shared Folder.

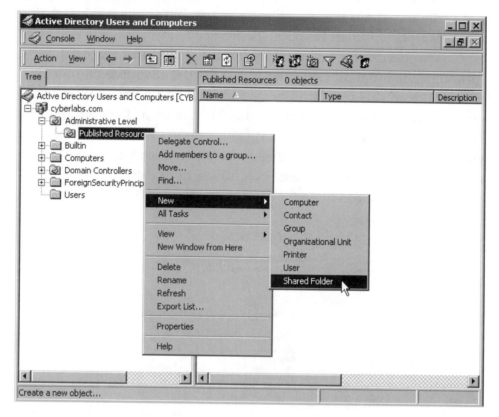

The Name box in the dialog will be the name of the resource as it appears in the Active Directory. This name can include spaces, so if a phrase is a better description than a single word, you may use it here. The Network path box is simply the UNC (Universal Naming Convention) location of the share.

You can publish a shared folder on a server that does not exist because the Active Directory does not check to see if either the server or the share is available on the network. While this functionality is helpful for offline configuration purposes, it does pose a problem if you are prone to typographical errors. You should check each share that you create to ensure that the location is correct. However, you can change the network location at any time for a published resource, so any errors, or even file migrations, can be rectified after a share has been published. The Active Directory does not verify if a share has a duplicate entry. If a share has more than one description, it can be published twice.

The properties for a shared folder are shown in Figure 10.3. Although the originally selected Name for the resource cannot be changed from this window, you are able to add a description or change the location. (You can change the name in the contents pane of the Active Directory Users and Computers window.) Additionally, you can click KEYWORDS and designate a set of keywords that will return this share when a user executes a query looking for this share. The Keywords dialog is shown in Figure 10.4.

Figure 10.3 Shared folder properties.

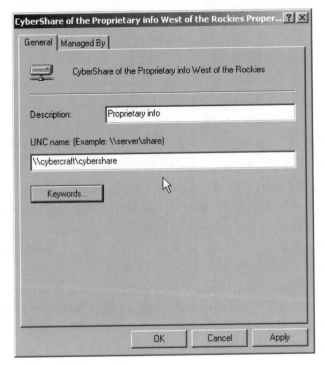

Figure 10.4 Keywords for shared folders.

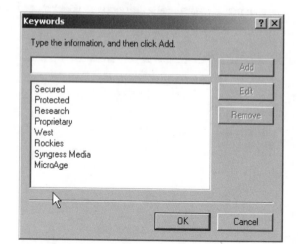

Browsing and Querying for Shared Folders

For those who lived through the change from NetWare 3 to NetWare 4, they soon found that even the most user-friendly changes to the interface into the network required a hand-holding session with end users to assist them through the first couple of times. It is likely that users will need a boost when they start using the Active Directory too.

If the users have Windows 2000, they can use the My Network Places icon to lead them to the network. By browsing the Entire Network and then looking through the Directory, they can browse through the Active Directory until they reach a shared resource, as shown in Figure 10.5.

If the user double-clicks a shared resource, the files appear even though they are not part of the Active Directory tree, as illustrated in Figure 10.6. The Active Directory functions in such a way that when you open a published folder, it will locate it in the hierarchy of the "Microsoft Network" and open it there. The published folder is a pointer, not a copy or stored information. In this way, files can be location independent, and users do not need to know on which server a share is located.

Figure 10.5 Browsing for shared resources.

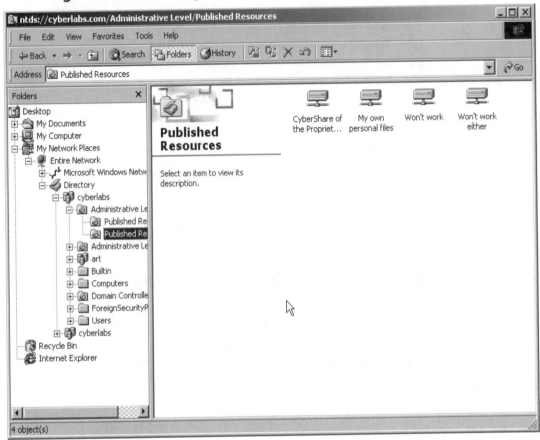

Querying the Active Directory for shared folders can be done
through the Find utility on a Windows 2000 Professional client or a
Windows client that has the DS Client installed. Open the My
Network Places icon in Windows 2000 Professional (Network
Neighborhood in other Windows clients), right-click the domain, and
select Find. Then in the resulting dialog, click the Find drop-down
box and select Shared Folders. If you wish to look throughout the
entire forest for the shares, or in another domain, you can click the
In drop-down box and select Entire Directory or the target domain.
You do not need to know the name of the resource, but you can use
keywords to narrow your search, as shown in Figure 10.7.

Figure 10.6 Shares appear as part of the Active Directory until they are opened.

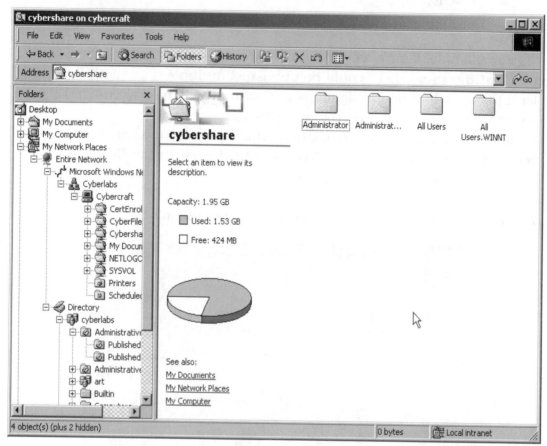

If you want to find shares with a more focused control over the field details, click the Advanced tab. There are five fields that you may use: Description, Keywords, Managed By, Name, and Network Path. Even though the Name and Keywords are available on the first tab, this dialog allows a search looking for exact matches or partial matches for the field's contents. The options include:

- Starts with
- Ends with
- Is (exactly)

- Is not
- Present
- Not Present

For example, if a Network Administrator took advantage of the fact that the same share could be published multiple times with different names, in different domains and with different keywords and descriptions, and then moved a share to a new server, the Administrator would need to locate all the copies of the shared resource within the directory. This could be done with the Network Path field, as shown in Figure 10.8.

Figure 10.7 Using keywords to execute a simple search.

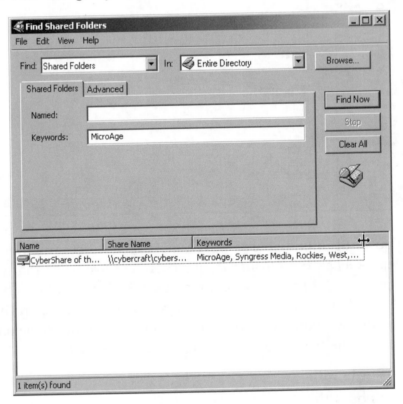

Figure 10.8 Using an Advanced search to locate multiple shares.

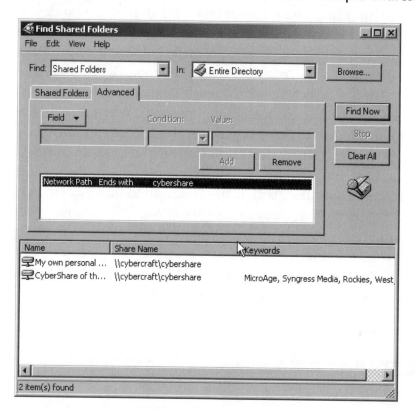

Overview of DFS and EFS

Understanding the Distributed File System (DFS) and the Encrypted File System (EFS) will assist in managing a Windows 2000 network. DFS creates a single logical file system tree that can access files and folders residing on multiple servers in various locations. There are two configurations for DFS:

- Standalone
- Fault-tolerant

When DFS is standalone, it has little to do with the Active Directory because the DFS topology is stored on a single computer. When DFS is fault-tolerant, however, the DFS topology is stored within the Active Directory, where it takes advantage of multi-master replication to provide redundancy for the DFS topology.

To create either type of DFS, use the Distributed File System console. The Distributed File System console is located under Administrative Tools. To create a new Dfs root, right-click Distributed File System and select New Dfs Root... This opens the New Dfs root Wizard. Click NEXT at the introduction screen. When storing the DFS topology in the Active Directory, select the "Create a fault-tolerant Dfs Root" option. Next, the wizard prompts for the Domain to host Dfs, a server to host Dfs, a share for the Dfs root, and a name for the Dfs root. To create another root, in the Distributed File System console, right-click the hosting domain and select New Root Replica Member, as shown in Figure 10.9. After that, complete the filesystem tree by adding Dfs Links, which are the names that users see when connecting to DFS. Note that you are able to hide the Dfs root by right-clicking the root and selecting Remove Display of Dfs Root.

Figure 10.9 New Dfs link.

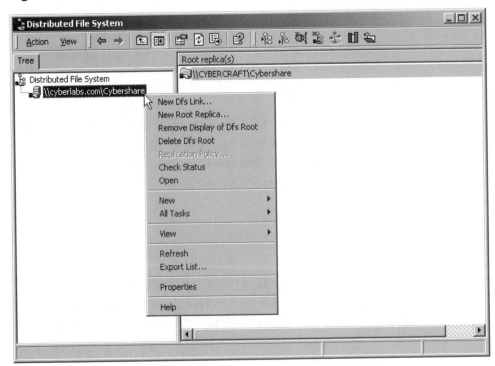

EFS uses a strong public key cryptographic system to encrypt files. A new feature of Windows 2000, it is a highly desirable feature for users who carry laptops or communicate across the Internet. It is preferable to use the Certificate Authority (CA) service when using EFS. If a CA is available, it can be used to sign the public key; otherwise, EFS self-signs the key. CA stores certificates within the Active Directory.

Encrypting a folder starts with viewing its properties in the Windows Explorer. Click ADVANCED and select "Encrypt contents" to secure data. The folder and its contents will be encrypted, but the user who encrypted it will be able to access the file transparently. Only when access by an unauthorized person is attempted will the encryption be apparent. A command-line utility called cipher.exe can be used to encrypt or decrypt files as well.

The only people who are able to access an encrypted file are the user who encrypted it and the data recovery agent. A data recovery agent is an authorized user who can be added to the Domain or Local security policy, or to the group policy object for a computer.

Publishing a Printer in the Active Directory

Printers are published in the Active Directory through the Add Printer Wizard of a Windows 2000 computer. The default behavior for a shared printer is a listing in the Active Directory.

To verify whether a printer is shared in the directory, right-click the printer object and select Properties. Click the Sharing tab. Verify that the box for List in Directory is checked, as shown in Figure 10.10.

If a legacy Windows NT printer must be shared in the Active Directory, you can right-click any container, select New, and then Printer from the popup menu. Enter the UNC name for the shared printer.

Another method of publishing printers from non-Windows 2000 networks is through the use of the script in Winnt\system32\pub-prn.vbs. This Visual Basic script can be executed with the syntax:

Figure 10.10 Windows 2000 printers listed in Active Directory.

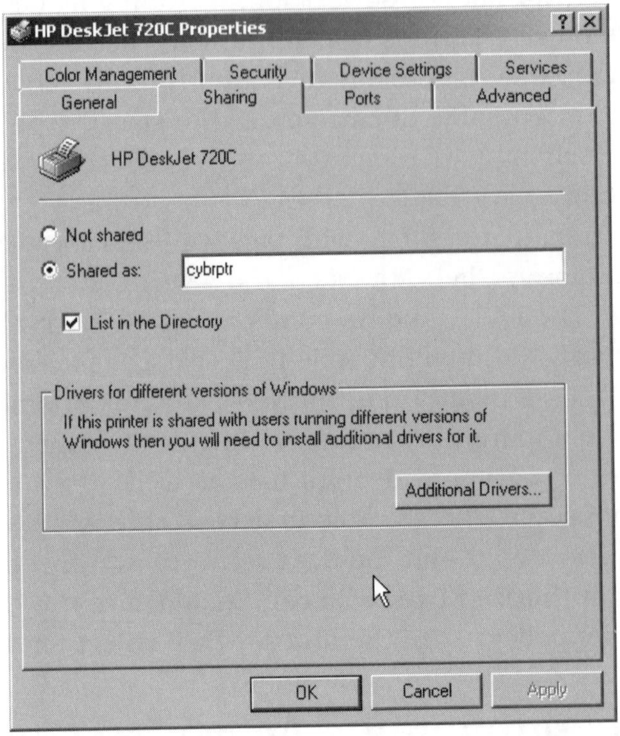

```
cscript pubprn.vbs servername ldap directory services path
```

For example, executing the command:

```
Cscript pubprn.vbs \\printserver  LDAP://cn=printers,dc=root,dc=com
```

will publish all the printers located on the server named Printserver into the Active Directory OU named Printers within the domain root.com.

Interfacing with Active Directory

It's no secret that there are directory services other than the Active Directory. There are many different ways of accessing these directories. Some methods are based on protocols, others are based on application programming interfaces (APIs). Using these methods, two or more directory services can be synchronized. Understanding how these items work will assist in managing and synchronizing multiple directory services.

- Active Directory Services Interface (ADSI)
- Remote Procedure Calls (RPC)
- Windows Sockets (WinSock)
- Distributed Component Object Model (DCOM)
- Exchange Server Active Directory Connector (ADC)
- Microsoft Directory Service Synchronization for Novell (MSDSS)

ADSI

ADSI is an API for the Active Directory that is made up of a set of COM programming interfaces. ADSI is intended to be used by Network Administrators to automate Active Directory tasks, and by developers to connect their applications to the Active Directory. ADSI has been adopted by vendors to enable connectivity between their directories and any ADSI-enabled application.

Four ADSI objects are capable of extending a directory service schema. They are called schema management ADSI objects.

- **Schema container:** Contains the target directory service schema.
- **Class container:** Defines object classes for the target directory service.
- **Property object:** Defines object attributes for the target directory service.
- **Syntax object:** Further defines the syntax used for a property object.

In addition to schema management objects, ADSI has directory objects that represent the directory service components. There are two types of directory objects: container and leaf objects. Container objects include namespaces, country, locality, organization, OU, domain, and computer. Leaf objects include users, groups, aliases, services, print queues, print devices, print jobs, file service, file shares, sessions, and resources.

To manipulate a property value, ADSI uses two commands: GetInfo to read information about a directory service object and refresh cache from the directory, and SetInfo to establish new information for a directory service object to ensure it is written to disk.

ADSI uses its own naming convention so that the object can be identified regardless of which namespace it will be ported to. For example, the directory is identified in a string called AdsPath along with the container and object names. A user named Joe in an Active Directory OU named Sales and a domain called CyberLabs.com would have an AdsPath of:

```
LDAP://cn=Joe,ou=Sales,dc=Cyberlabs,dc=com
```

If you wanted to use ADSI to log on to Active Directory, you could use a script similar to the following:

```
Dim dsobj As IADsOpenDSObject

Dim dom As IADsDomain

Set dsobj = GetObject(LDAP:)

Set dom = dsobj.OpenDSObject(LDAP://DC=Cyberlabs,DC=COM, MyUser, password,
ADS_SECURE_AUTHENTICATION)
```

Another ADSI script can be used to run a backup of Windows 2000 computers.

```
Set cntnr = GetObject(LDAP://OU=W2Kpro, DC=Cyberlabs, DC=COM)

Cntnr.Filter = Array(computer)

For each comp in cntnr

        Comp.BackupNow()

Next
```

RPC

RPCs are a Session-layer API that makes remote applications appear to be executing locally. The activity of an RPC is completely transparent to the end user. At the Session layer, RPC is able to run over other lower-level protocols such as IPX, Vines, NetBEUI, and TCP/IP. RPCs may use other interprocess communications to access remote systems, including named pipes and WinSock.

An application that uses RPCs can place portions of the application on different computers. This is the definition of true client/server networking, in which a server can execute part of the processing and the client executes the remainder. The components of an RPC enabled application include the items listed in Table 10.1.

Table 10.1 RPC Components

Component	Component Full Name	Function
Proc Stub	Remote Procedure Stub	Packages the calls to be sent to a remote server by RPC RT
RPC RT	RPC Run Time	Manages the communications between local and remote computers
APP Stub	Application Stub	RPC RT sends RPC requests to APP Stub, which then unwraps the package and sends the call to a remote procedure
Proc	Remote Procedure	The procedure called by the network

Windows Sockets

Windows Sockets, also known as WinSock, is a standard interface based on the original Berkeley Sockets interface specification. What Sockets intended to do was enable multiple applications to be able to access and use the same network connection. The result managed to send data across a network from two or more separate applications. WinSock standardized this system further, and can work over the NetWare-compatible (IPX) protocol, as well as TCP/IP.

DCOM

DCOM, or the Distributed Component Object Model, is actually a form of network-aware object linking and embedding. It has grown to be a software development system where software objects can be reused and/or replaced. Each object represents multiple sets of functions, with each set being considered an interface. The reason why more than one interface can be supported by a DCOM object is that any change or addition to an interface can only be done with the creation of a new interface.

Exchange Server Active Directory Connector

One useful thing for an Administrator is the ability to synchronize accounts between two systems. Doing so cuts the work in half. Exchange Server was capable of synchronizing mailboxes with Windows NT accounts. However, with an upgrade to Windows 2000, Exchange Server can no longer use the same mechanisms to synchronize accounts. Active Directory can be synchronized with Exchange Server using the AD connector.

The technical requirements for deploying the Exchange Server Active Directory connector are as follows:

- For each Active Directory domain, plan to have at least one Active Directory Connector server.

- Exchange Server 5.5 must be installed with Service Pack 2, at a minimum.

- Exchange Server's LDAP port must be changed to a port number that will not conflict with Active Directory.

- If upgrading a Windows NT domain, first complete the upgrade to Windows 2000 before implementing the connector in order to avoid duplicate accounts.

- Whenever possible, place the Active Directory connector server on the same subnet as the Exchange Server bridgehead to Active Directory.

If a single Active Directory domain is connected to a single Exchange site, the requirements are simplified: A single Active Directory connector with two primary connection agreements (each connection agreement is configured from its starting point), one pointing at Exchange from Active Directory, the other pointing at Active Directory from Exchange. Even though the connection agreement is configured from a starting point, it can designate either one-way or two-way traffic. Select two-way if you are unsure which your connection should be.

When two Active Directory domains are connected to a single Exchange site, a decision must be made as to which domain will be the primary connection for Exchange. To avoid confusion over which is the master over the connection, always designate the domain closest to the root of the Active Directory forest to be the primary connection.

When there are multiple sites and multiple domains, there can be any number of complex arrangements for connections. In these situations, planning is essential to ensure that redundant connections do not end up creating multiple duplicate accounts in either Exchange or Active Directory. There should only be one primary connection pointing to each Active Directory domain. Likewise, there should only be one primary connection pointing to each Exchange Server site.

Bridgehead servers should be designated for the connections between Exchange and Active Directory. When designating a bridgehead server for Exchange, select any servers that are solely used as gateways or "connector servers" first. After that, select a server that is well-connected to the network and has available resources for the connection processing overhead. When designating a bridgehead server for Active Directory, select a Global Catalog (GC) server first, a DC second, and a member server last. Also select a server that is well-connected to the network and has available processing resources.

To install the Exchange Server Active Directory Connector, look on the Windows 2000 Server CD-ROM for the \valueadd\msft\mgmt\adc directory.

Execute the setup.exe program to begin the Active Directory Connector Installation Wizard. When prompted for the component selection, select both the Microsoft Active Directory Connector Service and Microsoft Active Directory Connector Management components. Specify the install folder for ADC. Finally, designate a service account to manage the connection, and then finish the wizard.

There will be a new program in the Administrative Tools menu called Active Directory Connector Management. This is the program used to configure the connector. Open it, right-click the Active Directory Connector Management object, and select Properties from the popup menu. The default properties for information originating in Exchange and for information originating in Active Directory will be available in this dialog after creating a new connection agreement. To create a connection agreement, right-click the Active Directory Connector for your server, select New, and then Connection Agreement.

After configuring the connector, you can create new users in Active Directory or new mailboxes in Exchange, or change information to verify that communication is taking place.

Novell Directory Service Synchronization

Microsoft Directory Synchronization Services (MSDSS) is a connector between Novell's Novell Directory Services and Microsoft's Active Directory that enables synchronization from either directory service to the other. MSDSS also connects to legacy Novell NetWare bindery servers, but will only send data to those binderies in one direction. It will not receive updates from a Novell NetWare bindery server.

MSDSS requires that there is at least one Active Directory DC to manage the MSDSS synchronization. It also requires a Windows 2000 machine, whether it is a Professional, Server, Advance Server, or DataCenter Server version, that is running both the MSDSS client and the Novell Client32 redirector. This second machine acts as a gateway between the two directory services, taking information in the form of updates from one directory service and passing it on to the other. Because the gateway runs the Novell Client32 redirector, MSDSS is capable of synchronizing passwords between the two directory services while maintaining a secure environment.

Summary

Published resources are network shares or printers that are enabled for access via the Active Directory. After being published, a resource can be either browsed or queried from an Active Directory aware application. For example, a file resource can be viewed from below the Directory location in the My Network Places icon on any Windows 2000 PC when the user has access to it.

Published resources should be placed in containers that are meaningful to the users who access them. Whenever possible, a resource should be published in the containers of the users that access the resource the most.

Windows 2000 printers are published by default when they are created as network printers on Windows 2000 servers. If a Windows 2000 printer has been unpublished, and it is desired for that printer to be published, the Administrator can change the Sharing properties for that printer, making certain that the check box to List in the Directory is checked.

To publish a legacy NT printer, the Administrator can right-click in any container in the Active Directory Users and Computers console, select New, then Printer. After supplying the location and description, the printer is published as an object.

To publish a folder in the Active Directory, it must first be shared as a resource on the network. Then, the Administrator can right-click any container in the Active Directory Users and Computers console, select New, then Shared Folder. After supplying the location of the share and new name for it, the folder is published as an object.

RPC, DCOM, and WinSock are all part of a developer system for network-aware Windows applications. These work alongside the Active Directory Services Interface to provide a method for both Administrators and developers to manage and extend the Active Directory.

FAQs

Q: When I right-click a container and select New | Printer, I receive a dialog for a printer share. I put in the printer share, but then receive an error saying that this is a Windows 2000 printer and must be listed elsewhere. What am I doing wrong?

A: Nothing. The printer object that shows up in the popup menu for containers is a pointer to legacy Windows NT printers. The Active Directory does check to make sure that the printer is available before publishing it in the directory, and it also checks to make sure that the printer is a legacy Windows NT printer. Windows 2000 network printers are listed in the Active Directory by default when their print queue is created in the Printers folder. The Sharing tab for a Windows 2000 printer's properties will show whether the printer is shared or not.

Chapter 11

Plugging into Active Directory

Microsoft may have developed the Active Directory, but they did not create it in a vacuum. Microsoft made every effort to ensure that the Active Directory would be representative of Internet standards, and be able to interoperate with third-party applications.

Microsoft's Metadirectory

Many enterprise networks have a common set of business requirements for their networked systems, including:

- Single logon and synchronized passwords across systems to simplify network access from the user's perspective, which translates directly to a reduction in support needs.

- Ease of propagating human resources information throughout multiple systems when a user is hired, thus providing network access; and when a user is fired, thus providing a measure of security.

- Single global address book that contains current information for other users, including their e-mail addresses regardless of the messaging system used.

Metadirectories have become more prevalent in networking because of the proliferation of directory databases. The average enterprise has about 10 directories residing in their multiple network operating systems, electronic messaging, databases, groupware, PBX telephone systems, and infrastructure operating systems. For example, when a new employee is hired, a company may need to enter that employee's data into an HR database, a security badge database, the PBX voice mail system, an electronic messaging application, a proxy server, Novell Directory Services, a NetWare bindery, a legacy Windows NT domain, the Active Directory, and so forth.

A metadirectory is somewhat different from a synchronization method of updating directories. Synchronization is the process of ensuring that when an Administrator makes a change to one database, that change is synchronized across all other databases. This is like multi-master replication among dissimilar databases. As unlikely as it seems, this is a common system already developed for many messaging systems. It enables global address books from different vendors to be synchronized when a change is made to one of those vendors' directories. This type of synchronization is traditionally implemented through gateway or connector software.

A metadirectory, on the other hand, is a superset of all directories. Primarily, these directories manage identity information, but many of them extend into other resource information, such as data, files, printers, shares, applications, telephone information, policy rules, and so on. Not all directories contain the exact same extent of information, but most have a commonality in the identity of users who are allowed to access this information, as shown in Figure 11.1.

Figure 11.1 Identity management with a metadirectory.

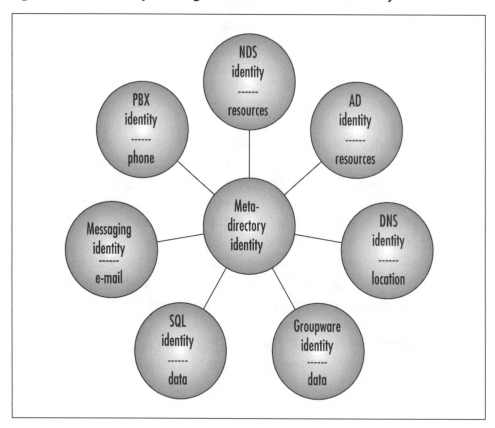

The metadirectory is actually a directory itself, or an index, of all the information that can be synchronized between these various databases. There are two approaches to metadirectory products:

- Identity information index
- Single point of administration

The identity index approach enables centralization of the common identity information from the various databases mapped to each other. In the early development of metadirectories, this approach is most common. The single point of administration approach includes a further extension into the security aspects of the various directories by including the resource information and the rules that apply to how users are granted access to those resources. Regardless of which approach is used, the capability of managing identity from a single point is a major administrative process improvement over the problems incurred through managing an average of 10 directories containing information about the same user identity.

The challenge with metadirectories is to establish rules to manage the updates when they can be initiated from any one of the directories. The question at hand is, "which directory owns that particular identity attribute?" For example, is it more sensible to have the messaging database own the e-mail address or the SQL database? Probably the messaging database should own that piece of information. That means, if an Administrator made a change to the e-mail address on a SQL database, and another Administrator made a change to the messaging database, the change that would win is the messaging database e-mail address. This is done by establishing the messaging database as the Master of the e-mail address attribute, whereas other databases are slaves to the messaging master.

Microsoft acquired Zoomit Corporation, a company that developed metadirectory technologies, in 1999. This acquisition enables Microsoft to implement a metadirectory that will be able to access and interact natively with the Active Directory, and be able to work with other directory services. Such directories would likely include:

- Messaging address books
- DNS and DHCP databases
- Third-party directory services
- Database directories
- Mainframe and minicomputer account managers

In essence, a metadirectory enables an Administrator to have a single interface into multiple directory services, and manage those directory services using intelligent rules. The metadirectory must be able to integrate with those other directory services in a way that can maintain integrity across directories, and translate between different types of data representing the same value. For example, the e-mail address in one directory might be given two fields: a string representing the user ID and a string representing the Internet domain. A different directory might keep the e-mail address in a single field as a string value. Phone numbers can include area codes and symbols in one directory, represented by a string value, but they could be a seven-digit phone number in another directory with no symbols and represented by a number.

The metadirectory must be able to understand these values and map them between directories. This can be done by using a native API for each directory, or by using a common protocol to access each directory (such as the Lightweight Directory Access Protocol, or LDAP) and then manipulating the data to ensure that the data is correct in each directory that the metadirectory touches.

The optimal architecture for a metadirectory is one in which the metadirectory is the central connecting point between all the other directory services (see Figure 11.2). If a directory service were connected to others in a serial fashion, it would be less likely that the metadirectory could apply business rules regarding the ownership of values in the data (see Figure 11.3).

Figure 11.2 Hub and spoke metadirectory.

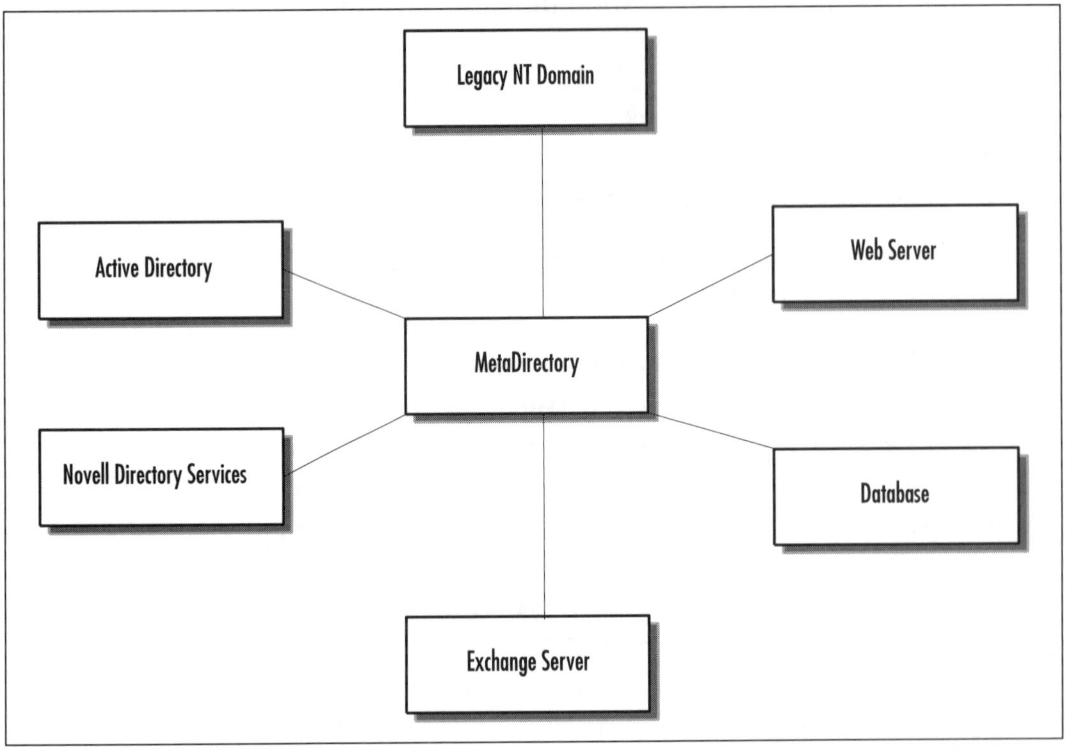

VIA Architecture

VIA is the name of the metadirectory product that Microsoft acquired when they bought Zoomit. It can run as a service or a console on a Windows NT 4 or Windows 2000 Server. To access the VIA metadirectory, a client can be a:

- Web browser
- LDAP client
- Zoomit Compass client

The VIA "metaverse" database connects to multiple directories through management agents that work in a bidirectional flow that can be scheduled by the Administrator. There are management agents currently available for the following directories. Future versions and updates may contain additional management agents.

- Banyan VINES
- GMHS (BeyondMail and DaVinci)
- Lotus Notes
- Microsoft Exchange Server
- Microsoft Mail
- Microsoft Windows NT domains
- Microsoft Windows 2000 Active Directory
- Netscape Directory Server
- Novell NetWare bindery
- Novell Directory Services
- Novell GroupWise (4.*x* and 5.*x*)
- SQL databases, via ODBC
- X.500 directories, via LDAP, such as ISOCOR, ICL, and Control Data

Figure 11.3 Serial directories.

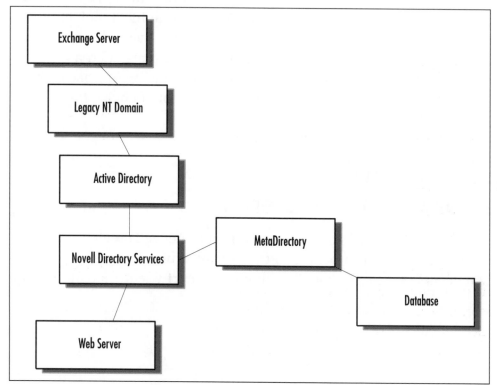

Additionally, a "report" management agent is available for reporting on the metaverse, and a "generic" management agent is available to use in creating a custom version for a different database.

The metaverse can synchronize directories to the attribute level. In fact, new objects can be created in any directory or the metadirectory, or attributes can be changed, and then those objects and attribute changes will be propagated to the metadirectory (if made from a different directory). From the metadirectory, they will be propagated to the rest of the connected directories.

VIA also supports ownership of data to the attribute level. This further maintains the referential integrity of the data when there are two or more different sources for identity information.

Mission Critical's Migration Tool

Microsoft has licensed the Mission Critical application for migrating users from one domain of either Windows NT or Windows 2000 to a Windows 2000 domain only. This utility will be called Active Directory Migration Tool (ADMT). ADMT is a graphical tool with wizards and an easy-to use console. It can easily move users, computers, and Local groups between domains. While tools such as ClonePrincipal are capable of providing the same result, because of its interface it is likely that ADMT will be a tool of choice for many Administrators.

Deploying Active Directory-Enabled Clients

Windows 2000 Professional is the ultimate Active Directory-enabled client. It was built to belong to that architecture. Because of Windows 2000 Professional's enhanced security features and other improvements, many organizations will combine a Windows 2000 Server rollout with a Windows 2000 Professional rollout. However, there are others that will not. For those organizations, the goal is to successfully integrate clients with the Active Directory, and to access resources located on Windows 2000 Servers.

Best Practices

In general, a prudent approach to project management will enable better success with any Windows 2000 rollout, regardless of client types. This includes:

- Planning the locations of domain controllers/DNS servers in respect to clients

- Planning sites to enhance users' perception of network performance

- Considering the deployment of Active Directory-enabled applications

- Establishing appropriate administrative roles and boundaries for sets of clients

- Ensuring that business requirements are met by the technical solution that is implemented

Deploying DSClient

The DSClient file is located on the Windows 2000 Server CD-ROM under Clients\<ostype>. For example, if installing the client for Windows 95 or Windows 98, the directory is \CLIENTS\WIN9X. The executable is named DSClient.exe. When you execute this command, you will see the Directory Service Client Wizard, as shown in Figure 11.4.

There is not much to the installation process. The wizard offers a couple of dialog screens that explain the DSClient installation, and after copying the appropriate files, the machine prompts to be rebooted. The DSClient can be executed in quiet mode, without requiring any user intervention, by using the /Q switch with the dsclient.exe command.

Figure 11.4 Directory Service Client Wizard Welcome screen.

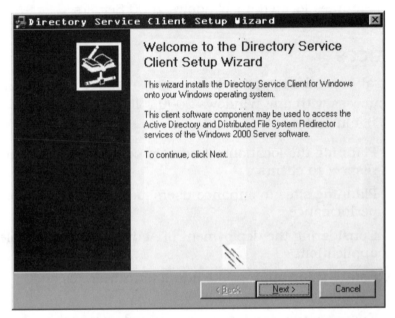

After installation, there are a few changes to the client workstation. The main change is in the Find menu, shown in Figure 11.5, to which a "People" option has been added.

Figure 11.5 DSClient finding people.

The Find command has an added menu that can look in various directories, including the Active Directory. This is illustrated in Figure 11.6.

Figure 11.6 Active Directory is added to the Find options.

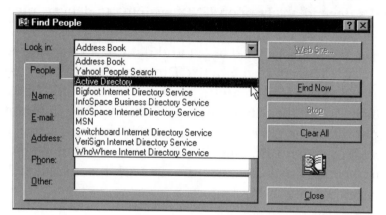

Cisco

The Active Directory presents a comprehensive distributed directory service. It is scalable, uses standard technologies that are familiar on the global Internet, and is integrated with the Windows 2000 network operating system. Cisco has built a product called Cisco Networking Services for Active Directory (CNS/AD) that is built upon the Active Directory's scalable and extensible architecture. CNS/AD provides an integration point between the Active Directory and the Cisco Internetworking Operating System (IOS). The result is a directory-enabled internetworking solution.

It is expected that CNS/AD will provide an architecture for use by third-party products, but CNS/AD also provides a basis for a suite of Cisco solutions, Cisco Service Management System (CSM), that address a service provider's four areas of operations:

- Planning
- Provisioning
- Monitoring
- Billing

Since these services are directly applicable to service providers, such as those providing access to the Internet (ISPs), Cisco has further taken the Active Directory and ported it to UNIX systems. Many ISPs depend solely upon UNIX systems to deliver Internet access services. By providing a UNIX type of solution, CNS/AD can provide the common Cisco schema and data to all network systems.

This new extension of the Active Directory provides a basis for an intelligent network. Users can be provided services that are differentiated solely by the identity of the user himself. This differentiation is transparent to the users. The directory provides an elemental role in the intelligent network, since it provides a dynamic glue between users, applications, policies, and the network resources such as servers, printers, and even routers.

CNS/AD

Policy-based networking has been around for many years. For instance, a policy for networking could state "All traffic from MAC address X will receive the highest priority to reach MAC address Y." A policy like this could be executed on a router or server with a simple rule. This type of rule exists on a single network segment and applies to the Data Link layer (layer 2) of the OSI reference model. At layer 3, the rule can apply to a logical IP address. Using a logical address allows some mobility for that address to move around from machine to machine, if needed, since the user could potentially change the IP address on any machine she visited. However, that is not a likely scenario.

The flexibility of a logical network address is not enough for an Administrator to be certain that the correct user was receiving the correct level of service. The most useful type of policy would be one that could be tied to the person using the machine, regardless of which machine. In this scenario, a policy would need the ability to plug in to a directory service, like the Active Directory, to match the identity of the user to the IP address of the machine that the user has logged on to, and then to send the policy to the networking infrastructure equipment (routers, hubs, and switches) to flag that user's traffic for priority, or Quality of Service (QoS). This type of rule would be more user friendly, as well as capable of following the user anywhere on the internetwork. For instance, the rule might state "All traffic from Vice President George Doe will receive the highest priority." Then VP can travel to Alaska from Florida, yet receive the same QoS when he logs in to the directory service. This system is independent of physical location, as shown in Figure 11.7.

Figure 11.7 CNS/AD and Quality of Service.

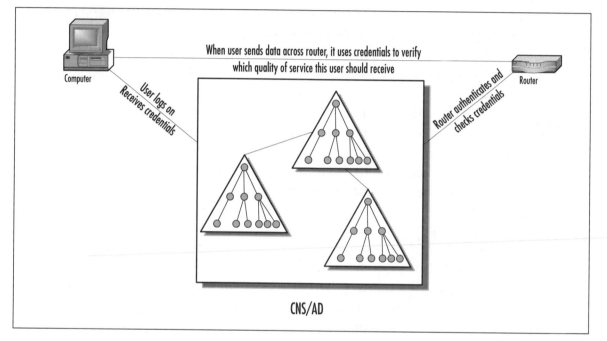

When policies are stored in a dynamic database, they are not only flexible and simple to execute, but reflect more accurately the results that a Network Administrator is trying to gain. For example, an Administrator can manually configure several routers to provide a higher QoS to traffic originating from a certain IP address. This address can be manually assigned to a specific computer used by a specific user. If, however, the user uses another computer, or the QoS is only supposed to be enabled during certain hours, the Administrator will be required to reconfigure everything to meet these business requirements. With CNS/AD, a policy can automate this, thereby saving the Administrator a lot of work. QoS policies are one of the main draws for using CNS/AD.

One of the main benefits of CNS/AD is that Cisco's IOS features can be managed from a policy standpoint in a central location. This is highly desirable for an enterprise that has multiple Cisco routers, since a single point of administration (the Active Directory) can be accessed and used rather than the alternative choice: using Telnet (or a Web browser if the IOS version supports it) to access individual routers with their IP addresses.

By extending the Active Directory, information and policy used by network services can be stored. These items can be linked to user accounts or other objects, such as computers, in order to specify the users' or computers' access to them. In a case where a person used videoconferencing on a different user's computer, this linking process will still enable that person to have the QoS granted to him for videoconference data (assuming he logged in as himself). An Administrator has fundamental control over the policies, and does not need to control the dynamic nature of the users and resources that those policies may apply to.

What CNS/AD Does

CNS/AD is a set of extensions to the Active Directory that provide a foundation that may be used by network-aware applications and even existing IOS applications, such as the CiscoAssure policy server. These extensions will enable:

- Storage and management of secure information from authenticated resources, such as routers or users

- Processing of events from resources, such as time-critical alarms or application events

- Maintenance of information about network resources' current state, such as router statistics

In order to function, each user and resource must authenticate to the Active Directory. The Active Directory-provided credentials supplied upon authentication determine security options such as which user can access data or which machine can process which events. A process in which a user and router both authenticate to the Active Directory illustrates how the user is governed by both his credentials and the router's policies when he needs to access the router.

CNS/AD supplies a high-speed transaction-based cache that stores and replicates transitory data (such as router statistics) and low-latency data. Low-latency data is any type of data that can propagate quickly across a network and usually carries a low overhead, such as DHCP data, which is based upon UDP (user datagram protocol). UDP has a much smaller header than TCP because UDP's header doesn't require the fields needed for reliability (which TCP provides). Otherwise, UDP performs the same basic function at the Transport layer.

The following are two examples of the way that CNS/AD may be able to assist a network manager on a real-world network.

- A research and development manager for a company that has contracted to develop a new technology logs in to his network. While executing normal file and print services, CNS/AD enables standard security measures established by the Administrator for those services. However, when the manager logs in to the R&D database, CNS/AD authenticates the manager and then turns on IPSec encryption during the session, plus grants him a higher QoS for that session. These policies apply to the session end to end through each infrastructure component that sits between the manager and the R&D database server. Because they are all connected logically through the Active Directory, the system is able to apply the policies throughout an internetwork.

- An ISP provides services to thousands of consumers. A demand from several of its top corporate clients for faster, more reliable services has placed the ISP in jeopardy of losing a large percentage of its business. The ISP implements CNS/AD. It then creates several policies that grant users' accounts a QoS in a matrix of Platinum, Gold, Silver, and Bronze, in which a Bronze user receives the least amount of service quality and Platinum receives the highest.

Then the ISP grants the top accounts Gold services and offers them a Platinum account for a premium charge. All other accounts are granted Bronze services with upgrades available for premium charges. The result is that the ISP can grant a higher quality of service to clients who have paid for the privilege or who are too valuable to lose. When users authenticate to the ISP's Active Directory, they are granted the appropriate QoS based on their level and current network conditions.

Fastlane Technologies

Fastlane Technologies began creating network administration tools in 1993. The original focus of the tools was to automate tedious functions, and to solve problems surrounding Banyan networks. Then Fastlane began to create software focused on Windows NT network administration. In 1997, they created an "Enterprise Directory Management" engine called Active DMS. This was quickly followed by products that assisted with domain migrations, network reporting, and NT administration, based upon that Enterprise Directory Management engine.

Fastlane Technologies creates software that can be used for Active Directory migrations and for directory management. Fastlane's tools make daily network administration much less tedious and repetitive by providing ways to delegate, script, and automate repetitive tasks. Fastlane has a lifecycle for their products' usage in the Windows 2000 migration cycle (see Figure 11.8).

DM/Reporter

A best practice for executing a Windows NT to Windows 2000 migration is to clean up the existing user accounts and machine accounts in the NT SAM prior to the migration. This will avoid unnecessary processing and reduce the time it takes to migrate the data. DM/Reporter is a tool that can discover which accounts are no

Figure 11.8 DM/Lifecycle.

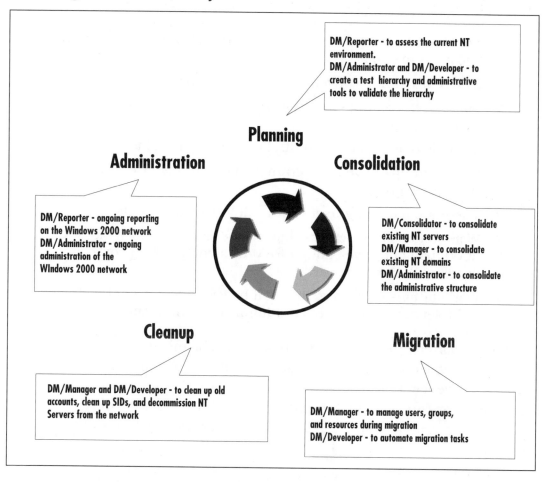

DM/Reporter - to assess the current NT environment.
DM/Administrator and DM/Developer - to create a test hierarchy and administrative tools to validate the hierarchy

Planning

Administration

Consolidation

DM/Reporter - ongoing reporting on the Windows 2000 network
DM/Administrator - ongoing administration of the WIndows 2000 network

DM/Consolidator - to consolidate existing NT servers
DM/Manager - to consolidate existing NT domains
DM/Administrator - to consolidate the administrative structure

Cleanup

Migration

DM/Manager and DM/Developer - to clean up old accounts, clean up SIDs, and decommission NT Servers from the network

DM/Manager - to manage users, groups, and resources during migration
DM/Developer - to automate migration tasks

longer valid. DM/Reporter can provide much more detailed information than accounts, which makes it an excellent ongoing administrative tool as well.

DM/Reporter uses Active DMS to access directory service data, and displays that data in a report based on Seagate's Crystal Reports software. Many reports are provided within the DM/Reporter product as standards, and an Administrator can customize his own reports to suit his needs.

DM/Reporter shines best when migrating to Windows 2000 from Windows NT. There can be a multitude of problems that must be fixed in a Windows NT environment that is going to be upgraded to Windows 2000, including:

- There are inactive or invalid accounts in the NT security accounts manager.
- Different naming conventions have been used.
- Some user accounts have passwords that violate security requirements.
- Multiple domains contain duplicate account names.
- Global groups have been granted rights to resources, rather than Local groups.
- There are too many users with Administrative rights.
- Workstations and servers that will be upgraded to Windows 2000 may not have enough RAM or a compatible processor or network interface card (NIC).
- Workstations or servers that will be upgraded are not at the right service pack or are running incompatible applications.

DM/Reporter can expose these types of problems and many others. This enables the migration team to identify problem issues before experiencing problems with the Windows 2000 migration. The Administrator can take the information from DM/Reporter and make the necessary changes to the accounts or the machines as needed.

DM/Administrator

Network delegation is the process of granting users the ability to perform management functions for a portion of the directory. For example, an Administrator may grant a manager rights to administer users in his own group first. The problem in the past has been that this type of delegation has been granted through creating multiple domains or by adding many people to the Administrators groups.

DM/Administrator mitigates these problems by enabling a specific task-by-task delegation, and even per-user delegation. So, whereas in Windows 2000 you have the flexibility of selecting which organizational unit (OU) and which rights a user should have over certain user accounts and resources, with DM/Administrator you can select a subset of users within an OU or several users across OUs that a user can have rights to administer.

The most effective use DM/Administrator has for a Windows 2000 migration, however, is in maintaining a standard administrative interface before, during, and after the migration has completed. The DM/Administrator software can be used to create a test hierarchy as an overlay structure on top of an existing Windows NT 4.0 network. Multiple, different test hierarchies can be created simultaneously to validate the most optimal hierarchy for the Administrators to use.

Once a hierarchy has been selected, the Administrators can use DM/Administrator to manage the network. This application can be used to delegate administration to other groups, with only the required rights needed, during the migration from NT 4 to Windows 2000.

After the Windows 2000 migration has completed, the DM/Administrator can be used to administer the network. This can prevent the need for delegated Administrators to have access to Administrative consoles such as the Active Directory Users and Computers or Active Directory Sites and Services. If using the DM/Administrator application throughout the migration, Administrators will be familiar with the management tasks since they are executed through the same interface.

DM/Manager

DM/Manager is a migration tool that uses a project approach to migrating to Windows 2000. The DM/Manager lets an Administrator create a project, select the items to be migrated, and then perform the migration.

DM/Manager can import a scripted selection of user objects from other data sources as well. All that is required is a source file and a separate file to describe the source's structure. If populating the Windows 2000 domain with user accounts from a Human Resources database, for example, a delimited text file can be extracted with the user information. Another text file simply describes the location of the fields that will be populated. It does not matter if the user's first-name field is before or after the last-name field, since the second text file will describe its location and place the information into the correct user account attribute in the new Active Directory objects.

During the project, the Administrator may need to view certain aspects of the users or resources. DM/Manager has the capability of looking at these items. Figure 11.9 shows the groups within a domain, both Global and Local groups, and their members.

Figure 11.9 Viewing groups.

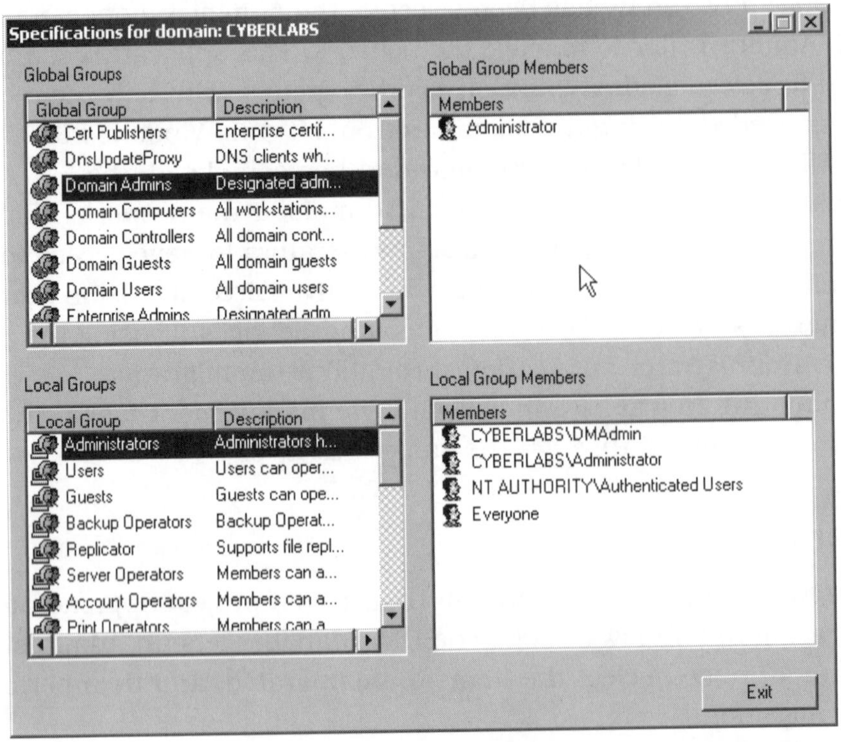

SIDHistory issues exist when migrating a user account. SIDHistory is the new functionality within Windows 2000 to migrate a user account along with the token it originally had to access resources. This feature can shorten the time to migrate since there is no need to reestablish rights to resources for each user that is migrated. The user still has the SID that identifies it as a member of the Windows NT groups, and so the user keeps those rights while those Windows NT domains and groups remain. Problems begin to build when the user is granted new rights to existing resources. If the user eventually is granted the identical rights to the same resources, then the user's token is double what it would otherwise be. What happens if the user account is migrated to another domain and retains the SIDHistory again? The result is *token bloat,* or an excessive number of rights within a single token. Simply viewing resources' Access Control Lists (ACLs) and planning to migrate accordingly can help make a decision whether to retain SIDHistory. DM/Manager enables this process and several others, as shown in Figure 11.10.

Figure 11.10 Viewing the ACLs.

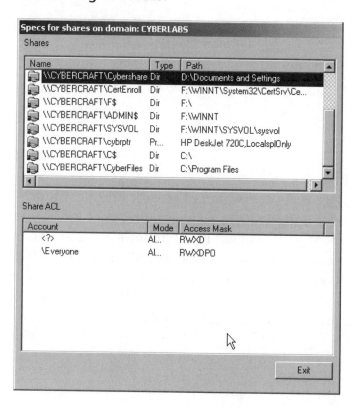

Windows NT did not have any way of migrating Windows NT primary domain controllers (PDCs) or backup domain controllers (BDCs) between domains or, changing their status from DC to server, and vice versa. The only way of doing this, without a third-party tool, was to reinstall the Windows NT Server. When these server changes are needed before the Windows 2000 migration is begun, DM/Manager includes a tool to do this, as shown in Figure 11.11.

Figure 11.11 Migrating Windows NT domain controllers.

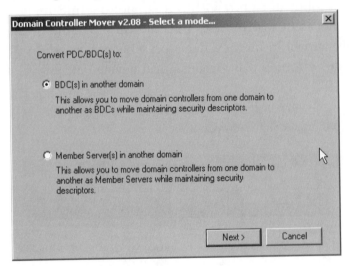

DM/Developer

DM/Developer is for the serious Network Administrator. DM/Developer is basically a software developer kit for cross-directory management with "hooks" into Windows NT and Windows 2000 Active Directory. There are several established scripts that enable the translation of multiple directories into shareable information. DM/Developer can not only script administrative tasks, but it can assist in managing across multiple directory services.

DM/Consolidator

The DM/Consolidator product is new to the Fastlane suite. It makes a complex task, consolidating two servers into a single box, into a simple one. DM/Consolidator enables the Administrator to move data from one server to another, yet enable users to retain the same rights they had on the original server to the data now on the other server. This considerably shortens the time it takes to merge two servers into a single one. Many corporations may discover that one or more of their servers do not meet the minimum hardware compatibility requirements for Windows 2000. In that case, they may decide to simply migrate the data to another server in preparation for upgrading to Windows 2000. DM/Consolidator makes this mission as brief as possible.

SAP

Microsoft works with independent hardware and software vendors in ensuring that their operating system will work with the hardware and software that consumers will be purchasing. SAP is one such software vendor. SAP has a client that locates servers by searching for an application's information stored in the Active Directory database. This client is a directory service interface within SAP's Computing Center Management System (CCMS).

CCMS can monitor and manage R/3 (SAP's highly acclaimed program) and other SAP components. CCMS does not require the Active Directory in order to function, and can work independently as the management application for R/3. However, if a Network Administrator wanted to integrate the R/3 account information as a part of the Active Directory, CCMS can interface to it using LDAP.

Summary

The Active Directory will not stand alone in the network as a directory service. As time goes by, an enterprise may add other applications and systems that integrate with the Active Directory. There may be some directories that cannot be integrated or synchronized directly with the Active Directory. If the network grows with multiple directory services, it may simplify processes to use a metadirectory.

A metadirectory is a database that serves as an index of other directories. This index can propagate data throughout the various directory services. It can synchronize data between them. Microsoft purchased Zoomit Corporation, which produced a metadirectory called VIA. VIA is now a Microsoft metadirectory that can access Active Directory information. In addition to being a standard metadirectory, VIA can apply business rules in order to place owner-ship of data for certain directories over others.

Microsoft has released a directory services client (DSClient) for legacy Windows machines. This client is located on the Windows 2000 CD-ROM. Installing DS Client is simple and quick, and makes a few small changes to the Windows interface, such as the Find fea-ture to enable browsing of the Active Directory.

Cisco has created a direction in partnership with Microsoft to create a directory-enabled network infrastructure. This system is called Cisco Networking Services for Active Directory (CNS/AD). CNS/AD is an extension of the Active Directory that allows infra-structure equipment using the Cisco Internetworking Operating System (IOS) to authenticate to the Active Directory. In addition to authenticating, routers can apply rules, or policies, to traffic that is passing over them depending on either who (which user account) or what (which directory-enabled application) is sending that traffic.

Fastlane Technologies has a suite of applications that can help in preparing for a migration to Windows 2000, and administer the Active Directory after the migration has completed. These applica-tions include:

- **DM/Reporter,** which reports information about the Windows NT or Windows 2000 accounts and resources

- **DM/Administrator,** which can create a test hierarchy as a superstructure over existing Windows NT domains, and can be used to delegate administrative tasks

- **DM/Manager,** which takes a project approach to migrating from Windows NT to Windows 2000

- **DM/Developer,** which scripts tasks even across different directory services

- **DM/Consolidator,** which can merge two servers into a single server

SAP has included a Lightweight Directory Access Protocol (LDAP) directory service interface with its management application for R/3. This interface can access the Active Directory so that R/3 becomes a directory-enabled application.

FAQs

Q: Is Microsoft's Directory Synchronization Service (MSDSS) for Novell NetWare a metadirectory?

A: No. MSDSS is not a metadirectory, since it does not create a centralized index that connects the Active Directory to others. Instead, it works more closely to a multi-master replication scheme, since no single directory owns any data.

Q: Is there a DSClient for Windows 3.1?

A: No. There is no DSClient for Windows 3.1. There is a single DSClient for both Windows 95 and Windows 98, and a DSClient is expected for Windows NT 4.0.

Q: How does CNS/AD change the way in which a user interacts with the network?

A: Users should not experience any overt changes to the way that they work on the network. Instead, CNS/AD works transparently through the Active Directory. The results users see when they access directory-enabled applications or require a higher Quality of Service (QoS) will improve since the users will no longer be required to be in a single place to use that service.

Chapter 12

Active Directory for Windows 2000 Fast-Track

Solutions in this chapter:

- What Active Directory Is, and Why You Need to Know About It

- Important Features and Design Changes

- Industries and Companies Affected by Windows 2000

- Advantages and Disadvantages of Active Directory

- Active Directory Summary Points

Welcome to the fast track. Details and technical secrets can be found elsewhere in this book, but this chapter can get you started on understanding Active Directory today.

What Active Directory Is, and Why You Need to Know About It

The Active Directory is a multi-master database, or directory service, of user accounts and network resources available to all participating Windows 2000 Servers. It is a directory service for a network that can tie user accounts to resources in order to assign access to those resources for those users.

Directory services, in general, have several capabilities:

- Enable single sign-on
- Enable a single point of administration
- Provide an enterprisewide viewpoint of a network

The fact is, directory services can deliver these goals when they are implemented in a network with a limited number of other types of systems. Those systems must be enabled for the directory service in order to access it and use its capabilities. With multiple types of systems ranging from the infrastructure to applications available today, it is likely that there will be multiple systems around and that they all must be managed in different ways.

Microsoft has answered the directory service challenge by creating the Active Directory as a Standards-based system, accessible via the Active Directory Services Interface API and standard protocols such as LDAP (Lightweight Directory Access Protocol).

Windows 2000 is packed with new and important features. The Active Directory itself offers features that are new to the way a Microsoft network works.

- Ability to promote and demote domain controllers (DCs)
- Granular, policy-based administration

- Organizational unit (OU) hierarchy offers decentralized administration
- Improved security

Demote a DC

One of the less touted, but most useful features of an Active Directory DC is the ability to demote a DC to a standard server and promote it into other domains or to the same domain, as needed. Domain restructuring is a powerful and flexible tool for enterprises that experience high growth and change. The same command used to install the Active Directory, DCPROMO.EXE, is the one used to remove it.

Policy-Based Administration

Active Directory also offers policy-based administration using group policies that, although similar to legacy Windows 9x and NT 4 System Policies, can be applied to a hierarchy. The hierarchical organization of resources within Active Directory makes this an exceptionally useful tool, with capabilities that flow down to a granular level. Policy-based administration is part of the Intellimirror feature of Windows 2000, in which group policies are used to establish a user's or a computer's environment when it authenticates to the Active Directory.

Decentralized Administration

The use of OUs enables the Active Directory for decentralized administration within a single domain. In prior versions of NT, people who needed access to a few administrative capabilities were simply added to the Administrators or Domain Admins groups. Or, they were granted an entirely new domain. The result was an extensive list of domains and bloated administrative groups. By enabling administrative delegation to the attribute level on OUs, these previously fractured domains can be merged into one domain and the bloated administrative groups can be reduced.

Improved Security

Active Directory uses Kerberos for a secure method of trusting domains within a forest. Kerberos trusts are bidirectional and transitive. They are automatically created where they are needed within a forest, which subsequently reduces administrative overhead.

Active Directory can be integrated with Certificate Authority (CA) services so that encryption can be used transparently on the network. These features are available within Windows 2000 if they need to be implemented.

Important Features and Design Changes

Several essential features of Windows 2000 are enhanced by the Active Directory that make the Active Directory capable of being an enterprisewide directory service:

- Scalability of forests, domains, OUs, and sites
- Extensibility of the schema
- Multi-master replication
- Intellimirror
- Kerberos trusts
- Use of standard protocols
- Accessibility to resources

Scalability of Forests, Domains, Organizational Units, and Sites

The components of the Active Directory enable it to scale from a small-sized network to a global network. This is accomplished through forests made of domains, domains made of OUs and sites that unite the logical Active Directory with the physical network.

A description of all the components of Active Directory is available in Chapter 1, "Introduction to Active Directory." Installation is discussed in Chapter 2, "Migrating from NT 3.51 and NT 4 to Active Directory."

A forest is the largest division for an Active Directory database. Each separate forest has its own global catalog (GC), schema, and configuration that is shared by all its domains. The schema, which lists all the possible object types for a forest, and configuration, which contains the site topology, are copied onto all DCs. The GC, which is an index of all user accounts and network resources in the forest, is copied onto all designated GC DCs. There can be multiple forests within a network, if there are reasons to have separate GCs, schemas, or configurations.

For details about forests, see Chapter 4, "Designing a Domain Structure," and Chapter 6, "Building Trees and Forests."

Forests are comprised of domains and domain trees. A domain tree is a set of domains that have a contiguous DNS (Domain Naming System) namespace, as shown in Figure 12.1. Each domain is a partition of the Active Directory database. A copy of the domain partition is housed on every DC within a single domain. Each domain partition contains its own users, groups, resources, and set of OUs. A domain is given a single DNS name, such as domain.com.

For more information on DNS naming, and domains, see Chapters 3, 4, and 5.

OUs are containers for objects within the domain partitions. Objects represent user accounts, groups, and resources in the database. Each OU can contain other OUs, nested into a hierarchy, or tree structure. The hierarchy lends itself to many uses, such as delegation of administration and application of group policy. A sample OU hierarchy is illustrated in Figure 12.2.

Figure 12.1 Domain tree.

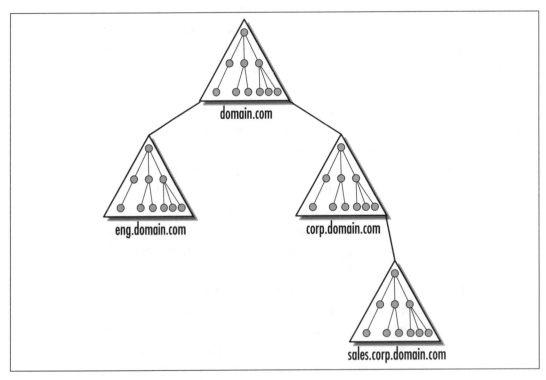

Figure12.2 OU hierarchy.

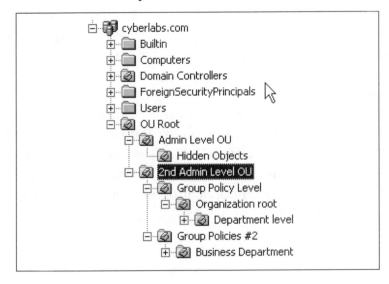

For more information on OUs, check out Chapter 4, "Designing a Domain Structure."

Sites are collections of well-connected IP subnets. Sites are used to localize traffic. When users contact a DC to authenticate or query the Active Directory, they attempt to contact one within their own site. Sites are also used to manage the replication traffic.

Replication traffic is uncompressed within a site. Between sites, replication traffic is compressed. The site topology is automatically created by the Knowledge Consistency Checker (KCC) within a site. It is established as a bidirectional ring of no more than three hops between DCs. When there are more than three DCs, there are additional connections to ensure that the ring replicates updates quickly. Between sites, the site topology must be created by a Network Administrator. This is done by creating sites, site links, site link bridges, and connection objects, and assigning IP subnets to sites in the Active Directory Sites and Services shown in Figure 12.3.

Figure 12.3 The Active Directory Sites and Services console.

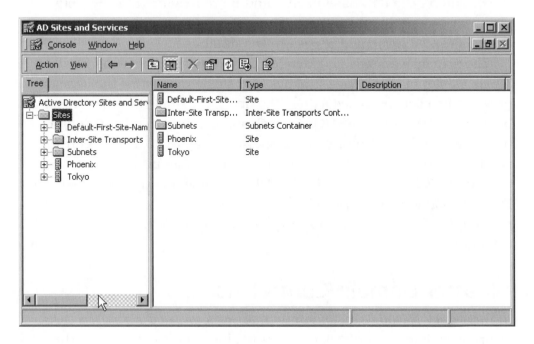

Replication and sites are discussed in Chapter 8, "Planning and Implementing Sites."

Extensibility of the Schema

The schema is the list of the objects that can be created within an Active Directory forest, and the attributes that any objects can have. Objects are user accounts, group accounts, and network resources. Attributes are descriptive values for the objects. For example, a person named Ulysses Ser would be represented by a user object "USER," assuming the naming convention was first initial concatenated with the last name. The first name attribute of "USER" would be "ULYSSES," and the last name attribute of "USER" would be "SER."

The schema can be extended to include new objects and attributes. This extensibility can enable an application or corporation to customize the Active Directory for its uses. The possibilities are endless. If an application for Time and Billing extended the Active Directory, it might add attributes to user objects for a billing rate. Furthermore, the database itself could be represented in the Active Directory by a time and billing object. Then, the users and groups can be granted or denied access to the database.

The schema can only be extended on a designated schema Flexible Single Master of Operations (FSMO). The single master for the schema prevents conflicts from occurring. The first DC installed in the forest is, by default, the schema FSMO. The schema can be extended through the Schema Administrator console shown in Figure 12.4. This console is not available by default on a DC; instead, it must be added later by executing REGSVR3Z SCHMMGMT.DLL and opening up the console in the Microsoft Management Console.

Chapter 7, "Modifying the Schema," discusses the schema and extending it.

Multi-Master Domain Controllers

In the legacy NT domains, each domain was granted a single PDC, or primary domain controller, which held a read/write copy of the Security Account Manager (SAM). All other servers that participated

Figure 12.4 Schema console.

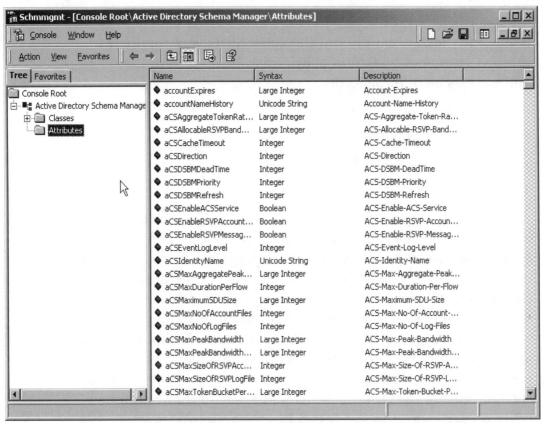

as DCs were BDCs, or backup domain controllers, which held read-only copies of the SAM. Any changes that must be made to the security database are confined to a PDC in this arrangement. BDCs simply offer an authentication "boost" when they are placed close to users who are logging on. If a problem occurs that forces the PDC to not be accessible, no one can change passwords or add computers to the network, or execute any functions that make changes to the domain's SAM until one of the BDCs is promoted to a PDC or the PDC is brought back online. Active Directory, instead, makes all DCs equal, and changes can be made on any DC. After a change is made, the Active Directory synchronizes all the DCs using replication.

Intellimirror

Intellimirror is a feature in which the user's environment and files intelligently follow him around the network. This is conducted through group policy. Group policies can be applied to the following, and are executed in this order:

- Local group policy
- Site group policy
- Domain group policy
- OU group policy

The Local group policy exists on the local computer. Site group policies are linked to a site but exist on a single domain, and the site must contact that domain in order to execute the policy. Domain group policies are applied to a single domain. OU group policies are applied to an OU. A user will execute group policies in each OU from the top of the domain down to the OU where his own account is located.

Each group policy consists of two portions, a User configuration and a Computer configuration. When a workstation first authenticates to the Active Directory, Active Directory applies the Computer configuration of the group policies that apply to that computer. When a user logs on to the Active Directory, Active Directory applies the User configuration of the group policies that apply to that user. Even though the group policies may be housed together, they are applied independently. This independence enables a user's environment to intelligently follow him around the network.

The remaining part of Intellimirror is the ability to have redirected folders. This means that a user can transparently access files from a folder that appears to be local but is actually located on a network server. Those files can be backed up, and can be moved around the network without the interupting the user's daily productivity. Offline folders further enable the user to retain a copy of those files locally, which means that remote users can use network files when they are disconnected from the network.

The Group Policy Editor is used to create and edit group policies. This console is illustrated in Figure 12.5.

Figure 12.5 Group Policy Editor.

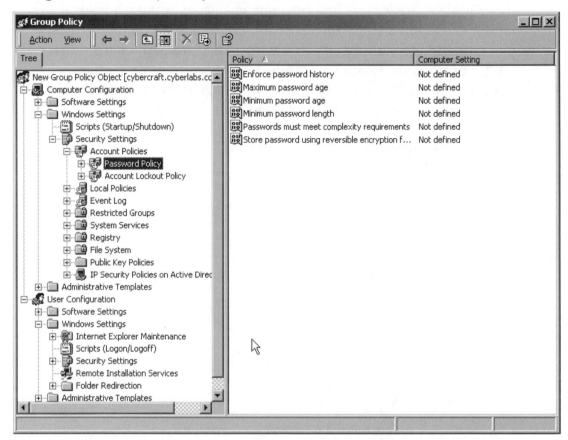

More about Intellimirror's group policy is available in Chapter 9, "Intellimirror."

Kerberos Trusts

Kerberos is an open-standard security protocol developed for the Internet. It provides a network authentication service. The Active Directory uses Kerberos to verify the identity of users and network resources. Instead of relying on the network operating system or trusted IP addresses to authenticate the users and resources, Kerberos uses credentials to validate the identity and authenticate the user or resource to the network.

This process is used between domains through Kerberos trust relationships. Unlike legacy trust relationships (which were made explicitly and were only in a single direction and nontransitive), Kerberos trusts are created automatically within a forest. They are both bidirectional and transitive. For example, if a forest consisted of three domains—root.com, trunk.root.com, and tree.com—a kerberos trust would be created between tree.com and root.com, as shown in Figure 12.6.

Figure 12.6 Transitive Kerberos trusts.

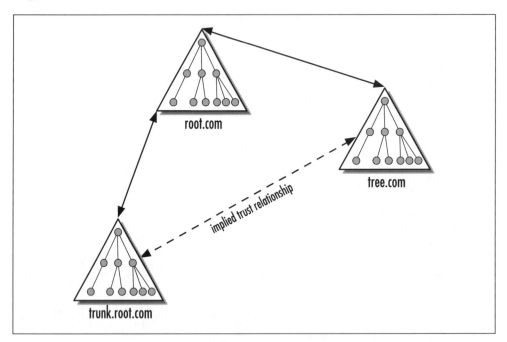

Because the trusts are transitive, it is implied that trunk.root.com and tree.com trust each other. This enables users in either domain to access resources in the other domain, but only if they have been granted access to those resources. In order to view the trust relationships for the Active Directory, use the Active Directory Domains and Trusts console shown in Figure 12.7. Domains and trusts are described in Chapter 6.

Figure 12.7 Active Directory Domains and Trusts console.

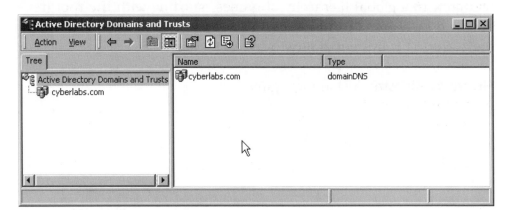

Use of Standard Protocols

Microsoft has made Windows 2000 and the Active Directory Internet-ready by integrating the TCP/IP protocol stack. This stack was originally created for ARPANET and commonly made part of the UNIX operating system. Since ARPANET evolved into the Internet, TCP/IP is now the most widely used, open-standard protocol stack in the world.

Two of the protocols from the TCP/IP protocol stack that are specifically used with Active Directory are LDAP and DNS.

LDAP is a protocol that enables clients to access information within a directory service. LDAP was created after X.500, a directory service standard protocol, because of the high overhead and subsequent slow response of "heavy" X.500 clients. Hence the name "lightweight." LDAP clients are able to access the Active Directory, which opens the Active Directory up to clients other than those that access Windows 2000 in a standard fashion.

DNS is a hierarchical naming system for domains. Since each computer is granted an IP address, and since IP addresses are difficult to remember, names were given to computers to make it easier for users to find and connect to resources. The naming system grew to a global hierarchy of names, starting with the root (represented by a dot ".") and adding new domains and subdomains thereafter. This system is illustrated in Figure 12.8.

Figure 12.8 Domain Naming System.

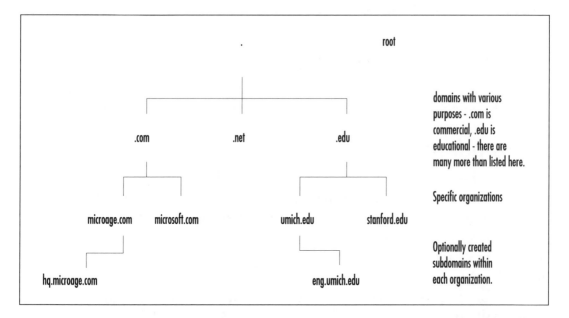

DNS is used by the Active Directory as a locator service. It holds service records indicating the DCs on the network. Not only do computers use DNS to locate resources, when DCs need to contact other DCs, they use DNS. The Active Directory requires DNS to exist on the network or else it will not function correctly.

DNS naming is discussed in Chapter 3 "Active Directory Naming Strategies."

Accessibility of Resources

The Active Directory enables resources to be accessible to users on the network. Whereas resources such as files and printers are available through standard sharing, the Active Directory allows the resources to be organized and given searchable descriptions.

Therefore, if a user is searching for a folder created for the Accounting department, the user can search with the word "Accounting" and find appropriate resources. These capabilities are not present in standard network shares. The search dialog is depicted in Figure 12.9.

Figure 12.9 Searching for resources in the Active Directory.

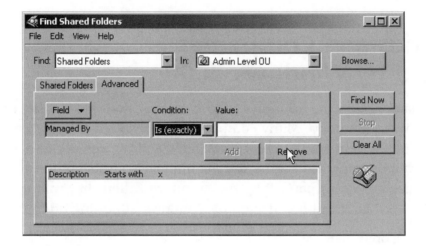

See Chapter 10, "Publishing," for more information on publishing Active Directory resources.

The Active Directory is capable of being integrated with other applications. This can be accomplished through its extensibility and common protocols and interfaces. Accessing the Active Directory is demonstrated by

- Metadirectories such as Microsoft's VIA
- Schema extensions such as Cisco Networking Services
- Management utilities such as FastLane's DM/Suite
- Integrated databases such as SAP's R/3

To find out more about plugging in, see Chapter 11, "Plugging into Active Directory."

Resource accessibility is not merely the availability of resources and capability of plugging into the Active Directory, it is also the ability to access resources fairly quickly after a disaster has occurred. Many features of Windows 2000 support the recovery of the Active Directory and shared resources. These range from back-ups to the file replication system, from UPS support to RAID.

Disaster recovery issues are described in Chapter 13, "Disaster Recovery for Active Directory."

Industries and Companies Affected by Windows 2000

It is hard to imagine an industry or company that will not be affect-ed by Windows 2000. Many companies have waited to install a new operating system simply because Windows 2000 was announced. They will be impacted by the new technology's performance and administrative ease caused by the standardization that rolling it out will bring. Many will be affected by Windows 2000, including:

- Consumers
- Technology vendors and partners
- Consultants and integrators
- Competitors
- Customers

Technology Vendors and Partners

Both hardware and software manufacturers were involved with the creation of Windows 2000 since it was first conceived as Windows NT v5.0. The need for technology partners is due mainly to the oper-ating system needing to support the hardware and applications that would potentially be used on it.

3Com is a hardware manufacturer that worked closely with Microsoft. Hardware manufacturers in general only benefit by ensuring that their products work with a new operating system. 3Com develops many types of technologies, but one of their mainstays is their connectivity equipment. They make routers, hubs, switches, modems, and network interface cards (NICs), among other things. 3Com has had to ensure that the drivers for their hardware are compatible with Windows 2000. If a NIC driver is not compatible, a server would not be able to communicate on the network. In addition, 3com creates NICs that contain Pre-eXecute boot Environment (PXE) capabilities. They worked with Microsoft to ensure that Windows 2000's Remote Installation Service would function with their NICs.

FastLane Technologies is an Independent Software Vendor (ISV). They have developed management utilities for Windows NT. With the advent of Windows 2000, FastLane has created new management utilities and upgraded existing utilities for Windows 2000. Many ISVs are doing either or both in preparation for the change in users' technology needs due to their use of Windows 2000.

Cisco and Microsoft announced a partnership specifically around Active Directory. This partnership is unusual since infrastructure has historically been separated from the higher-level networking applications. This partnership is strictly due to the Windows 2000 directory service implementation.

Competitors

There are several competitors for Windows 2000 Active Directory; Novell, RedHat, and Netscape all come to mind.

Novell has experienced a long-time reputation of having a best-in-class directory service (Novell Directory Services, or NDS) and a solid networking operating system (NetWare). There is clear competition between Windows 2000 Server and NetWare for the network operating system market, and that competition is made more fierce with the introduction of Microsoft's Active Directory. There are some white papers on both Novell's (www.novell.com) and Microsoft's (www.microsoft.com) Web sites that compare NDS to Active Directory.

There is also another, friendlier side of this competition. Both Microsoft and Novell seem to realize that they will most likely have customers with integrated networks of both network operating systems. Novell has utilized the Active Directory Services Interface (ADSI) for interoperability, and Microsoft has created Directory Synchronization Services (MSDSS) for NetWare.

Red Hat develops Linux, an open-source version of UNIX. Linux has been positioned as a competitor for Windows NT. Even though there are directory services for various UNIX versions, the position that Linux holds will be somewhat tenuous unless a comparable directory service is created for it.

Netscape has developed a directory service for its Internet suite of applications. Netscape's directory service is a direct competitor for Active Directory, since the Active Directory is Internet-ready.

It will be interesting to see what happens as the competition continues among these vendors!

Customers

Microsoft created two similar programs, the Rapid Deployment Program (RDP) and the Joint Deployment Program (JDP). Both of these programs require active involvement with customers and resellers. Customers are given beta copies of software and, with their reseller, they begin the planning process for deploying Windows 2000 in their networks. All are granted a beta ID and access to newsgroups discussing the Windows 2000 beta software and issues.

The projects are closely watched by Microsoft. Microsoft learns about real-world client requirements and discovers challenges that clients face when rolling out the software. This learning experience is shared with all RDP or JDP members through conferences, which provide large learning labs and university-like lectures about various features and case studies.

Even those customers who do not participate in such programs will benefit from them. The experience is captured, and responses to the challenges are prepared for customers who implement Windows 2000 later on.

And . . . Microsoft Itself

Microsoft was immensely affected by its own development of Windows 2000 Server and Professional. Not only was the programming project one of the most extensive (with contributions from literally hundreds of programmers and partners over a series of years) for an operating system, but Microsoft followed it up by, well, eating its own dog food.

Microsoft was one of the first corporations to run a pure Windows 2000 environment in production. In fact, Microsoft upgraded the servers in its Redmond domain to Windows 2000 Server beta 3 as a production test of its solidity. The fact that Microsoft would place thousands of users on a system that had not completed its programming cycle says a lot!

Advantages and Disadvantages of Active Directory

Rarely will anyone find a perfect solution in any technology. There will always be adjustments and changes, or resistance from users during its implementation. People are the users of the technology, and they will either embrace new technology or resent it—and have many reasons to do so. Let's take a look at what could possibly be a benefit or a challenge with Active Directory.

Advantages with the Active Directory

If you have a current Windows NT network, or one in which all the servers are stand-alone, the Active Directory is a huge advantage for you. It will provide a single location for administration of the network, and will automate the way domains and servers communicate. Users will have a single logon to the network and enhanced security when they access resources. Since Active Directory can be implemented with little interruption to the user's view of the network, users will have an easy transition to the new system.

An obvious advantage to the Active Directory for anyone who has implemented Windows NT Servers is the ability to easily promote and demote DCs. Legacy NT Servers must be completely reinstalled if they need to be promoted to DCs or demoted to servers. With Windows 2000, Active Directory DCs can be promoted and demoted as required by executing DCPROMO.EXE.

For anyone with Windows 2000 Professional workstations, using the Active Directory offers a way to manage those workstations with group policies. This can reduce the overall cost of managing the network.

The hierarchical tree is a flexible, intuitive model for network resource organization. Not only is this superior to a flat container for resources, but it can be used to delegate administration. This offers existing Windows NT networks the ability to restructure into a smaller number of domains, thus reducing management costs.

The Active Directory is scalable and enables growth for organization's. It is flexible enough to be structured for any organization's requirements. Domains can contain millions of objects, rather than thousands, and can be automatically trusted in a forest using secure Kerberos trusts.

Problems with the Active Directory

Integration with Windows 2000 is a challenge for many organizations with existing networks. If a network consists mainly of Novell NetWare or UNIX servers, implementing Windows 2000 may be difficult to accomplish. One of the reasons is that the Active Directory cannot be separated from Windows 2000 and implemented as a separate product. If intending to implement Active Directory, at least one Windows 2000 DC must exist. And, if intending to use it to organize all resources, a method of synchronization or a metadirectory must be implemented for all the other network operating systems on the network.

Little management for non-Windows clients is a problem. Group policies are Windows-centric. If an organization has a significant percentage of Macintosh, UNIX, or other clients, the Active Directory will not add many benefits to managing clients or users.

Even for client management of Windows workstations, the Active Directory does not offer an integrated method of remotely controlling the workstation for administrative purposes. To do this, other software products must be installed.

The architecture for Windows 2000 intended to enable a single forest for any organization. The problem with it, however, is that any need to have separate schemas or GCs will force additional forests on the network. This will further add an incremental amount of network traffic and administrative overhead.

Forests and domains cannot be easily merged. If a corporation purchases another corporation that has an Active Directory forest, it will need to undergo a complete migration project in order to combine both forests into a single forest. This type of restructuring, while doable, is not a simple task.

Many existing DNS servers may not meet requirements for Active Directory to function. The Active Directory requires Service Resource Records to be supported by the DNS servers. This is a relatively new feature for DNS. Many organizations use UNIX BIND or other DNS servers that do not support this feature, and may wish to continue using their DNS servers. To implement Active Directory, this will not work and there may be a conflict, especially if one group manages DNS servers and another group manages the network file, Web, and print servers.

New technology implementations usually result in changing the way people do things. In essence, a new technology project is always a form of business process reengineering, and business process reengineering always meets some resistance. Users are not comfortable with new ways of doing things. In a way, they are faced with the idea that the way they did business before was not "as good" as the new process, and if they were proud of their work, it can be somewhat demoralizing. Implementing Active Directory, luckily, will have little impact on end users unless the project is combined with a rollout of Windows 2000 Professional. However, it will greatly impact the Network Administrators and any users who were previously granted administrative authority. If existing domains are restructured, Administrators who previously were in charge of their own domain will now be faced with sharing or only having authority over a portion of a domain.

These are major challenges when implementing Active Directory, and they should be considered thoroughly before deploying the new systems.

Active Directory Summary Points

The Active Directory is a directory service for Windows 2000 Server, and provides a hierarchical, extensible system to organize and store user accounts and resources.

This is an important upgrade for the legacy Windows NT domain architecture. The new architecture consists of a hierarchy of domains, using DNS (Domain Naming System) names, that are implemented within a forest. A forest forms the boundary for domains that share a common schema, configuration and global catalog (GC). Domains are database partitions of user accounts and network resource objects. They are similar to legacy domains except they are able to contain more objects and have multi-master domain controllers (DCs). Within each domain, the Administrator can create a hierarchy of organizational units (OUs). This hierarchy can be used to delegate administration, hide objects, apply group policies, and organize objects. Sites are provided as a method of optimizing network traffic.

The Active Directory database contains an extensible schema, which is a listing of the types of objects contained within it. This enables the Active Directory to respond to business requirements of organizations and to integrate with applications.

Active Directory uses a standard set of protocols based on the TCP/IP protocol stack, and is Internet-ready. These protocols include LDAP and DNS.

There are both advantages and disadvantages to the Active Directory. Clients will find challenges in implementing a new technology, but many will also find advantages in reducing administrative overhead.

FAQs

Q: How does DNS interact with Active Directory clients?

A: The client workstation contacts a DNS server. The DNS server locates domain controllers (DCs) within the client's domain. The client is provided with a DC that also exists within the client's site, if available. The client then contacts the DC. The DC authenticates the client to the Active Directory. When the user logs on to the workstation, the process repeats except that the Active Directory provides the location of the user's domain if it is different from that of the client workstation's domain. When either a client workstation or a user cannot contact a DNS server, it won't be able to find its DC, and will subsequently be denied access to the network.

Q: Should we install Active Directory now, or should we wait until the technology has matured?

A: This is dependent completely on your business requirements and your existing network. If this is a question that you cannot answer immediately by yourself, it may be best to have a consultant review your network and your business requirements with you and determine the best time and deployment strategy for you. However, if you have already decided that you will be implementing Active Directory but do not know exactly when to start, it is probably best to begin a planning project and a pilot deployment of the software as soon as you are able. This will only make a full deployment more successful because of your experience with the Active Directory.

Chapter 13

Disaster Recovery for Active Directory

Solutions in this chapter:

- Modeling a Site to Enable Recovery
- Using Windows 2000 Features to Avoid Disasters
- Backing Up a Domain Controller
- Restoring the Active Directory

Disasters come in many forms. They can range from a corruption of mission-critical data to a total destruction of a company's sole office building along with all systems within it. Regardless of the extent of the destruction, the end result is an interruption in business along with some loss of revenue.

Introduction

Not only is there a range for disasters, there is also a range for disaster recovery plans. Generally, these can extend from a plan to store backup tapes offsite to a plan to move critical personnel to a hot standby site that is ready to begin working immediately upon their arrival. When developing your disaster recovery plan, you must estimate the likelihood of a disaster and the scope of destruction that a disaster might have. It may be more likely that you will experience a virus spread by e-mail than a hurricane if your office is located in a desert and you are connected to the Internet. But don't dismiss the possibility of natural disasters; Nature has its own way of making itself known.

For example, if your building is located in an area that experiences hurricanes, establish a plan that will mitigate the disastrous effects of a hurricane and that is also realistically in line with the loss of revenue that may occur. If you have a small branch office that generates $30,000 profit per month, the plan should not exceed the revenue-generating potential of the office over a period of time during which the disaster's effects could be fixed. If the hurricane damage can be repaired within three months, then the disaster recovery plan should not cost more than $90,000 to implement, since it would effectively be saving only that much. However, if the office is a multimillion-dollar generating campus with hundreds of employees, then a more extensive disaster recovery plan can be executed.

For further information on general disaster recovery techniques and planning best practices, check out these Web sites:

- http://admin5.hsc.uth.tmc.edu/ishome/dr/drwhy.html
- http://www.paaet.edu.kw/Info/HomePage/shaheen/ security.htm
- http://www.disaster-survival.com/Planning_Overview.html

Modeling Sites with Disaster Recovery in Mind

When planning Active Directory, keep disaster recovery preparation in mind. Sites offer a clear enabler of disaster recovery if their structure is implemented according to your disaster recovery plan. Let me explain: If there is a planned cold standby or hot standby office (cold standby offices are available to begin business after being set up and data and personnel have been transferred to them, and hot standby offices have recent data and available personnel to staff them should an emergency take place), an Active Directory structure can be implemented in that office with an up-to-date copy of all identity information and resource information simply by placing appropriate DNS, DHCP, Global Catalog (GC) and domain controller (DC) servers for each domain that will use that standby site in addition to a link from the production network to the standby site.

For instance, fobya.com is run by a company that has planned a standby site for disaster recovery. The Network Administrator establishes two sites within the fobya.com domain, one for the main office and one for the standby office. The company that sponsors the standby office establishes a T1 line between fobya.com and their data storage warehouse that houses the fobya.com standby servers. For the standby site, fobya.com places a server that manages DNS and DHCP, and a second server that acts as a DC and GC server. The fobya.com office maintains several servers and ships data backups to the warehouse on a weekly basis. The Administrator then sets replication to occur every 30 minutes because the servers can handle the extra processing and there is no other data traveling across the site link. The configuration is similar to Figure 13.1.

Figure 13.1 fobya.com single-domain site model for disaster recovery.

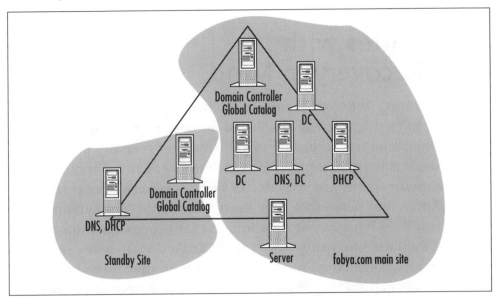

Dealing with a single production office means that a Network Administrator must manage to a single point of failure. But what happens if fobya.com grows to include multiple domains placed around the globe? Figure 13.2 shows the domain configuration for fobya.com after it has merged with other companies and become a global entity. In the new fobya.com forest, each domain exists in a separate country.

If the Network Administrator creates a second recovery site for each of the domains, he or she will need to establish two links from that recovery site: one to the domain that will be recovered, and a second link to some other site. The reason for the dual links is that if a site crashes, the standby site will lose its link to the forest unless it has that second link.

Because the sites are in different countries, the likelihood of a disaster wiping out more than one site is extremely small. Using

Figure 13.2 fobya.com global site and domain configuration.

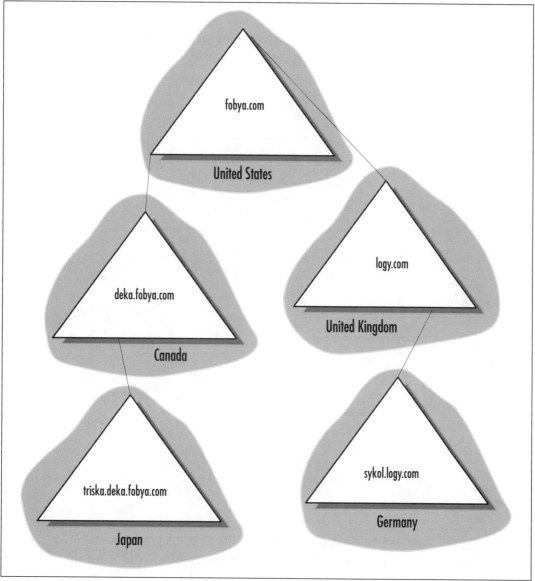

standby sites for each domain may not be feasible. Instead, the Network Administrator can configure sites in a way that provides redundancy and backup of the domain information in a different site. The Network Administrator can place a DC from one domain into a site that houses most of another domain. The result would be similar to Figure 13.3.

Figure 13.3 Modeling multiple domains and sites for disaster recovery.

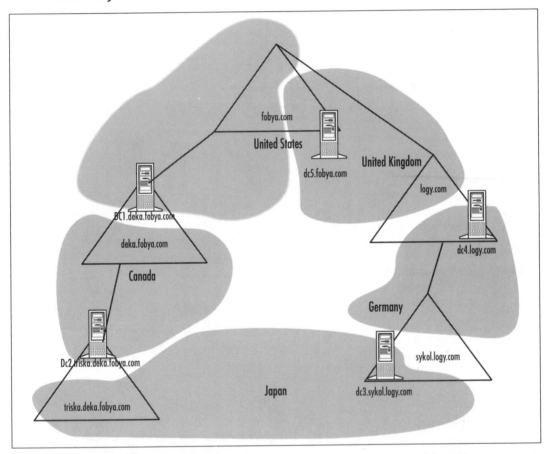

Figure 13.3 ensures that the destruction of a single location, such as Japan, would not cause a complete loss of all the domain information for the triska.deka.fobya.com domain. There will be an incremental increase in traffic between sites when domains span sites, since more data (from the domain partition) than the GC, schema, and configuration will be traveling across the wire.

Avoiding Disasters

Many small disasters can be avoided through effective implementation of Windows 2000 features along with the appropriate hardware to support those features. Disaster avoidance can diminish the consequences of disasters. The following items contribute to disaster avoidance and recovery:

- Uninterruptible Power Supply (UPS)
- Redundant Array of Inexpensive Disks (RAID)
- Daily backup of data to removable media
- Offsite storage of removable media
- Clustered servers
- Antivirus

Universal Power Source

A UPS provides power if an electrical failure occurs. Windows 2000 supports UPS power supplies. A UPS is added by configuring the UPS service in the Power Options applet within Control Panel. Most UPS manufacturers create their own UPS management programs. The basic UPS features supported by the Windows 2000 UPS service areas follows:

- Detect power failures
- Detect low battery
- Shutdown from the UPS

When a UPS detects a power failure, it notifies the Windows 2000 Server, usually via a serial cable connected to the server's com1 or com2 port. Windows 2000 maintains a configuration for the UPS that tells it how to act in the event of a power failure. In most cases, a UPS should be used to shut the server down in such a way that it will not cause data corruption, rather than to provide continuous power until the battery is exhausted.

RAID

There are several versions of RAID, the following being the most common:

- **RAID 0:** A striped disk array without fault tolerance and requires a minimum of 2 drives.
- **RAID 1:** Mirroring, which requires two disks.
- **RAID 5:** Striped data with parity across disks, which requires three or more disks.

These are all configurable through Windows 2000 software or through hardware from manufacturers. A manufacturer's hardware RAID solution is recommended because it offloads processing and management from the operating system to a separate piece of hardware in the server. If you want to implement mirroring RAID 1 or software RAID 5 in Windows 2000, use the Computer Management utility in the Administrative Tools menu. The disk configuration can be found under Storage\Disk Management, as shown in Figure 13.4.

In order to implement software RAID 5, the disks must be in dynamic mode. If they are not, right-click each disk and select Upgrade to Dynamic Disk from the popup menu. RAID 5 volumes are created by clicking on the dynamic disk's unallocated space and selecting "Create volume" from the popup menu, and then following the dialog sequence through the RAID 5 volume creation path.

A RAID 5 array appears as a Failed Redundancy if one of its disks is offline, missing, or has errors. In order to recover a failed RAID 5 volume, first attempt to repair the disk by right-clicking it and selecting Reactivate Disk. If the disk is unable to be recovered, remove it from the system and replace it with a new disk. Then right-click the failed disk's RAID 5 volume and select Repair Volume from the menu. Select the new disk from the dialog, and click Oĸ. The array should be recovered.

Figure 13.4 Configuring disks in the Computer Management console.

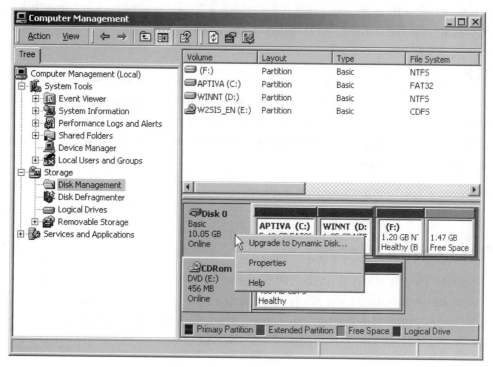

Clustering

Clustering is a group of independent servers called nodes that work together to provide fault tolerance to any single system failure within the group. There are two requirements to implementing clustering:

- The software and hardware that creates a cluster
- The software that manages the cluster

If there is a failure of one server in a cluster, a different server will continue to provide network services after a failover sequence is completed.

Windows 2000 Advance Server supports clustering. This can be deployed with the Windows 2000 cluster services or with a manufacturer's application. When the Windows 2000 clustering is installed, a new program utility is added to the Administrative Tools menu called Cluster Administrator. A command-line utility called cluster.exe will also manage the server. Clustering is recommended for systems that must be available on a 24 x 7 basis.

NOTE

Whenever possible, use hardware-based fault tolerance solutions. Manufacturers provide extended capabilities that increase the fault tolerance and reduce the performance hit that implementing such solutions may cause.

File Replication Service

The File Replication Service (FRS) is a fault-tolerant system automatically configured on each DC. Since it is dependent upon DCs, you must have the Active Directory installed to use it. FRS automatically replicates the contents of the SYSVOL share between all DCs.

Distributed File Service (Dfs)

Dfs offers the capability of creating a fault-tolerant root within the Active Directory and adding up to 128 replicas across the network. A redundant system can only be implemented when the fault-tolerant Active Directory root is used; a standalone Dfs implementation cannot offer any redundancy. The Dfs utility is shown in Figure 13.5.

Figure 13.5 Dfs console.

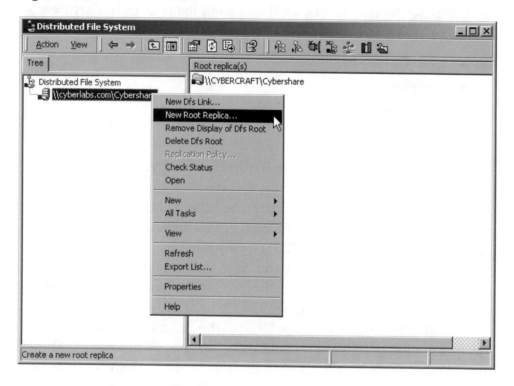

The Active Directory Database File Structure

Each DC contains a set of files that hold its portion of the Active Directory. The file structure is a fault-tolerant transaction-based database, which is based on ESE (Extensible Storage Engine). Transactions occur in a short sequence of actions:

1. The Administrator creates an object, which initiates the transaction.
2. The transaction is written to a log file.
3. The transaction is then committed to a database buffer.
4. The transaction is completed when the database on the disk is written.

Several files are involved in this process. The NTDS.DIT file is the database file that stores all the objects for that DC's partition of the Active Directory. There are also several log files:

- Transaction logs
- Checkpoints
- Reserved logs
- Patch files

Transaction log files can reach 10MB in size. A current transaction log, called edb.log, is used until it reaches the 10MB limit. At that point, the log is saved as a separate file, edb00001.log—where the numerical position of the filename is incremented as new full logfiles are saved—and the edb.log is emptied for new transactions. Circular logging will not create the past transaction log files, such as edb00001.log, edb00002.log, and so on. Instead, it will rewrite over the current transaction log. The circular logging can be turned on to reduce the number of log files on the hard drive. Avoid circular logging as a practice. The default behavior of Windows 2000 Active Directory is to not execute circular logging. However, you can change the default behavior through a registry key:

`HKLM\CurrentControlSet\Services\NTDS\Parameters\Circular Logging`

Set the circular logging to a 0 to turn circular logging off, and to a 1 to turn circular logging on.

There is a checkpoint file named edb.chk, which is stored in the same directory as NTDS.DIT. This file holds the pointers to the transactions in the transaction logs that have actually been written to the database. The file literally checks the point at which the log file and the database are consistent.

Two reserved log files, res1.log and res2.log, are also placed in the same directory as NTDS.DIT. These files are each 10MB in size and will become log files if there is not enough space on the disk to create a new edb.log file. Any outstanding transactions are copied from memory into the reserved logs and then the Active Directory will shut down with an "out of disk space" error.

Patch files are used to track transactions written to the Active Directory database during backup. Split transactions are those that are written across multiple database pages. A split transaction can be written to a portion of the Active Directory database that has already been backed up. The backup process is as follows:

1. A patch file with a .pat extension is created for the current database written to disk.

2. Backup begins.

3. Active Directory split transactions are written both to the database and to the patch file.

4. The backup writes the patch file to tape.

5. The patch file is deleted.

Do not delete log files. The Active Directory will automatically run a Garbage Collection process to delete unused objects, delete unused files, and defragment the database. When files are manually deleted, the Active Directory can become corrupted. Garbage collection will take place on a 12-hour interval basis.

Offline database management is performed with the NTDSUtil.exe program. To run the offline database tool, start the server and at the initial boot menu screen press F8. Select the Directory Services Repair Mode option, and then run the ntdsutil.exe tool.

Backup

Windows 2000 has a Backup utility program found in the Programs\Accessories\System Tools menu. This utility is shown in Figure 13.6.

The Backup utility provides the following features:

- Data backup of files, folders, Active Directory, and system information

- Scheduled backups

- Storage of backup data on networked systems and removable media

- Data and Active Directory restoration
- Emergency repair disk creation

Figure 13.6 Backup.

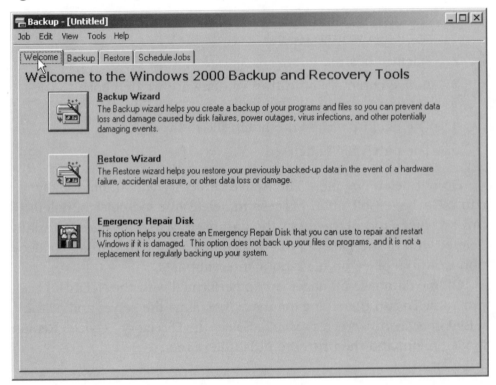

To create a backup job, you will select the files and folders to back up, the location to place the backed up data on, and options such as data verification or compression of the data. One of the new items in the Backup utility is the System State data. System State data refers to the server's registry, component services Class Registration database (storing COM data), startup files, Certificate services data, Active Directory, and SYSVOL. Whenever creating a backup that is intended to be able to repair a server, select the System State in addition to the data that is being backed up. The System State data is selected by checking it off, as shown in Figure 13.7.

Figure 13.7 Checking off System State data.

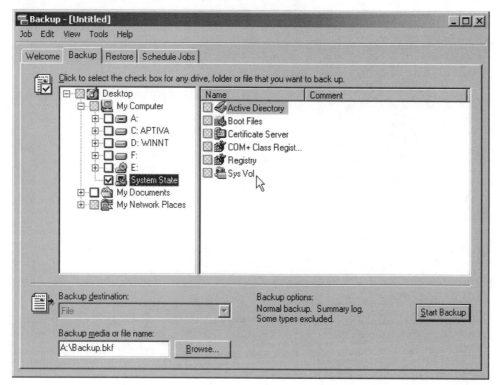

The Backup utility does support a scheduled backup. This is a common feature in many backup utilities, where a backup automatically executes after standard business hours and is completed when Administrators return. Scheduling backups to occur after standard business hours reduces the impact to network performance that a backup may cause.

Creating an Emergency Repair Disk

In Windows 2000, the emergency repair disk is included as a backup option, rather than a separate application. Emergency repair disks contain minimal system data, although typically enough to get a downed server to restart. To create an emergency repair disk, select the option in the Backup utility as shown in Figure 13.8. The Backup utility will prompt for a diskette to be placed in the default drive A:.

Figure 13.8 Create an Emergency Repair Disk.

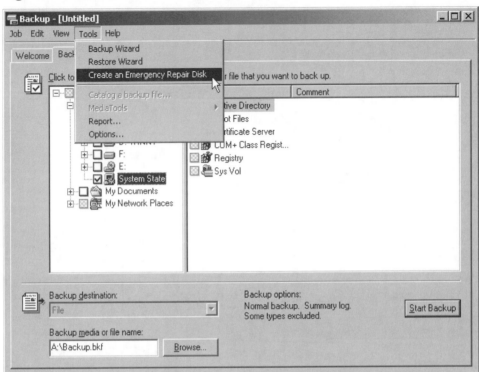

Recovering a Failed Domain Controller

When a DC fails, there is typically more to be restored than just files and folders. There are two issues involved:

- Transactions may not have been written to disk, but were written to log files for the Active Directory.

- Data in the Active Directory databases on other DCs may have had additional changes since the failure.

This means that the log files must be used to bring the written transactions to a current state. It also means that when the Active Directory database is brought online, it must be synchronized with the rest of the domain and forest. To ensure that this happens, make certain to restore the System State data. After that is restored, an automatic consistency check occurs on the DC's Active Directory database and then indexes it. After that, replication takes place and the Active Directory is updated with the latest information, and file replication services restore the latest data versions from other DCs.

> **WARNING**
>
> If the DC has a corrupted Active Directory database, you must use the Directory Services Restore Mode startup option before restoring the System State data.

Authoritative Restore of Deleted Objects

It is going to happen at some point. Someone will delete an organizational unit (OU) filled with user accounts or other objects. It will be an accident, of course, but an accident that you will need to fix quickly. The place to start is restoring your last backup. But there will be a problem...

When you restore deleted objects from the Active Directory, those objects will be deleted—actually become tombstones—the next time replication takes place. The reason that this happens is that the objects have been marked for deletion in another DC's replica of the Active Directory, and replication will redelete them in the database you just restored. This is normally the behavior you want, except in the case of accidents.

To prevent this behavior, you can execute an authoritative restore. This process will enable the objects that are restored to resist deletion when replication occurs. Each object that is restored in this manner will be marked as "authoritative." The authoritative attribute prevails over the tombstone attribute when replication next occurs. To perform this operation:

1. Boot the computer.
2. At the startup screen, press F8 for Advanced startup options.
3. Select Directory Services Restore mode.

4. Restore the System State data of a backup that contains the objects that you want to restore.

5. After restoration has finished, close Backup.

6. Run NTDSUtil.exe.

7. Type **authoritative restore** at the prompt.

8. Type **restore subtree** and the distinguished name of the object or OU (for example, restore subtree ou=labs,ou=eng,dc=microage,dc=com).

9. Exit the NTDSUtil program and restart the computer normally.

Startup Options

There are several options available when Windows 2000 starts. These can assist in returning a failed server to normal operations in different ways. Table 13.1 lists the startup options.

Table 13.1 Startup Modes

Startup Option	Function	Purpose
Debugging Mode	Sends the debug data to another computer through a serial cable.	Only use this when you need to do high-level debugging or are sending a report to a debugging expert.
Directory Services Restore mode	Allows restoring of the Active Directory and SYSVOL files.	Use this whenever you need to do offline defragmenting of the NTDS.DIT file using the NTDSUtil.exe utility, or when you need to restore or repair the Active Directory on a DC.
Enable Boot Logging	Creates an ntbtlog.txt file in the systemroot showing all device drivers loaded during startup.	Use this if you want to find out which device drivers are loading. This is helpful if you suspect one of them is causing problems on the server.

Continued

Startup Option	Function	Purpose
Enable VGA Mode	Runs Windows 2000 using a standard VGA driver.	Use this if you accidentally selected the wrong display driver and it will no longer load properly. When in this mode, you can change the display driver and then test it by rebooting normally.
Last Known Good Configuration	Starts up Windows 2000 with the last configuration that a full logon was executed on.	Use this if you changed the server's configuration and the server will no longer get to the point of a logon screen. Or, if you have reached the logon screen, but really don't want to save your changes, reboot instead of logging on and select this option.
Safe Mode	Runs Windows 2000 with the most basic drivers, creates a log file.	Use this if the server will not function properly and you suspect a device driver of some type is causing the problem. If it starts properly in Safe Mode, it is most likely a new device driver.
Safe Mode with Command Prompt	Runs Windows 2000 with the most basic drivers at a command prompt rather than the GUI, creates a log file.	Use this if you want to change that device driver by copying over a file from a command prompt. This option is rather handy.
Safe Mode with Networking	Runs Windows 2000 with the most basic drivers, loads networking drivers, creates a log file.	Use this if you need to get the server into a file and print sharing mode and you have been able to get the server into Safe Mode, or if you want to test that the network device driver is not the one that has caused the server to stop functioning, if it has this option will not work.

The Recovery Console

The Recovery console does not automatically install on a Windows 2000 machine, nor does it have to be installed to be used. It can be executed from the Windows 2000 CD-ROM using the Recovery Console option when given the Repair Options screen. If you want to install the Recovery console, open a command prompt and execute:

```
<cdrom drive>:\i386\winnt32 /cmdcons
```

When you use the Recovery Console option, you can configure a service to start or stop when the server boots—a handy tool for corrupted services that cause a server to hang before logons can begin. You may also copy files to the NTFS hard drive, which is handy in case one of the files on the hard drive has become corrupted. (Previously, this could only be attempted with a third-party tool that could access an NTFS drive from a DOS prompt.) Finally, you can manage files, folders, partitions, and disk drives, even deleting and recreating partitions and formatting them. Interestingly, you cannot access the floppy drive from the console. However, changing partitions and formatting them should be a last resort when you have a server with errors.

Summary

When designing the Active Directory, a part of the design should take into account the plans for disaster recovery. Because each DC holds several partitions of the Active Database—at a minimum, the schema, configuration, and the domain in which they belong—with some DCs containing a copy of the GC, they can become a point of failure if they are all held within the same physical location. If all the controllers in a single domain were held in a single building, the loss of that building would become the loss of that domain as well. Sites can be designed by adding an extra site for each standby office, or by maintaining at least one DC in another location.

Windows 2000 Server, Advanced Server, and DataCenter Server support hardware that can help avoid disasters. RAID uses multiple disks to provide redundancy for data so that if one hard drive fails, the others can essentially continue providing services. UPS provides a source of power in the event of a power outage, and further can shut a server down properly without causing data corruption. Clustering is a solution that provides redundancy for the entire server. If a server is in a cluster and it fails, the cluster undergoes a failover procedure that enables another server within the cluster to take over the processing for the failed unit.

Windows 2000 also includes a file replication service (FRS) that can provide redundancy for data. FRS is executed automatically. Additionally, using the Distributed File System (Dfs) with a redundant root in the Active Directory can provide fault tolerance for files, with additional replicas of data placed throughout the network. Redundant data can be used in the case of a downed server carrying a different replica of the same data.

The Active Directory database consists of several file types:

- The database itself—ntds.dit
- Checkpoint files—edb.chk
- Transaction logs—edb.log
- Patch files—*.pat
- Reserved log files—res1.log, res2.log

The patch files are used during backup. The checkpoint and log files are used to indicate which files have been written to disk and which have not.

The Windows 2000 Backup utility can be used to both back up and restore the Active Directory. The key to this process is to back up the System State data.

If restoring the Active Directory, an authoritative restore created with the NTDSUtil.exe utility can restore deleted objects and ensure that they persist after replication takes place.

FAQs

Q: I have many files named edb000xx.log on my Windows 2000 Server and I would like to delete them to free up space. Can I delete them from Windows Explorer?

A: No. These log files are essential for ensuring that data is able to be restored to a current state. When a backup is performed, log files will be deleted automatically. If the log files are manually deleted, they may cause corruption to the Active Directory.

Q: When browsing the registry, I noted that a Circular Logging key was set to 0. Should I change it to 1 in order to make sure that circular logging is not used?

A: No. The default behavior of the Active Directory is to have circular logging turned off. If circular logging is turned on, then past log files are not created. If these past log files are not created and a disaster does occur, it is probable that some Active Directory data will not be able to be restored.

Appendix A

Secrets

- Lesser Known Management Shortcuts

- Under-Documented Functions/Procedure

- For Experts Only

Lesser Known Management Shortcuts

Upgrading DNS and Supporting DNS Dynamic Update Protocol

When you upgrade DNS from Windows NT 4.0 to Windows 2000, DNS does not automatically support dynamic updates. In fact, Windows NT 4.0 DNS does not support DNS Dynamic Update Protocol, so if you plan to use this feature, you should upgrade your NT 4.0 DNS first. The DNS Dynamic Update features must be manually changed in the new DNS Management Console.

1. Click Start | Programs | Administrative Tools | DNS.
2. If not running DNS on the local server, connect to the computer running Microsoft DNS.
3. Right-click on the zone that you want to support Dynamic Updates, and select Properties.
4. The General tab has a drop-down box for Dynamic updates—select whether any dynamic update will be accepted, or if only trusted updates will be.

Creating a Custom Microsoft Management Console (MMC)

One of the most annoying things to do is to change from one console to another in order to manage the Active Directory. Luckily, the MMC is customizable. To create an MMC console that contains all the options that you need to manage Active Directory:

1. Click Start | Run, and **MMC,** and click Oĸ.
2. Click the Console menu and select Add/Remove Snap-in.
3. Click Aᴅᴅ.

4. In the resulting dialog, select each of the consoles that you will want to use most often. (I recommend that you at least select Active Directory Users and Computers, Active Directory Sites and Services, DNS, and Computer Management.) You can always add or remove snap-ins from the console later.

5. Click Close, and then OK when you have finished.

6. Click the Console menu and select Save or Save As. If you want the console to be available on this computer for any user, save it to the C:\Documents and Settings\All Users\ Start menu or Desktop folders.

7. If you are creating a custom MMC for a user and want the console to appear in user mode rather than author mode, click the Console menu and select Options. Drop down the box that states Author mode and select a User mode. Then clear the box that enables the user to save changes to the console. This will lock the console into a mode that is more secure than the default.

PDC Emulation and Native Mode

When a Windows 2000 Active Directory is working in mixed mode, it has a FSMO that is set to act as the "PDC Emulator." The PDC Emulator takes on the tasks of a primary domain controller (PDC) to down-level Windows NT backup domain controllers (BDCs). This is an intuitive role for a PDC Emulator to play.

What is interesting is that the PDC Emulator does not go away after the Active Directory is changed over to native mode. Instead, the PDC Emulator remains as a primary check point for password changes. When a password is changed in the Active Directory, the PDC Emulator is preferred to receive this replication traffic first. The reason that this role exists is to manage situations in which replication of password changes may take several hours to complete across an entire Active Directory database.

For example, if a password is changed, it will be replicated as a changed password to the PDC Emulator. Then, if the user attempts to log on at another domain controller (DC), which has not yet received the update to the Active Directory including that user's password, the DC will not immediately reject the logon. Instead the DC contacts the PDC Emulator and checks with it first to make sure that the password is correct. The PDC Emulator FSMO gets all password changes immediately. This should drive placement of that FSMO in a central location, well connected to the other subnets. A DC can be set to not contact the PDC Emulator if the PDC Emulator role owner is not in the current site. If the AvoidPdcOnWan registry entry in HKEY_LOCAL_MACHINE\CurrentControlSet\Services\Netlogon\Parameters\ is set to 1, the password change reaches the PDC Emulator *nonurgently*, through *normal* replication.

The PDC Emulator in the root domain of the forest provides one other function, regardless of which mode the domain is in: the authoritative time source for the forest. This root domain PDC Emulator is the one that should be set up with an external time source in order for the forest to use an external time provider. The hierarchy of time providers is as follows:

- Client workstations and member servers use the authenticating DC as a time provider.

- DCs in a domain use the PDC Emulator of their own domain as the time provider.

- Each PDC Emulator will use the PDC Emulator of its parent domain, or the forest's root domain if they are the top of a domain tree, as its time provider.

- The root domain's PDC Emulator is the top of the hierarchy and can be used to connect to external time sources.

How Active Directory Prevents Unnecessary Replication

The bidirectional loop created for replication gives multiple paths for DCs to send and receive updated information. As a result, there is both fault tolerance and enhanced performance. A less desirable result could be that multiple instances of the same update are sent to the same DC. Active Directory prevents this through *propagation dampening*.

In Figure A-1, there are three servers that are direct replication partners to each other in a bidirectional ring. (They each have connection objects beneath their NTDS Settings for the other two servers.)

Figure A-1 Server replication ring.

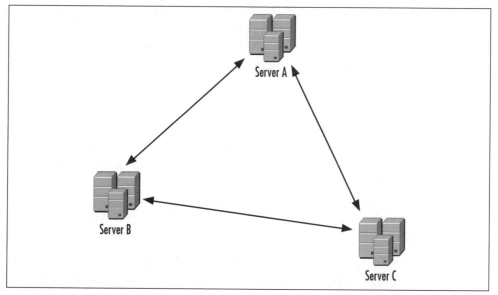

When an object in the Active Directory is updated on Server A, it changes the object's Update Sequence Number, or USN. Replication occurs to both Server B and Server C since they are both direct replication partners. Servers B and C detect that Server A had replicated the change to both, so they do not send the update to each other.

To make this process work, the Active Directory uses two vectors:

- Up-to-date vector
- High watermark vector

The up-to-date vector is comprised of pairs of server USNs. The high watermark vector is the highest USN stored for each object. Propagation dampening occurs because each DC keeps track of its direct replication partners' high watermarks.

Under-Documented Functions/Procedure

How an LDAP Query Accesses Active Directory

The lightweight directory access protocol (LDAP) query will start in the domain where the query was generated. In the Active Directory forest using LDAP, each domain knows about the other domains within their own trees, so LDAP gets referred within a single tree. To use an expanded scope including domains with other namespaces in a forest, the Global Catalog (GC) must be used.

The LDAP referral process for an LDAP query acquires an authoritative answer first. In the following example, the LDAP client is asking for information about an Active Directory object within a sister domain.

1. The LDAP client queries DNS for an LDAP server in the current domain.
2. DNS responds with a DC in the current domain.
3. The LDAP client queries the DC for information about an Active Directory object.
4. The DC refers the client to the parent domain.
5. The LDAP client queries DNS for an LDAP server in the parent domain.
6. DNS responds with a DC in the parent domain.

7. The LDAP client queries the parent DC for information about an Active Directory object.

8. The parent DC refers the client to another of its child domains.

9. The LDAP client queries DNS for an LDAP server in the sister domain.

10. DNS responds with a DC in the sister domain

11. The LDAP client queries the sister DC for information about an Active Directory object.

12. The sister DC responds to the request.

Software Installation

In group policy, assigning an application and publishing an application not only differ from each other, but have different attributes when applied to a User Configuration's Software Installation package compared to a Computer Configuration's Software Installation package. The resulting behavior is summed up in Table A-1.

Table A.1 Assigning vs. Publishing Details

Assigned or Published	User or Computer Configuration	Result
Assigned	User	Users will see a program icon "advertisement" on their desktop or Start menu when they log on. The program will not install until either that icon is double-clicked or a file that has an extension associated with that program is executed.
Assigned	Computer	When the computer starts up and the group policy object is applied, the applications assigned to a computer are automatically installed. Any user who logs on to the computer will have that application automatically.

Assigned or Published	User or Computer Configuration	Result
Published	User	When the user logs on, the group policy object enables the user to Add or Remove the program via the Add/Remove Programs icon in Control Panel. Additionally, if the user invokes a file with an extension that is associated with the program, the program will install. When the user logs off the machine, if the user never installed the application, the Add/Remove programs icon will not remain for the next user unless that user has the same group policy applied. If the user installed the application, it will not be available to other users.
Published	Computer	When the computer starts up, the group policy object is applied so that the program appears in the Add/Remove Programs icon in Control Panel as an option. Additionally, if a file is invoked that has an extension associated with the program, it will be installed and available to all users. These items do not change, regardless of who logs on to the computer.

Group policy software distribution appears to be dependent upon the Windows Installer. Not so. If you have a custom application to install that does not use the Windows Installer, you can create a .zap file to do the job. There are some limitations to using a .zap file, so if you have the option of using Windows Installer, you will be better off doing so.

- You cannot assign a zap file.
- Your users will probably be required to answer setup questions, and they must have the local permissions for installing software on their computer.

- You do not get the benefits of the "auto-repair" functionality that Windows Installer provides. Instead, if the application cannot start, it will typically try to reinstall itself.

.zap files are text files that are similar to standard .ini files. A .zap file will let you install many applications through group policy, even if they can't be installed with the standard Windows Installer. They have two standard headings:

- **[Application]** Describes the name of the file, the setup command, and other application information.

- **[Ext]** This is an optional section in the file that lists the extensions that this application will use.

How to Create and Configure a Dfs Root

1. Click Start | Programs | Administrative Tools | Distributed File System.

2. Once in the Dfs console, right-click on the distributed filesystem and select New Dfs Root.

3. The Create New Dfs Root wizard will start. After clicking Next at the Welcome screen, the wizard will prompt for the type of Dfs root. It is preferable to create a fault-tolerant Dfs root since that is integrated into the Active Directory. If not desired, however, select "Create a standalone Dfs root."

4. The next screen of this wizard will prompt for the server to host the Dfs root.

5. After that, the wizard will prompt for the share that will be the Dfs Root Volume. If you prefer, you can create a new share, rather than selecting an existing share.

6. You will then be asked for a Dfs root name, which can be different from the share name.

7. Setting up the root is not the only task to complete. Next, Dfs links and replicas can be added. This is done by right-clicking on the root, (or subsequently added Dfs links), and selecting New Dfs Link from the pop-up menu, or new replica. Since the paths to the links use UNC naming conventions, you can add Dfs Links and Replicas throughout the network by indicating \\servername\sharename.

Informational Message

At server startup time, there may be an NTDS Event number 1094 stating "Disk write caching on drive E: has been disabled to prevent possible data loss during system failures." This message will only appear for drives that contain the Active Directory and the log files. (Remember, the log files and the Active Directory should not be placed on the same physical disk.) For any drive that has soft write caching enabled, the Active Directory will disable it and leave this message.

Renaming

A domain cannot be renamed. However, if you demote and repromote each of the DCs into a new domain, and then either recreate accounts, or migrate them to the new domain, and finally join clients to the new domain, you will achieve the same effect. Do not attempt this with a domain that has child domains. If this is the case, you will need to migrate all the child domains first, and then attempt the parent domain.

The only way you can rename a DC is to demote the DC, rename it, and then repromote it. If there are no other DCs in the domain, all the user accounts will be lost.

Quick Application of an Updated Group Policy

If you have created a new group policy and want to see if it works, you can apply it to the local machine with a quick command. In order to quickly refresh the group policy without logging off and logging on again, for a computer configuration, run the following command from a command prompt on the local machine:

```
secedit /RefreshPolicy MACHINE_POLICY /Enforce
```

In order to quickly refresh the group policy for a user's configuration, run the following command from a command prompt on the machine where the user has logged on:

```
Secedit /RefreshPolicy USER_POLICY /Enforce
```

DNS Migrations

If the existing DNS server does not support SRV resource records (SRV RRs), the only options available to the Windows 2000 are to upgrade the DNS server to a version that does support SRV RRs, or to migrate to Windows 2000 DNS. The method of migrating to Windows 2000 DNS is dependent upon the final DNS configuration.

If the existing DNS server is authoritative for the domain that Windows 2000 will be in—for example, domain.com—then the migration strategy should be:

1. Review the existing DNS zone information and make sure that it is current. If any changes need to be made, then make the changes.

2. Perform zone transfers with any other secondary DNS servers so that all are current.

3. Install the Windows 2000 DNS server as a secondary server for the domain.com zone.

4. Perform a zone transfer so that the Windows 2000 DNS server becomes current.

5. Promote the Windows 2000 DNS server so that it is a primary DNS server for the domain.com zone.

6. Test that the Windows 2000 DNS server is primary for the zone by making a change to it and performing zone transfers from the other secondary servers.

7. Remove any secondary DNS servers that do not support SRV RRs.

If there is no way to remove the existing DNS server as a primary server, for whatever reason, there is another option: to delegate the Windows 2000 zones that contain the SRV RRs. These zones are actually created as subdomains. If the DNS domain is domain.com, the zones that must be delegated are:

- _msdcs.domain.com
- _tcp.domain.com
- _udp.domain.com
- _sites.domain.com

The reason that each of these subdomains begins with an underscore is so that those organizations that do have hostnames or domain names that use "msdcs" or "tcp" for example, will have conflicts when these domains are created automatically. It is much rarer for an organization to create domains with underscores (the _ symbol) at the beginning, so these names are fairly safe from causing conflicts. So, to use this technique, the migration strategy is:

1. Review the existing DNS zone information and make sure that it is current. If any changes need to be made, then make the changes.

2. Perform zone transfers with any other secondary DNS servers so that all are current.

3. Add the delegated zones to the existing DNS server and point it to the Windows 2000 DNS server.

4. Install the Windows 2000 DNS server as a primary server for the _msdcs.domain.com, _tcp.domain.com, _udp.domain.com, and _sites.domain.com domains.

5. Make sure to include the A record for the parent domain's host.

DNS Best Practices

Delegate a zone for each Active Directory domain. Then place DNS servers, which are authoritative for each Active Directory domain, near their own domain's DCs.

When there are multiple domains within a forest, and the forest root domain is separated from any of the child domains via slow links, create a delegated _msdcs.domain.com zone, then make DNS servers across those WAN links secondary servers to the _msdcs.domain.com zone. This will avoid extra traffic across the WAN.

Configure all clients to query more than one DNS server, even if the second of those servers exists across a WAN link. This practice will avoid errors in the case of a downed DNS server. "Clients," as used here, describes each Windows 2000 DC, member server, each network-aware TCP/IP printer, each workstation, and any other type of IP host that does not provide DNS services.

For Experts Only

Add a Server to Two Different Sites Simultaneously

Using the Active Directory Sites and Services console will allow you to configure a server as a member of a single site. If you want a server to be available in multiple sites, you will need to use a different method—this is by design. Having a server as a member of two or more sites may result in poor network performance, so only use this as a last resort.

Begin by logging on to the server that you want to be a member of more than one site. Make sure to use an Administrator's name and password. Then, click Start and then Run. Type **regedt32**, and click O<small>K</small>.

In the Registry Editor, navigate to HKLM\System\
CurrentControlSet\Services\NetLogon\Parameters. Select the Edit
menu and choose Add Value.

In the resulting dialog box, type the name **SiteCoverage** and
select the type of REG_MULTI_SZ, then click OK. After that, enter
the names of each site of which the server will be a member, each
site name on a new line with the identical spelling and capitalization
used. After the last entry, press SHIFT and ENTER to move to the next
line, and click OK to finish.

Now the server is a member of more than one site, but it will not
show up in the Active Directory Sites and Services console. You can
manually create the server objects by right-clicking on each additional site and selecting New, and then selecting Server. Place the
NetBIOS name of the server in the space provided, and click OK.

Once the server object has been created, right-click on it and
select Properties from the popup menu. In the section under
Computer, click CHANGE. Select the correct server from the ones
available on the network. This capability is useful when a site exists
without a DC. It allows a DC in another site to become the preferred
logon DC.

Removing Phantom Objects

A phantom object is one that has been removed from the Active
Directory, but for some reason still appears as an object within it.
This type of error can happen when a command has not completed
properly (the server lost power, received an unrecoverable network
packet during the change to the Active Directory, etc.), and is trou-
blesome since the Active Directory does not truly reflect the current
network configuration. This is not a difficult problem to solve.

First, note the full path of the object, such as
cn=object,cn=ou,dc=domain,dc=com. Then boot the DC into DS
Repair Mode. Start NTDSUtil.exe. Type **Files** and press ENTER.
Remove the object using its full path. Run a Header check, and then
run an Integrity check. After these complete, reboot the server normally and initiate replication.

Sometimes an object is left as a logical placeholder in the Active Directory, even though its physical component has been removed. For example, if a DC is removed from the Active Directory and does not appear in the Active Directory Users and Computers console (or when you run NTDSUtil), it may still appear in the Active Directory Sites and Services console. When this happens, you can safely remove that object by right-clicking on the server object and selecting Delete from the popup menu.

Phantom Domains

When an Administrator demotes the last DC for a domain, he or she should select the option for "This server is the last domain controller in the domain." This will remove the metadata for the domain from the Active Directory forest. If the Administrator does not select it, the metadata for that domain must be removed.

1. Log on to the domain naming master FSMO DC as a member of the Enterprise Admins group and force replication to take place.

2. Open a command prompt, type **ntdsutil,** and press ENTER.

3. Type **metadata cleanup,** and press ENTER.

4. Type **connections,** and press ENTER.

5. Type **connect to server nameofdomainnamingmasterFSMO,** and press ENTER.

6. Type **quit,** and press ENTER.

7. Type **select operation target,** and press ENTER.

8. Type **list domains,** and press ENTER. You will see a list of domains associated with numbers.

9. Type **select domain numberofdomain,** and press ENTER.

10. Type **quit,** and press ENTER.

11. Type **remove selected domain,** and press ENTER.

12. Type **quit,** and press Enter until you have exited the NTDSUTIL.

Transferring FSMO Roles

Moving the RID master, which is a single designated DC in an entire forest that provides the relative ID (RID) portion of the SID to other DCs, entails one of two methods.

1. In the Active Directory Users and Computers console, right-click on the domain and select Connect to Domain Controller from the popup menu.
2. Select the DC that will be the new RID Master, and click Ok.
3. Right-click on the domain again, and select Operations Masters from the popup menu.
4. Select the Rid Pool tab
5. Click Change at the bottom of the dialog.
6. Click OK

Or, using NTDSUTIL, the Administrator can do the following to change the RID master:

1. Log on as a member of Enterprise Admins to any DC.
2. Open a command prompt, type **ntdsutil**, and press ENTER.
3. Type **roles**, and press ENTER.
4. Type **connections**, and press ENTER.
5. Type **connect to server servernameofnewRIDMaster**, and press ENTER.
6. Type **quit**, and press Enter.
7. Type **transfer rid master**, and press Enter.
8. You will be prompted by a dialog to transfer the role. Select YES.
9. Type **quit**, and press ENTER until you have exited NTDSUTIL.

The PDC Emulator is a computer that acts as the PDC for Windows NT BDCs in a mixed domain. It also handles password changes and has authority for time for its domain. To change the PDC FSMO role:

1. In the Active Directory Users and Computers console, right-click on the domain and select Connect to Domain Controller from the popup menu.

2. Select the DC to be the new PDC Emulator, and click OK.

3. Right-click on the domain and select Operations Masters from the popup menu.

4. Click the PDC tab.

5. Click CHANGE, and Click OK.

Or, using NTDSUTIL, the administrator can do the following to change the PDC Emulator:

1. Log on as a member of the Enterprise Admins group on any DC.

2. Open a command prompt, type **ntdsutil**, and press ENTER.

3. Type **roles**, and press ENTER.

4. Type **connections**, and press ENTER.

5. Type **connect to server servernameofnewPDCEmulator**, and press ENTER.

6. Type **quit**, and press ENTER.

7. Type **transfer pdc**, and press ENTER.

8. You will be prompted by a dialog to transfer the role. Select YES.

9. Type **quit**, and press ENTER until you have exited the NTDSUTIL.

The Infrastructure master is responsible for managing the group to user references. This will ensure that users are able to access resources. To change the Infrastructure master, do the following:

1. In the Active Directory Users and Computers console, right-click on the domain and select Connect to Domain Controller from the popup menu.

2. Select the DC that will be the new Infrastructure master, and click OK.

3. Right-click on the domain, and select Operations Masters from the popup menu.

4. Click the Infrastructure tab.

5. Click CHANGE, and click OK to confirm.

To do this same change with NTDSUTIL, execute the following:

1. Log on as a member of the Enterprise Admins group on any DC.

2. Open a command prompt, type **ntdsutil,** and press ENTER.

3. Type **roles,** and press ENTER.

4. Type **connections,** and press ENTER.

5. Type **connect to server servernameofnewInfrastructureFSMO,** and press ENTER.

6. Type **quit,** and press ENTER.

7. Type **transfer infrastructure master,** and press ENTER.

8. You will be prompted to transfer the role. Select YES.

9. Type **quit,** and press ENTER until you have exited NTDSUTIL.

There is only one domain naming master FSMO per forest. This designated DC ensures that any domain added to the forest has a unique name. To change the server that handles this role, first make sure that the new DC is also a GC server.

1. In the Active Directory Domains and Trusts console, right-click on the Active Directory Domains and Trusts root, and select Connect to Domain Controller from the popup menu.

2. Specify the name of the DC that will be the next domain naming master FSMO (remember, it must also be a GC server), and press ENTER.

3. Right click on the Active Directory Domains and Trusts, and select Operations Masters from the popup menu.

4. Click CHANGE.

5. Click OK to confirm.

To execute this same process using NTDSUTIL:

1. Log on to a DC as a member of the Enterprise Admins group.

2. Open a command prompt, type **ntdsutil,** then press ENTER.

3. Type **roles,** and press ENTER.

4. Type **connections,** and press ENTER.

5. Type **connect to server servernameofnewdomainnamingmasterFSMO,** and press ENTER.

6. Type **quit,** and press ENTER.

7. Type **transfer domain naming master,** and press ENTER.

8. A dialog will appear to confirm the role transfer. Choose YES.

9. Type **quit,** and press ENTER until you have exited the NTDSUTIL.

The schema master is the one DC upon which the schema can be changed. There is only one schema per forest. To change this role, you must use the Active Directory Schema Manager console.

1. Log on to a DC as a member of the Schema Admins group.

2. Start the Active Directory Schema Manager console and right-click on the Active Directory Schema root.

3. Select Change Domain Controller from the popup menu.

4. Specify the name of the DC that will be the new schema master, and click Ok.

5. Right-click on the Active Directory Schema, and select Operations Master from the popup menu.

6. Click CHANGE.

7. Click OK when a dialog confirms the role transfer.

The change of the Schema Master FSMO can be accomplished using NTDSUTIL.

1. Log on to a DC as a member of the Enterprise Admins group.

2. Open a command prompt, type **ntdsutil**, then press ENTER.

3. Type **roles**, and press ENTER.

4. Type **connections**, and press ENTER.

5. Type **connect to server servernameofnewSchemaMasterFSMO**, and press ENTER.

6. Type **quit**, and press ENTER.

7. Type **transfer schema master**, and press ENTER.

8. Select YES for the dialog regarding the role transfer.

9. Type **quit**, and press ENTER until you have exited NTDSUTIL.

Troubleshooting Tips

Avoiding Errors When Migrating a Domain

Do not try to add a Windows 2000 server as a DC into a Windows NT 4.0 domain that has a Windows NT 4.0 PDC. The Windows 2000 DC will automatically emulate the PDC for that domain and cause conflicts.

Remote Procedure Call (RPC) Errors

A strange but true fact: When you receive an RPC error, you are most likely having problems with DNS. Or worse, there is a hardware problem, or an IP address is not applied to the network interface, or some other lower-layer problem. RPC is the session-level protocol that runs procedures transparently on remote hosts. It can run over multiple lower-layer protocols including TCP/IP. It uses DNS to find remote services. DNS depends on IP addressing, which further depends on the Physical and Data Link layer protocols such as Ethernet or Token Ring, and those lower-layer protocols can only function if the network interface is working and connected to a functional network. So, the order in which to troubleshoot an RPC error is this:

1. Run NetDIAG.

2. Check your DNS server's configuration (DNSCMD on a Windows 2000 DNS Server).

3. Verify that your workstation's network interface has an IP address (you can use WINIPCFG or IPCONFIG on most Windows machines).

4. Check to make sure the network interface card (NIC) is functioning. (If the NIC has lights, are they green? Did you run the vendor diags?)

5. Check the network cable.

6. Check the hub and switches to make sure that they are functioning.

Index

A

I

M

O

U

IP Security for Microsoft Windows 2000 Server

Solutions in this chapter:

- **Introduction**

- **Network Encroachment Methodologies**

- **IPSec Architecture**

- **Deploying Windows IP Security**

Introduction

Security issues are of paramount importance to the network administrator. In the past, networks were lone entities. These lone networks typically ran NetBEUI in small workgroups of fewer than 200 computers and were not connected to any other networks. The major security concerns in an isolated environment typically revolved around employees located at the site. You could focus your security efforts on local access controls, such as locking down floppy drives on employee workstations, and checking briefcases and handbags for printed materials.

Today's network is very different from the isolated NetBEUI network. It is likely that your network is connected to other networks via dedicated leased lines, the Internet, or your organizational remote access server.

Each of these points of access represents an ever-increasing security risk. Previously, electronic documents had to be copied to a floppy disk or printed in order to leave your premises; now, it is as easy as sending an e-mail attachment over the Internet. The organization's prized database can just as easily be posted to electronic newsgroups. Hackers can snoop the network and gain usernames and passwords that allow them to bypass normal access controls. Innocent experimenting by fledging systems engineers and power users can corrupt or destroy data just as effectively as the most malignant of hackers.

Effective network security standards are the sum total of a well-planned and -implemented security infrastructure. These measures include hardware security, file and folder access controls, strong passwords, smart cards, social security, physical sequestration of servers, file encryption, and protection of data as it moves across the wire within the organizational intranet and outside the organization.

This chapter focuses on protecting the integrity and confidentiality of information as it moves through the network. First, it looks at some of the common security risks incurred as data moves across the wires. The next section discusses the basics of cryptography and how they function within the framework Microsoft's new IPSec capabilities. The last and most comprehensive section covers the specifics of implementing IP security in your network.

Network Encroachment Methodologies

Hackers can use a number of methods to circumvent your network security and gain access to information, including:

- Snooping
- Spoofing
- Password compromise
- Denial of service attacks
- Man-in-the-middle attacks
- Application-level attacks
- Key compromise

Snooping

Most data sent over the network is in clear text. Individuals with a network sniffer such as the Network Monitor program that comes with Systems Management Server, or third-party programs such as Sniffer Pro, can easily read the clear text messages as they traverse the network.

Some server applications that maintain their own username and password lists allow for the logon information to cross the network in free-text format. The network snooper, using easily accessible sniffing programs, can plug into an available port in a hub or switch and access this information. The use of clear text makes it easy for the snooper to access information. Such information might include: credit card numbers, Social Security numbers, contents of personal e-mail messages, and proprietary organizational secrets.

Spoofing

The source and destination IP address are prerequisite for establishing sessions between computers on a TCP/IP-based network. The act of IP spoofing involves falsely assuming the identity of a legitimate host computer on the network in order to gain access to computers on the internal network. Another term for spoofing is *impersonation*. The intruder is impersonating a computer with a legitimate IP address. A common spoofing-based attack is the TCP/IP Sequence number attack.

TCP/IP Sequence Number Attack

The Transmission Control Protocol (TCP) is responsible for reliability of communications on a TCP/IP-based network. This includes acknowledgment of information sent to the destination host. In order to track bytes sent over the network, each segment is given a sequence number. A sophisticated attacker can establish the sequencing pattern between two computers because the sequence pattern is not random.

First, the attacker must gain access to the network, and then the attacker must connect to a server and analyze the sequence pattern between the server and a legitimate host it is communicating with at the time. The TCP/IP Sequence Number attacker then will attempt a connection to the server by spoofing (falsely assuming) a legitimate host's IP address. In order to prevent the legitimate host from responding, the spoofer will start a denial of service attack on the legitimate host.

Since the legitimate host cannot respond, the spoofer will wait for the server to send its reply and then will respond with the correct sequence number. The server now believes that the spoofing computer is the legitimate host, and the spoofer now can begin data transfer.

Password Compromise

Users who have illegitimate access to network passwords can access resources they are not otherwise able to use. There are a number of ways an attacker can gain knowledge of passwords:

- **Social Engineering.** The attacker contacts an individual using an assumed identity, and then makes a request for a password from an individual who has access rights to the information of interest.

- **Sniffing.** Many network applications allow the username and password to cross the network in clear text. The attacker can use a network sniffer application to intercept this information.

- **Cracking.** The cracker uses a number of different techniques to gain illegal access to passwords. Examples of cracking techniques include dictionary attacks and brute force attacks.

If an administrator password is compromised, the attacker will then have access to all resources on the network that are protected with access controls. The intruder now has access to the entire user account database and can use this information to access all files and folders, change routing information, and alter information unbeknownst to users who are dependent on that information.

Denial of Service Attacks

There are a number of different denial of service attacks. All these techniques have in common the ability to disrupt normal computer or operating system functioning on the targeted machine. These attacks can flood the network with useless packets, corrupt or exhaust memory resources, or exploit a weakness in a network application. Denial of service attacks include:

- TCP SYN attack
- SMURF attack
- Teardrop attack
- Ping of Death

TCP SYN Attack

When computers on a TCP/IP-based network establish a session, they go through the three-way handshake process:

1. The originating client sends a packet with the SYN flag set to ON. This host includes a sequence number in the packet. The server will use this sequence number in the next step.

2. The server will return a packet to the originating host with its SYN flag set to ON. This packet will have a sequence number that is incremented by 1 over the number that was sent by the requesting computer.

3. The client will respond to this request with a packet that will acknowledge the server's sequence number by incrementing the sequence number by 1.

Whenever a host requests a session with a server, the pair will go through the three-way handshake process. The attacker can take advantage of this process by initiating multiple session requests that originate from bogus-source IP addresses. The server keeps each open request in a queue as it is waiting for step 3 to occur. Entries into the queue are typically emptied every 60 seconds.

If the attacker is able to keep the queue filled, then legitimate connection requests will be denied, so service is denied to legitimate users of e-mail, Web, ftp, and other IP-related services.

The Global Knowledge Advantage

Global Knowledge has a global delivery system for its products and services. The company has 28 subsidiaries, and offers its programs through a total of 60+ locations. No other vendor can provide consistent services across a geographic area this large. Global Knowledge is the largest independent information technology education provider, offering programs on a variety of platforms. This enables our multi-platform and multi-national customers to obtain all of their programs from a single vendor. The company has developed the unique CompetusTM Framework software tool and methodology which can quickly reconfigure courseware to the proficiency level of a student on an interactive basis. Combined with self-paced and on-line programs, this technology can reduce the time required for training by prescribing content in only the deficient skills areas. The company has fully automated every aspect of the education process, from registration and follow-up, to "just-in-time" production of courseware. Global Knowledge through its Enterprise Services Consultancy, can customize programs and products to suit the needs of an individual customer.

Global Knowledge Classroom Education Programs

The backbone of our delivery options is classroom-based education. Our modern, well-equipped facilities staffed with the finest instructors offer programs in a wide variety of information technology topics, many of which lead to professional certifications.

Custom Learning Solutions

This delivery option has been created for companies and governments that value customized learning solutions. For them, our consultancy-based approach of developing targeted education solutions is most effective at helping them meet specific objectives.

Self-Paced and Multimedia Products

This delivery option offers self-paced program titles in interactive CD-ROM, videotape and audio tape programs. In addition, we offer custom development of interactive multimedia courseware to customers and partners. Call us at 1-888-427-4228.

Electronic Delivery of Training

Our network-based training service delivers efficient competency-based, interactive training via the World Wide Web and organizational intranets. This leading-edge delivery option provides a custom learning path and "just-in-time" training for maximum convenience to students.

Global Knowledge Courses Available

Microsoft
- Windows 2000 Deployment Strategies
- Introduction to Directory Services
- Windows 2000 Client Administration
- Windows 2000 Server
- Windows 2000 Update
- MCSE Bootcamp
- Microsoft Networking Essentials
- Windows NT 4.0 Workstation
- Windows NT 4.0 Server
- Windows NT Troubleshooting
- Windows NT 4.0 Security
- Windows 2000 Security
- Introduction to Microsoft Web Tools

Management Skills
- Project Management for IT Professionals
- Microsoft Project Workshop
- Management Skills for IT Professionals

Network Fundamentals
- Understanding Computer Networks
- Telecommunications Fundamentals I
- Telecommunications Fundamentals II
- Understanding Networking Fundamentals
- Upgrading and Repairing PCs
- DOS/Windows A+ Preparation
- Network Cabling Systems

WAN Networking and Telephony
- Building Broadband Networks
- Frame Relay Internetworking
- Converging Voice and Data Networks
- Introduction to Voice Over IP
- Understanding Digital Subscriber Line (xDSL)

Internetworking
- ATM Essentials
- ATM Internetworking
- ATM Troubleshooting
- Understanding Networking Protocols
- Internetworking Routers and Switches
- Network Troubleshooting
- Internetworking with TCP/IP
- Troubleshooting TCP/IP Networks
- Network Management
- Network Security Administration
- Virtual Private Networks
- Storage Area Networks
- Cisco OSPF Design and Configuration
- Cisco Border Gateway Protocol (BGP) Configuration

Web Site Management and Development
- Advanced Web Site Design
- Introduction to XML
- Building a Web Site
- Introduction to JavaScript
- Web Development Fundamentals
- Introduction to Web Databases

PERL, UNIX, and Linux
- PERL Scripting
- PERL with CGI for the Web
- UNIX Level I
- UNIX Level II
- Introduction to Linux for New Users
- Linux Installation, Configuration, and Maintenance

Authorized Vendor Training
Red Hat
- Introduction to Red Hat Linux
- Red Hat Linux Systems Administration
- Red Hat Linux Network and Security Administration
- RHCE Rapid Track Certification

Cisco Systems
- Interconnecting Cisco Network Devices
- Advanced Cisco Router Configuration
- Installation and Maintenance of Cisco Routers
- Cisco Internetwork Troubleshooting
- Designing Cisco Networks
- Cisco Internetwork Design
- Configuring Cisco Catalyst Switches
- Cisco Campus ATM Solutions
- Cisco Voice Over Frame Relay, ATM, and IP
- Configuring for Selsius IP Phones
- Building Cisco Remote Access Networks
- Managing Cisco Network Security
- Cisco Enterprise Management Solutions

Nortel Networks
- Nortel Networks Accelerated Router Configuration
- Nortel Networks Advanced IP Routing
- Nortel Networks WAN Protocols
- Nortel Networks Frame Switching
- Nortel Networks Accelar 1000
- Comprehensive Configuration
- Nortel Networks Centillion Switching
- Network Management with Optivity for Windows

Oracle Training
- Introduction to Oracle8 and PL/SQL
- Oracle8 Database Administration

Custom Corporate Network Training

Train on Cutting Edge Technology
We can bring the best in skill-based training to your facility to create a real-world hands-on training experience. Global Knowledge has invested millions of dollars in network hardware and software to train our students on the same equipment they will work with on the job. Our relationships with vendors allow us to incorporate the latest equipment and platforms into your on-site labs.

Maximize Your Training Budget
Global Knowledge provides experienced instructors, comprehensive course materials, and all the networking equipment needed to deliver high quality training. You provide the students; we provide the knowledge.

Avoid Travel Expenses
On-site courses allow you to schedule technical training at your convenience, saving time, expense, and the opportunity cost of travel away from the workplace.

Discuss Confidential Topics
Private on-site training permits the open discussion of sensitive issues such as security, access, and network design. We can work with your existing network's proprietary files while demonstrating the latest technologies.

Customize Course Content
Global Knowledge can tailor your courses to include the technologies and the topics which have the greatest impact on your business. We can complement your internal training efforts or provide a total solution to your training needs.

Corporate Pass
The Corporate Pass Discount Program rewards our best network training customers with preferred pricing on public courses, discounts on multimedia training packages, and an array of career planning services.

Global Knowledge Training Lifecycle
Supporting the Dynamic and Specialized Training Requirements of Information Technology Professionals

- Define Profile
- Assess Skills
- Design Training
- Deliver Training
- Test Knowledge
- Update Profile
- Use New Skills

Global Knowledge

Global Knowledge programs are developed and presented by industry professionals with "real-world" experience. Designed to help professionals meet today's inter-
connectivity and interoperability challenges, most of our programs feature
hands-on labs that incorporate state-of-the-art communication components and
equipment.

ON-SITE TEAM TRAINING

Bring Global Knowledge's powerful training programs to your company. At Global
Knowledge, we will custom design courses to meet your specific network requirements. Call (919)-461-8686 for more information.

YOUR GUARANTEE

Global Knowledge believes its courses offer the best possible training in this field.
If during the first day you are not satisfied and wish to withdraw from the course,
simply notify the instructor, return all course materials and receive a 100%
refund.

REGISTRATION INFORMATION

In the US:
call: (888) 762–4442
fax: (919) 469–7070
visit our website:
www.globalknowledge.com

SYNGRESS SOLUTIONS...

MANAGING WINDOWS 2000
NETWORK SERVICES

Microsoft Windows 2000 Server integrates network services for companies and administrators to set up and manage networks, remote access, and extranets, as well as to manage other communications. This is the first book to focus exclusively on networking and integrated voice, video, and data on networks. Readers will learn how to deploy and integrate all Windows 2000 networking technologies within an enterprise network.

ISBN: 1-928994-06-7

$49.95

CONFIGURING WINDOWS 2000
SERVER SECURITY

Microsoft has incorporated dramatic new security changes in Windows 2000 Server, including Kerberos Server Authentication, Public Key Infrastructure (PKI), IP Security (IPSec), Encrypting File System (EFS), and Active Directory permissions. This book is an indispensable guide for anyone bearing the responsibility for the overall security of a Windows 2000 Server network.

ISBN: 1-928994-02-4

$49.95

WINDOWS 2000 SERVER
SYSTEM ADMINISTRATION HANDBOOK

As an NT System Administrator, you must quickly master Windows 2000 Server's new administration tools Don't be left behind on Microsoft Management Console (MMC), Active Directory, IP routing, Kerberos security, and the many other new features of Windows 2000 Server. This is the one book you'll need to quickly become proficient in configuring and running a Windows 2000 network.

ISBN: 1-928994-09-1

$49.95

CONFIGURING CISCO
VOICE OVER IP

Welcome to the brave new world of packetized voice! Learn to use the latest Cisco technology for integrating voice over ATM and IP. Determine the optimum service selection, equipment, and configuration of a voice-over-data network. Design branch and regional office voice connectivity using Cisco 3620/3810 multiservice equipment and configure Cisco 2600, 3600, and AS5300 routers for voice over IP.

ISBN: 1-928994-03-2

$59.95

solutions@syngress.com

SYNGRESS®